# SALT, LEAVEN, AND LIGHT

# Salt, Leaven, and Light

## THE COMMUNITY CALLED CHURCH

### T. Howland Sanks

*A Crossroad Herder Book*
The Crossroad Publishing Company
New York

This printing:2013

The Crossroad Publishing Company
www.CrossroadPublishing.com

Copyright © 1992 by T. Howland Sanks

Printed in the United States of America

---

**Library of Congress Cataloging-in-Publication Data**

Sanks, T. Howland.
    Salt, leaven, and light : the community called church / T. Howland
Sanks.
    p.  cm.
    ISBN 0-8245-1175-1; 0-8245-1666-4 (pbk.)
    1. Church.  2. Catholic Church—Doctrines.   I. Title.
BX1746.S243  1992
262—dc20
                                       91-39809
                                          CIP

*In Memory of*
*My Mother and Father*
*Kathleen D. and Thomas H. Sanks, Jr.*
*and*
*My Mentor and Friend*
*Harry W. Kirwin*

# Contents

# Part III
# CHALLENGES AND POSSIBILITIES

# Preface

Over the many years of teaching a course on the "Community Called Church" I have frequently been asked to recommend one book on the church for the interested, intelligent person who is not a professional theologian. I have also been asked what text I use in the course for graduate students and students preparing for ministry. I have never been able to answer either question. Although there are many fine books on the subject, no one of them integrates the historical, sociological, and theological approaches that I believe necessary for a complete understanding of the church. This volume is an attempt to meet that need.

For contemporary Christians, and Roman Catholics in particular, the church has become problematic for the many reasons I suggest in chapter 1. The Second Vatican Council, frequently called the "council on the church," opened up many new avenues of inquiry, new challenges, and new possibilities, but also raised many basic questions about the nature and mission of the church. The prevailing historical consciousness has made us aware of how conditioned all of our theological understandings are by time, place, and social location. Hence, any theological reflection on the church must take the historical background and situation into consideration if we are to deal responsibly with these new challenges and possibilities. These considerations have led to the structure of the book.

In Part I, I have tried to describe the context in which we reflect on the church at present, and to be honest and explicit about the methods necessary for this reflection. In Part II, I have tried to recall and retrieve the various self-understandings that the Christian community has developed throughout its history. This section is not church history as such, but rather the history of ecclesiology. In Part III, I have outlined the state of the question on five major issues confronting the Christian community at present. Underlying all these challenges is the fundamental question of the relationship of the church to the modern world. For an understanding of this relationship, I believe we need images that suggest neither subordination of one to the other, nor separation, but permeation. The church is in service to all humanity, as Vatican II asserted, and its mission is to transform all aspects of human existence. Hence, the title of the book, the biblical images of permeation: Salt, Leaven, and Light.

Several years ago, at the end of the course on the church, one of my students said, "At the beginning of the course I barely knew the church; now she is my friend." I hope the readers of this volume will share that experience.

Because I believe that language reflects and shapes our thinking, I have tried to use inclusive language throughout the volume. In citing authors from an earlier historical period, I faced the familiar dilemma of altering their works, indicating our current awareness of their lack of inclusive language by the use of *sic,* or allowing them to stand as they were written. I chose the third course and beg the indulgence of those readers who disagree with my choice.

I wish to acknowledge and thank many people, most importantly the students in my course "The Community Called Church," who, over the years, have contributed much to this volume, but especially my faculty colleagues who read individual chapters: John R. Donahue, John F. Baldovin, John A. Coleman, Allan F. Deck, James L. Empereur, George E. Griener, Sandra Schneiders, Louis Pascoe, Joseph A. Komonchak, Jay P. Dolan, Claude Welch, James B. Nickoloff, and two who read the entire manuscript, Roger Haight and John E. Linnan, for their time and very helpful comments and suggestions.

I originally intended to subtitle the book "The Self-Understanding of the Christian Community," but after some grumbling from my publisher I fell back on the title I had been using for my course on ecclesiology. It is taken, of course, from the title of Juan Luis Segundo's book, which was published in English in 1973 and to which I am deeply indebted. Finally, I wish to thank my research assistant, James P. Flaherty, and my editor, Frank Oveis, for their helpful suggestions and encouragement throughout the entire project.

# *Abbreviations*

CD     *Christus Dominus,* Decree on the Bishops' Pastoral Office in the Church (Vatican II)

DH     *Dignitatis Humanae,* Declaration on Religious Freedom (Vatican II)

EN     *Evangelii Nuntiandi,* Apostolic Exhortation (Pope Paul VI)

GS     *Gaudium et Spes,* Pastoral Constitution on the Church in the Modern World (Vatican II)

LG     *Lumen Gentium,* Dogmatic Constitution on the Church (Vatican II)

NA     *Nostra Aetate,* Declaration on the Relationship of the Church to Non-Christian Religions (Vatican II)

OE     *Orientalium Ecclesiarum,* Decree on Eastern Catholic Churches (Vatican II)

PO     *Presbyterorum Ordinis,* Decree on the Ministry and Life of Priests (Vatican II)

SC     *Sacrosanctum Concilium,* Constitution on the Sacred Liturgy (Vatican II)

UR     *Unitatis Redintegratio,* Decree on Ecumenism (Vatican II)

# PART I

# Context and Method

Chapter 1

# The Context
# of Our Reflections

The masters of suspicion have indeed permeated our culture! Over the years of teaching I have learned that, sooner or later, students will inevitably ask about the background of the author of an assigned reading. Who is he or she? Where is he or she coming from? What is her or his background? What region of the political spectrum does he or she represent? Where did he or she study? Live? Work? In short, we take it for granted today that everyone writes from a particular social location, perspective, background, or context, which sooner or later will be manifest in one's work. We know that we are all influenced by the culture and society in which we live and think. We cannot avoid this influence although we may transcend it. We can, however, bring it to consciousness and make it explicit, recognizing its limitations and possibilities. We also recognize that while our thinking and reflecting is particularized by its context, it is not thereby invalidated. The sociology of knowledge may relativize our thought, but it does not falsify it.

I write as a North American, Roman Catholic, twenty-five years after the Second Vatican Council and in the last decade of the twentieth century. The intended reader would share some of these characteristics also. I hope not to be too narrowly North American nor too exclusively Roman Catholic. In this chapter I will try to make explicit this context as I understand it and draw out the implications of the context for our reflections on the church.

## THE CONTEXT IN GENERAL

There are unarticulated assumptions and modes of thinking that characterize the so-called First World in varying degrees of intensity and with

3

necessary qualifications. I will attempt a general phenomenological description, aware of the risk of oversimplification and of the need for modification in specific areas.

## Secular: Pluralist, Relativist, Privatist

Those of us beginning this reflection live in a *secular* world, as opposed to a more sacral or traditional society of some generations ago. Many sociologists have written extensively over the last twenty-five years about the process of "secularization," so much so that although generally accepted as having some validity, the term has become so vague as to be almost meaningless.[1] In a survey of the sociological literature on the subject, John Coleman has pointed out that of the various qualities attributed to a secular society among sociologists there is a strong convergence: pluralism, relativism, and privatism.[2]

Traditional societies were unified, homogeneous, and monolithic. They were unified in the sense that all aspects of life — work, play, family, the economy, politics, etc. — were bound together (*religere, religio*) into a whole. Their world was in fact a *cosmos,* a unified and ordered whole. It was not fragmented or divided into discrete spheres. What was done in one area such as the economic (hunting or fishing) was related to and integrated with the domestic and religious spheres as well and vice versa. By contrast, a secular society has a plurality of spheres of activity and modes of thinking that are not integrated.

In addition to this plurality of spheres of activity and thinking, there is another sense in which a secular society is pluralistic. There is more than one way to organize and satisfy human needs and instincts. For example, our society tolerates a variety of ways of meeting our sexual needs; indeed, it is far more tolerant of practices that would have been considered deviant in more traditional societies, and even in our own society a few decades ago. We are also aware of and accept a variety of religious traditions and worldviews. We live with a plurality of ethnic and racial traditions, although with what success may be disputed. We enjoy a plurality of cultural expressions in art, music, food, and languages. In the United States this pluralism is taken for granted and lauded as fruit of our tradition of freedom. Not all would agree that such pluralism is an unmitigated good, but, although there is persistent racism and sexism and some recurrent bouts of nativism and chauvinism, no one would dispute that our secular society is in fact pluralistic.

---

1. The term "secularization" is not used here to describe a progressive decline in religious practice as the term is sometimes simplistically employed. Empirical evidence does not seem to confirm such a hypothesis, especially in the United States.

2. John Coleman, "Situation for Modern Faith," *Theological Studies* 39, no. 4 (December 1978): 601–32.

Such an experience of pluralism entails the second characteristic of a secular society: it is relativistic. Where a variety of ways of living, thinking, and acting exist side by side, any one of them is necessarily relativized. We know there is more than one way to be, and, hence, no one way can be absolutized. This relativism is not always consciously acknowledged or expressed, but it is always under the surface and produces a certain amount of anxiety and uncertainty. This atmosphere of relativism, even if unarticulated, casts doubt and suspicion on any claims to absolutism either by individuals or groups within the society. Tolerance of diversity is regarded as a virtue necessary for such a society to exist with any degree of harmony.

Such an experience of relativism in turn engenders the third characteristic of a secular society: privatization. This is perhaps most obvious in the realms of art and religion, which have become merely a matter of taste (*de gustibus*), of personal and private choice. In such areas we are inclined to retreat to what David Tracy refers to as "reservations of the spirit." But privatization is also evidenced in other spheres of life such as family and work. Family life is most often confined to the small nuclear family as opposed to the extended families and village life of more traditional societies. Indeed, we use the word "family" almost exclusively to refer to the nuclear family. Such small families tend to be isolated from relatives and even from neighbors in the large urban and suburban areas in which the vast majority of people live in our society. Work is also privatized in the sense that it has little to do with family life (how many children do not know what their fathers or mothers "do!") and even though carried out in large bureaucratic corporations is so specialized and segmented as to be almost incommunicable to those outside the specialized field.

Further, in a secular society many areas that once would have been considered matters of public policy or of the "common good" are now relegated to private decisions of individuals, such as family planning, sexual preference, or lifestyle. It is still disputed whether some issues or areas, such as abortion and homosexuality, are matters subject to public or private decision. The overall *geist,* however, supports the idea that what you do in the privacy of your own home or bedroom is nobody else's business. The right to privacy is regarded as a sacred right.[3]

There are other characteristics of a secular society that sociologists list but one that is frequently mentioned is the loss of control by institutionalized religion over many areas of human life that it regulated in traditional or more sacral societies. The state has taken control of and

---

3. For a perceptive discussion of this tendency see Richard Sennett, *The Fall of Public Man* (New York: Vintage, 1978), and Christopher Lasch, *The Culture of Narcissism* (New York: Warner Books, 1979).

responsibility for education, health care, regulation of marriage and divorce, etc. In this sense most modern societies, not just Western, are secular societies. The role of religion is greatly reduced compared to most traditional societies. Religion may still persist, as it does in the United States, but it is not the binding and dominating force that it was in traditional societies. Robert Bellah and others have argued that something called "civil religion" has replaced formal religion as this binding force.[4]

Undergirding and abetting these characteristics of a secular society is the sociological phenomenon of worldwide urbanization. The last fifty years have witnessed this not only in the developed countries of the Northern hemisphere, but on a massive scale in the less developed nations. The city of Lima, for example, has grown from a charming colonial city of about four hundred thousand people in the 1940s to a sprawling metropolis of over six million today. *Campesinos* move down from the Andes; thousands arrive every day. Now one-third of the entire population of Peru lives in Lima! This same phenomenon has occurred elsewhere in Latin America, in Africa, and in Asia. More traditional, that is, less secularized cultures, do not seem to have the resources to survive in urban areas. Traditional expressions of religion and ways of being church are only some of the victims of this rapid and massive urbanization.

## Modes of Thinking: Scientific and Historical

Let us turn now to the "modes of thinking" that characterize our society. By "modes of thinking" I mean the forms of knowledge or the unarticulated assumptions that undergird our knowledge. What passes for knowledge in our world? When do we say we "know" something? What counts for knowing? What is called "real"? What is called "true"? In our society, it is safe to say that the dominant forms of thought are scientific, technological, empirical, and objective, as contrasted with poetic, symbolic, personal, and existential. What is or seems to be objective, that is, based on empirical data, is what counts for knowledge in our world. We acknowledge only "hard facts" and statistical data as real knowledge. Insights, intuitions, impressions, or opinions are just that, but not really "knowledge." As Bellah says, "The new metalanguage is the language of facts, proven by scientific method to be truly, objectively there. Most of us, including most of those in the pews of our churches, give an un-

---

4. Robert Bellah, "Civil Religion in America," *Beyond Belief: Essays on Religion in a Post-Traditional World* (New York: Harper & Row, 1970), chap. 9.

thinking priority to the world of scientific fact as the world of the really real."[5]

Our knowledge is basically technical, i.e., geared to control, dominate, or manipulate. We seek knowledge to control our environment, the weather, or sources of food, transportation, and energy. Domination and control — rather than seeking to unravel mystery, create beauty, or delight the imagination and senses — are the goals of our research and exploration. This is not to deny the obvious fact that we do have "pure research" and poetry and art, but merely to say that the *dominant* form of knowledge in our society is scientific, technical, empirical, and objective. We have to *argue* that there is a cognitive aspect to art or religion; it is not taken for granted.

A second characteristic of our way of thinking and knowing is that it is historically conscious. At least since the middle of the nineteenth century, we have become increasingly aware of the historically conditioned character of our knowledge, language, and forms of expression. We are aware of development and change and therefore that all things have a history. The various species evolved, developed, changed; God did not create them as we now know them, contrary to our forebearers. Even those things that were once symbols of stability and immutability such as the Rock of Gibraltar and the very continents themselves have a history of change and movement. We now think in terms of moving tectonic plates rather than the "rock of ages"!

This historically conscious mindset is contrasted with what has been called the "ahistorical" or "classicist" mode of thinking, which assumed and claimed to know eternal or immutable essences, the very *nature* of things. In the classicist mode of thought, any changes were termed "accidents"; change was accidental and relatively unimportant compared to the essences, which were in themselves immutable. If such change, development, evolution is characteristic of nature, must it not also be true of other human experiences? Forms of language, institutions of government, of economy, of work, and other areas of human life also have changed and developed and therefore have a history. Change and development are no longer viewed as mere accidents but as constitutive of all human experience. Consequently, claims to immutability or timelessness just do not ring true in our ears.

An obvious consequence of such a mode of thinking is that we expect more change in the future. Things have changed and have a history and will continue to do so. We do not expect things to last or remain

---

5. Robert N. Bellah, "Christian Faithfulness in a Pluralist World," in Frederic B. Burnham, ed., *Postmodern Theology: Christian Faith in a Pluralist World* (New York: Harper & Row, 1989), 75. Bellah also points out that many contemporary intellectuals, philosophers, and scientists no longer accept this view of science, and I agree. My point is that this is still the *dominant* view of knowledge in our society.

the same. We witness "planned obsolescence" in which our buildings, for example, are designed to be remodeled or replaced in twenty years. We manufacture appliances with a planned life of five or ten years, after which we expect to replace them. "Durable goods" are defined as those designed to last three years or more. We make throwaway pens, cups, razors, and even cameras. Such a "throwaway" mentality seems to apply to personal relationships as well as things. Since we know that we change as persons, it is easy for us to say, "I am no longer the same person I was ten years ago when we were married," and so justify ending the relationship.

All things change; all things are therefore temporary. The notion of permanence, including permanent commitment, no longer has cultural support in such a historically minded society. We expect all things to end, including even the world as we know it — either by nuclear accident or environmental disaster. This is not the eschatological expectation of the ancient world but a purely natural, abiding awareness of our temporality. Again, such a sense of temporality, of change and development, of contingency, may not be consciously articulated or expressed, but it pervades the way we think and undermines any claims to the contrary by individuals or groups, including religious traditions.

In short, our consciousness is historical as opposed to classicist, evolutionary and developmental as opposed to static and permanent, temporary and contingent as opposed to eternal and absolute. We expect more change rather than less, expect all things and relationships to pass away rather than endure. There may be a hankering for permanence and endurance, and we may not particularly like the experience of constant change, but it is an all-pervasive experience and expectation. Some would say that this consciousness so permeates our being as to constitute our identity, our mode of being in the world.

## Conflictual and Interdependent World

Let us turn now from the characteristics of our mode of thinking to some other general features of the world in which we live that condition our reflections on the church. We have come to take for granted that our world is a divided and conflictual one. Although as I write, the division of the world into East and West, communist and capitalist, which has dominated our thinking for the last forty years, seems to have ended, there are other divisions that remain part of our mental furniture: North-South, developed-underdeveloped, center-periphery, oppressor-oppressed, dominant-dependent, haves-havenots. If the Cold War is over, the battle for control of the world's natural resources, such as oil and strategic minerals and other raw materials, will go on. Some form of division and conflict seems inevitable.

Concomitant with this awareness of division and conflict is a growing realization of how interdependent the world really is. The energy crisis of 1973 forced even the economically and militarily powerful nations to realize that they were still dependent on the oil-producing nations and could not ignore the demands of these nations for a fair price for their resources. The Third World debt crisis has forced the bankers and money-managers of the First World to face the fact of mutual interdependence. A one-sided and exploitative form of decision making in the board rooms of Europe and North America is no longer acceptable or feasible. We are just beginning to face the issue of global interdependence in the area of the earth's environment. Issues such as acid rain, the deforestation of the Amazon valley, and the depletion of the ozone layer have consequences that cut across national boundaries and affect us all. There is a growing awareness that such problems can be addressed only by cooperation on an international scale, for which we have no precedents and no real structures.

These are the characteristics of our context in general, sketched in broad strokes. These could certainly be qualified and specified, and there are others that each person could add, but let these suffice to make us aware of the unarticulated assumptions and the modes of thought that dominate our era. Let me turn now more specifically to the United States and then to the Roman Catholic community there.

## THE CONTEXT IN THE UNITED STATES

### Affluence

There are some characteristics of our context that are more particular to the United States and should be brought to our awareness. First, I would suggest the enormous affluence of the vast majority of the population. Even with an intolerable 32.5 million people (or 13.5 percent of the population) living below the poverty level and a seemingly permanent underclass, and with uneven distribution of income, still as a country we live in incredible comfort compared with two-thirds of the world's population.[6] The amount and variety of goods available to the general public astounds many foreign visitors and embarrasses some. The general availability of the necessities of life — of shelter, food, and clothing — is in stark contrast with many areas of the world. The ease of transportation and travel, of communication, of relocation for work or habitation, are all taken for granted in a manner that would amaze much of the present world and most of the past. I do not cite this out

---

6. Figures are from *Poverty in the United States 1987*, bulletin no. 163, issued February 1989 by the U.S. Department of Commerce, 7.

of chauvinistic pride or to suggest that it is an unmitigated good, but merely as a descriptive fact that we frequently forget or ignore. Indeed, astute observers at home and abroad have pointed out that a mindless consumerism and a crass materialism bordering on hedonism are qualities of life in the United States that are, in fact, dehumanizing and hardly universally admired. Nonetheless, the fact is that the country is extraordinarily affluent by comparison with most of the world, and most of the population describes itself as "middle class." Even though 29.6 percent of the personal wealth is controlled by only 2.8 percent of the populace, the overall self-perception is that of a middle-class country.[7]

## Individualism

A second characteristic of U.S. society about which much has been written recently is that we are highly individualistic as opposed to societies that are more community-oriented. The authors of *Habits of the Heart* argue persuasively that this is not just a sociological fact but a "cultural tradition" deeply imbedded in the American psyche.[8] They outline various strands in this tradition but divide it basically into two: "utilitarian individualism, appropriate in the economic and occupational spheres, and expressive individualism, appropriate in private life."[9] These have been variously symbolized by the enterprising young man who goes off to the West to make his fortune all by himself, Horatio Alger or the Marlboro man, and, in the private sphere, Walt Whitman or Henry Thoreau at Walden Pond. Citing de Tocqueville, they distinguish individualism from egoism: "Individualism is more moderate and orderly than egoism, but in the end its results are much the same. 'Individualism is a calm and considered feeling which disposes each citizen to isolate himself from the mass of his fellows and withdraw into the circle of family and friends; with this little society formed to his taste, he gladly leaves the greater society to look after itself.' "[10]

Another way to talk about this phenomenon of individualism in American society is to consider the value we place on our freedom and autonomy. To take just one example, I believe this freedom and autonomy, this highly valued individualism, manifests itself in our attitude toward mass transportation. We all want to go where we want when we want and not be dependent on others. So, we will put up with massive traffic jams and parking problems and pay any price for fuel, so we may

---

7. Cited in the Department of the Treasury, *Statistics of Income Bulletin* 7, no. 4 (Spring 1988): 31.
8. Robert Bellah et al., *Habits of the Heart: Individualism and Commitment in American Life* (Berkeley: University of California Press, 1985), chap. 2.
9. Ibid., 46.
10. Ibid., 37.

drive our own cars and not be dependent on busses or trains. I would suggest that the question is not only the cost of mass transportation or poor planning, but a deep-seated cultural value to be able to come and go with complete freedom and independence. If this is so, it is not surprising that so many issues in our society are framed in terms of the rights of individuals rather than in terms of the community's needs or of the common good. We will draw out the implications of this for our thinking about the church as a community below.

## Therapeutic

A third characteristic of U.S. culture that should be noted for its consequences on our reflections on the church is what Bellah and his coauthors have called the "therapeutic outlook." They argue that "today we are likely to see not only our marriages but also our families, work, community, and society in therapeutic terms."[11] This is an attitude not confined to the small percentage of Americans who see a therapist; rather it is a general outlook on life. It is a way of viewing all human relationships; a unique combination of closeness and distance. "For all its genuine emotional content, closeness, and honesty of communication, the therapeutic relationship is peculiarly distanced, circumscribed, and asymmetrical. Most of the time, one person talks and the other listens. The client almost always talks about himself and the therapist almost never does. The client pays a fee for professional services rendered, making it an economic exchange: the client's money for the therapist's time."[12] The therapeutic model has become the paradigm for all human relationships in our society whether consciously or not. The extended implications of this model for our society are drawn out by Bellah and his associates, but our concern is with its consequences for our reflections on the church and, more particularly, for ministry in the church.

I have drawn heavily on *Habits of the Heart* for this cultural analysis, but there are some problematic aspects to this work. First of all, the authors deliberately confined their research to middle-class Americans, and hence their reflections do not accurately portray the Hispanic or black minorities in our country. Are they equally as individualistic? Is everyone quite so affluent? Are they all so nuclear-family oriented? Has religion been relegated to the private sphere as much as some sociologists have imagined? Given these problematic aspects, nonetheless, I would submit that the general characterization of our society that the

---

11. Ibid., 113.
12. Ibid., 122.

book offers is correct and does influence how we think about ourselves and our church.

## Power, Moralism, and Messianism

A fourth and final feature of contemporary American society that has implications for how we think about the church is the way Americans generally see themselves vis-à-vis the rest of the world. Americans are acutely aware of their power, military, economic, technological, and cultural. They are ambiguous about its use, however. From the beginning, Americans have had a sense of mission, even of messianism. They were a "City Set on a Hill," on an "Errand in the Wilderness," with a "Manifest Destiny" to "Make the World Safe for Democracy," to cite a few familiar slogans. But they have also been wary of foreign entanglements. Historically, the United States has vacillated between isolationism and interventionism.

In addition to this awareness of power and wariness of its use, Americans generally see themselves as the "good guys," on the side of freedom, democracy, and human rights. They have a sense of responsibility to defend these values when and wherever they are threatened, although only the Carter administration explicitly made the defense of human rights part of its foreign policy. Although there have always been critics of this self-righteousness, it was most seriously called into question in the Vietnam war. For the first time, a large percentage of Americans wondered out loud about our national virtue. They want to be and to act morally, and this moral sense is generally presumed to be Judaeo-Christian in origin and form. Seeing themselves as the good guys, Americans expect and want to be liked abroad and care when they are not. In any event, they do expect that the United States will be a major actor on the world stage and on the side of justice and peace. This self-perception is shared by Catholics and Christians generally and affects their self-understanding in relation to the church universal.

## THE CONTEXT OF
## THE ROMAN CATHOLIC COMMUNITY

Let us now turn to the more particular context of the Roman Catholic community in the United States. Nothing could be more significant for the Roman Catholic community than the Second Vatican Council for determining its own self-awareness at this moment in history. Yet there are some factors that antedate the Second Vatican Council that still determine the self-consciousness of the church in the United States. As Andrew Greeley, among others, has pointed out, the Roman Catho-

lic community in the United States is still in some sense an immigrant
church. After all the years of assimilation, there is still a sense of being
guests in a host culture. Although the vast majority of Roman Catholics
are second-, third-, or even fourth-generation immigrants, nonetheless
that memory still pervades the mindset of most American Catholics. In
addition to that legacy, there are a vast number of *recent* immigrants
from Southeast Asia and Central and South America who are Roman
Catholics. The Hispanic population in this country is predicted to com-
prise about half of all Roman Catholics by the year 2000. However much
the Irish and Germans of the middle of the nineteenth century may have
assimilated to American culture, there is still a significant segment of
the Roman Catholic population that perceives itself as recent arrivals
on these shores.

A second characteristic, which might appear to contradict the first
and which Roman Catholics share with the U.S. population as a whole,
is that they are basically middle class. Since World War II the American
Roman Catholic population has moved massively into the middle class,
helped in part by the G.I. Bill, which sent many to college who otherwise
would not have made it there. They have also moved into the upper ech-
elons of business, the arts, and education, which had previously been
closed to them.[13]

By the time of the Second Vatican Council, American Catholics had
assimilated to the society and culture of the United States, a condition epitomized by the election of the first Roman Catholic president,
John F. Kennedy. While the symbolism should not be exaggerated, it was
a landmark in the "at-homeness" of American Catholics. The concomitant acceptance of Pope John XXIII by many non-Catholics who would
otherwise have found the papacy unacceptable made Catholics feel like
"real Americans" in a way that had eluded them as late as 1928. From the
beginning of the American experiment, Roman Catholics had lived with
the tension between learning what it meant to be American and being
Catholic.[14] By the early 1960s, they felt that they had finally figured out
what it meant to be American. At that very moment, with the beginning
of the Second Vatican Council, what it meant to be Roman Catholic became increasingly problematic. What had always been clear and distinct
was no longer so. I would respectfully submit that the Second Vatican
Council precipitated a crisis in the self-understanding of the American
Catholic community that has yet to be resolved.

Why was the Second Vatican Council such a traumatic (not too

---

13. We will discuss this in greater detail in chapter 10, but in general see Wade Clark
Roof and William McKinney, *American Mainline Religion: Its Changing Shape and Future*
(New Brunswick, N.J., and London: Rutgers University Press, 1987).

14. Jay P. Dolan, *The American Catholic Experience: A History from Colonial Times to
the Present* (New York: Doubleday & Co., 1985).

strong a term, I think) event for U.S. Roman Catholics? Since we will treat the Second Vatican Council at some length later in chapter 6, our purpose here is only to describe the context of our reflections on the church. The council introduced massive changes in practices, attitudes, and structures that had an immediate impact on the daily lives of Roman Catholics. Although there had been a fair amount of preparation on the level of theology in such areas as liturgy, ecumenism, and biblical studies, still the changes introduced by the council were sudden and unexpected by most practicing Roman Catholics. In the case of the liturgy, for example, arguments had been offered for years in favor of maintaining the use of Latin, saying that this preserved the universal character of Catholicism since one could go anywhere in the world and hear the same Mass; it was equally unintelligible everywhere! Further, Latin was another indication of the permanence and immutability of the faith. However much or little these arguments persuaded, when the vernacular was suddenly introduced, Catholics felt the loss of this vaunted universality and immutability. Some said that the church was being "Protestantized" since the Reformers had called for the use of the vernacular 450 years earlier and the Counter-Reformation had made a point of denying it!

Similarly, the Second Vatican Council's Constitution on the Liturgy urged that greater emphasis be placed on the liturgy of the word, the proclamation of Scripture and the homily, and recalled the nature of the Mass as a communal meal and not *just* a sacrifice. Hence it turned the altar to face the people rather than the wall and reintroduced the greeting of peace, usually, in the United States, in the form of a handshake.

Other forms of practical piety such as benediction, novenas, the rosary, and weekly confession seemed to, if not die of their own weight, at least quietly fade away. I would suggest that in fact they were quickly replaced by other forms of popular piety such as *cursillos*, charismatic prayer groups, marriage encounters, directed retreats for laypersons, and so on. But the suddenness and the lack of theological understanding for changes in eucharistic piety, for example, contributed in fact to a very unsettling and disconcerting experience for most Roman Catholics.

If the vast majority were unprepared for these changes in popular piety, they were even less prepared for changes in basic attitudes. I want to suggest three major shifts in attitudes that are difficult to document but that are nonetheless real. The first is a change in attitude from a sense of mystery to one of demystification and desacralization. This was experienced by the average Catholic in very practical terms: people were encouraged to talk, to greet one another in church, where before silence was the appropriate behavior in a "sacred place"; one need no longer

kneel at the consecration of the Mass; one could stand. The altar rail
was removed, thus taking away the clear line of demarcation between
the sacred and the profane realms. People were allowed to touch sacred things that had heretofore been prohibited to the noninitiated, as
with communion in the hand and offering the chalice; the veil was removed from the tabernacle — remember? As already mentioned, the
liturgy was now in the vernacular, automatically removing some of the
sense of mystery that Latin had preserved. Persons and things that had
been reverenced as sacred were now available to all the baptized. Things
were demystified and desacralized.

Second, although this term may be a little too strong, there were
tendencies toward democratization and greater participation. Although
the council spoke of collegiality only with regard to the college of bishops, it was quickly transferred to other levels of church organization.
If the pope could be expected to share governance with the episcopal
college, could we not equally expect the bishop to share governance
with his priests and the local pastor to share governance with a parish council? People were encouraged to participate in the life of the
church at all levels, whether or not we actually had the structures to facilitate this participation. The council had stressed that ministry in the
church was one of service, *diakonia,* not domination or the exercise
of power. It is not surprising, then, that people expected their pastors
to serve, not rule. The pastors, on all levels, had not been prepared
by their training or by their theology for this newly conceived role and
were frequently, though not always, reluctant to share responsibility and
power. Pastors often imposed the reforms of Vatican II with as much
authoritarian gusto as they had used in disciplining their flocks prior
to Vatican II.

The third major attitudinal shift introduced by Vatican II was an
unaccustomed "openness to the world." Throughout the nineteenth
and early twentieth centuries, as we will see, the church had reacted
with fear to developments in the modern world. Now, suddenly the
world was no longer seen as threatening, and, indeed, there was
something to be gained by dialog with it, as well as with Protestants,
non-Christians, and atheists. In effect, Vatican II said there *is* salvation
outside the church! For years, even centuries, since the Reformation
Roman Catholics had been schooled to avoid any contaminating contact with those of other religious traditions, to avoid *communicatio
in sacris* (participation in religious rites of non-Catholics), and certainly not to discuss serious religious issues with them. Now, suddenly,
they were encouraged to dialog with all those groups they had been
socialized to shun. There was no preparation for such a reversal of
course. In fact, there was no preparation for understanding change
at all!

Accompanying these shifts in practices and attitudes were incipient structural changes. The council urged greater participation in the governance of the whole church by the episcopacy, so Pope Paul VI created the Synod of Bishops as a consultative body. At the time, many thought that this was just the first step toward something like a legislative structure in the church. On the more local level, there were priests' senates or priests' councils and diocesan personnel boards that made decisions, or at least strongly advised the bishop, on appointments in the diocese — a realm that had previously belonged to the bishop alone. In parishes, pastors were expected to form parish councils and to seek the advice of parishioners with training and expertise in financial and other matters that, again, had been the private preserve of the pastors. Cooperation and collaboration, rather than top-down decision making, became the expected model.

The renewed emphasis that the council placed on the local church provided the impetus for such other still-emerging and controverted structures as national and regional episcopal conferences and base communities (*comunidades eclesiales de base*), of which we will say more later. In any case the expectations ran ahead of the structural changes and of the Roman Catholic community's ability to assimilate these changes.

Vatican II raised hopes and expectations, not all of which were fulfilled, and that spelled frustration for some. It also raised fears, not all of which were fulfilled, and that led to anxiety and uncertainty. The council precipitated a rapidity of change in an institution that had made an apologetic point of remaining the same! It urged accommodation and adaptation to the modern world, when only a century before such accommodation had been declared *anathema* (*Syllabus of Errors,* 1864). Whether or not the council should be called a reformation or a revolution, these changes in practices, attitudes, and structures constituted a major reversal of course. Thus, I believe, to call it a traumatic event in the consciousness of Roman Catholics is not unwarranted.

Although I have been focusing on the effects of the Second Vatican Council on the Roman Catholic community, I think the council had an impact on the whole Christian church. The ecumenical thrust of the council gave impetus to the bilateral dialogues and to much greater cooperation and association with other Christian communities. The context of our reflections on the church is a much more ecumenical one today than it would have been before Vatican II. It is impossible for us today to think only in narrowly Roman Catholic terms.

## IMPLICATIONS FOR OUR REFLECTIONS
## ON THE CHURCH

If, in fact, our world is as I have described it, i.e., secular, pluralistic, relativistic, and privatized; if, in fact, we think in a mode that is accurately described as scientific, technological, empirical, objective, and historically conscious; if, in fact, we expect change and development rather than permanence; if we take it for granted that our world is a divided and conflictual one, yet at the same time increasingly aware of our global interdependence, and responsibility — what are the implications for our thinking about the community called church?

If we, in the United States, are basically an immigrant population that has recently moved into the middle class; if we, as North Americans are especially individualistic, particularly concerned about our freedom and autonomy; if, in fact, our approach to both personal and community relations is aptly described as "therapeutic"; and if we see ourselves as actors on the world stage — what are the implications for our thinking about the community called church?

If, we as Roman Catholics, have been so traumatized by the experience of the Second Vatican Council that we suffer from frustration, fear, anxiety, and uncertainty; if we now live in a demystified, desacralized world; if, in fact, we are still struggling to be both American and Catholic, to incorporate the democratic experience into our Roman Catholicism; if we are learning to live with a changing and developmental view of reality — what are the implications for our reflections on the community called church? I want to suggest several as a preliminary starting point.

In a secular world, not only can we not take the existence and importance of the *church* for granted; we cannot take the existence and importance of *religion* for granted. Secularization is not just an objective phenomenon, as we will see in the next chapter, but a subjective one. We have internalized the perceptions of a secularized world, so that even we Christians who are reflecting on the self-understanding of the Christian community are not free from the effects of the secularization process in our own consciousness. Hence, we must come to some understanding of the nature and function of religion before we can discuss the self-understanding of the church. We are all too aware of the alternative visions of human life offered by Marxism, secular humanism, or a certain scientific positivism, and, indeed, we have consciously or unconsciously appropriated at least some aspects of these alternative worldviews. Hence, the apologetic argument for the importance and meaningfulness of religion is for our *own* benefit as well as that of non-Christians.

Those characteristics of a secular world described above — pluralism, relativism, and privatism — have also been internalized and are part of the mental furniture with which we approach our reflections on the church. A commitment to the Christian community is automatically problematic for those of us who are aware that there is more than one way to be, pluralism *ipso facto* makes commitment difficult. The relativization of any absolute claim by the church also makes commitment to it problematic for contemporary Christians. As we said above, absolutes are not culturally acceptable or intellectually very credible. The consequence is what we have called privatization; any commitment is a matter of personal choice, of taste, and nothing more. Hence, the claim of the community called church that Jesus is Lord, the final and absolute revelation of God, seems on the face of it to be excessive and unwarranted.

When we turn to the modes of thinking that dominate our culture — scientific, technological, empirical, and objective — we can see that a religion that claims to be mysterious, whose most fundamental affirmation, that Jesus was raised from the dead, is neither empirically verifiable nor falsifiable, can be dismissed as irrelevant to the "real" world. Other religious claims as well have come to be regarded as tautologies or, at best, expressions of emotional states or behavioral attitudes, but certainly not cognitive claims.

We have already indicated that a church that claims some kind of permanence and immutability is problematic in an age that assumes that change rather than immutability is the condition of the world. Similarly, the language of "divine origin," or *jus divinum*, is not at home in an empirically, scientifically, technologically oriented culture. These dominant thought forms also impel us to ask rather empirical questions about the history of the church and its workings today. We find theoretical or theological explanations of a pope's or a bishop's actions not wholly satisfying or credible. Further, the historical consciousness that characterizes our age reinforces such questions and forces us to situate the church in its context in each age and place. We are all too aware that the church, and not just a theological position, has been influenced by historical factors even in our own lifetime, e.g., its behavior in Germany in World War II or its posture in the Philippines at the end of the Marcos regime. We are ineluctably historically conscious, and hence any presumption that the church is above and beyond historical influences is unacceptable.

In a world that is divided and conflictual yet globally interdependent, we cannot accept the claims of the church in the First World as other than limited and distorted in relation to the Third World. Nor can we think that the church in the United States or Germany can go its own way independently of what is happening in Asia or Central America. These other cultures and religious traditions have seeped into our consciousness, and we cannot ignore them in our reflections on the community called church. We are aware that any assertions we make as Christians in the United States may have to be qualified by the experience of Christians in other continents as well as by the other world religions.

Having said this, however, we must recall the middle-class mindset that we share with most North Americans. Most of us who would engage in this reflection on the church are relatively comfortable materially speaking, relatively well educated, relatively unaffected by violence or disease. Thus, our appreciation of the experience of the Third World referred to above is, at best, a "notional" one, to use Newman's terminology. We are not necessarily representative of the blacks or Hispanics even in our own world. And we may have to recognize that, in fact, we have become more than a little materialistic and consumer-oriented.

Another characteristic of contemporary American society that affects our reflections on the community called church is the individualism described by Bellah and his colleagues. This cultural individualism, deeply embedded in the tradition, makes it difficult to think about or place high priority on community as such. Community is not something that is taken for granted in our society; it is something that must be striven for, something to be achieved. For many reasons, we do not assume that we *belong* to a community; rather, we have to construct one. The problem is on what basis are we to construct such a community. In another day and age, in more traditional societies, individuals had no doubt that they belonged to a community. Rather, they were at pains to free themselves from being absorbed in the community and to achieve some identity as individuals. We will discuss this more later, but one example is the expectation (excessive, I think) that the liturgy is or should be the main basis for building community in parishes in the United States. The liturgy may very well *contribute* to a sense of community in the church, but it cannot be the sole basis for building a community that lacks other bonds.

American individualism is further abetted by the mobility of the population, by age segmentation even within the family (e.g., people tend to spend more time with their peers than together as a family), and by the luxury of vast physical space that allows us to go off by ourselves and be alone, as contrasted with the physical closeness and crowdedness of a country like Japan. With such factors in the background and the mythos that is the base of our cultural individualism, community is hard to come by. Any reflection on the church as a Christian community is filtered through the lens of American individualism.

The third characteristic of U.S. culture to which we have referred, the so-called therapeutic approach, also has its impact on our thinking about the church, especially with regard to ministry. The therapeutic approach provides a model for interpersonal relationships in community that is a unique combination of closeness and distance. In the therapeutic model, one person pays a fee for professional services rendered. It is not a model of equal partners in dialogue; rather one speaks for his or her own benefit and pays the other to listen and react. In the American tradition discussed above it is utilitarian, but now "psychological benefits have replaced economic ones."[15] The relationship is a contractual one, as opposed to those other bases of human relationships in more traditional societies such as kinship, civic friendship, or religious commitment, not to mention service to another. The therapeutic model of human relationships is "at once intimate and instrumental."[16] How one thinks about a community called church, then, will be influenced by this model of human relationships. If "the purely contractual structure of the economic and bureaucratic world is becoming an ideological model for personal life," then the expectations of what a church should be will definitely be altered.

When it comes to an understanding of ministry in the Christian community, the therapeutic model suggests that ministers should be skilled healers with certain intrapersonal communication and listening skills and that the ultimate goal of the minister's work with individuals is their self-fulfillment rather than any kind of discipleship or apostleship. The model Christian becomes one who is self-fulfilled rather than the self-emptying one presented in Philippians 2! When such an implication is articulated, many of us would not accept it as our model. But Bellah and his colleagues are arguing that in fact it is a cultural model that has surreptitiously penetrated our middle-class society. We have, to some extent, absorbed this model, consciously or not.

These characteristics of U.S. culture — that it is secular, hence pluralistic, relativistic, and privatized, that it is highly individualistic, and that the therapeutic model pervades our individual and communal relationships — make the church problematic for us as North Americans.

For Roman Catholics, the radical reversal of course initiated by the Second Vatican Council only intensifies the problems posed by our social and cultural context. Changes in practices, attitudes, and structures, which came rapidly and without adequate preparation, have left many people very ambivalent about the church. The lack of clarity and certainty (corresponding to the relativism and historical consciousness in the culture as a whole) was felt most keenly by those who had committed themselves to the church most deeply — clergy and religious. The massive exodus from the priesthood and religious life after Vatican II is the most obvious example of this ambivalence. Many lay people also ceased to "practice" Catholicism, and we have seen a whole genre

---

15. Bellah et al., *Habits of the Heart*, 134.
16. Ibid., 122.

of literature about what it was like to grow up Roman Catholic before the council. The phenomenon of the "returning Catholic" has become widespread as I write.

For those Roman Catholics who strongly welcomed the changes of the council, who saw it as just the beginning, and who had high expectations of a soon-to-be-reunited Christian church spurred by the council's Decree on Ecumenism, there has been a dashing of hopes and frustration with the slow implementation of many of the council's initiatives. Under the present pope it has become common to speak of a "Restoration." For these Roman Catholics the church remains problematic.

The reign of Pope John Paul II has given encouragement to those who feel that the church needs to recover the pre–Vatican II sense of unity, certainty, and centrality of authority. These people feel that some of the changes initiated by the council have gotten out of hand and some retrenchment is necessary. For these Roman Catholics too the church is problematic.

In summary, all of the characteristics of our cultural context in general, of the United States in particular, and of the Roman Catholic community after Vatican II, make the community called church problematic. The source of the problem is the culture itself. But there are also problems with the church that arise from the personal experiences of individuals.

We are all familiar, I am sure, with such experiences: the insensitive priest or pastor who shows more concern for the Sunday collection than for the daily needs of his people, the overly strict or harsh confessor, the rigid discipline of some parochial school teacher, the unecumenical approach to mixed marriages, and other similar personal experiences. All such experiences contribute to making the church problematic for our contemporaries.

In addition to such individual and personal experiences, there is what I think is the most fundamental problem with the church today — the seeming contradiction between what the institutional church says and preaches and what it does, between theory and practice. Again, each of us has had some experience of such contradictions, but to mention some of the most obvious: the lack of social justice in the treatment of women and ethnic and racial minorities within the church itself, the lack of fairness and openness in the Vatican's dealings with theologians and scholars who articulate a view other than the one prevailing in Rome, the exercise of authority on many levels in a manner contradicting the Gospel injunction to serve and not to lord it over others as the pagans do, the scandal of the institutional church aligning itself with dictators and totalitarian governments.

For all of these reasons, cultural, personal, and institutional, the church is problematic for those of us who are reflecting on it. Why, then, bother? For Christians, it is a matter of our own self-understanding and, hence, is unavoidable. For non-Christians, the church remains one of the major forces shaping Western culture and is, at least, an object of curiosity. We are approaching this reflection as Christians, however, and so it is our own self-understanding as a community that will occupy us in the rest of this volume. How we go about this reflection will be the subject of the next chapter.

## RECOMMENDED READINGS

Bellah, Robert, Richard Madsen, William M. Sullivan, Ann Swidler, Steven M. Tipton. *Habits of the Heart: Individualism and Commitment in American Life*. Berkeley: University of California Press, 1985.

Roof, Wade Clark, and William McKinney. *American Mainline Religion: Its Changing Shape and Future*. New Brunswick, N.J., and London: Rutgers University Press, 1987.

# Chapter 2

# *The Method of Our Reflections*

Our reflections on the church are conditioned by our social and cultural context, as sketched in the previous chapter, but the method of our reflections is determined by the object of those reflections, that is, the church itself. I use the word not to refer to a particular local church or to a specific denominational group, but to the whole Christian community.

Whatever else may be said about the church, it is at least a *human* group, a social reality. As a human social group it may be understood like other human social realities with the help of social theory and social science categories. This particular social group has existed for some time, however, and therefore has a history. It is not only a human social reality; it is also a *historical* reality and hence can be understood with the aid of historical-critical methods. The church has a history, a tradition, a sedimented memory, and a full understanding of it requires a historical as well as a sociocritical approach.

Unlike most other human social groups, however, the Christian community has always understood itself to have a relationship to the transcendent, to God, as well as to the rest of the world. Other international social realities, like the United Nations, Rotary International, or IBM, do not include such a transcendent relationship in their self-understanding. Thus the church is not only a social and a historical reality; it is also a *theological* reality. Hence, a study of the various theological symbols as employed and transformed by early Christians is also necessary and appropriate for a full understanding of the community called church. To concentrate on only one of these approaches would be reductionism, whether sociological reductionism, historical reductionism, or theological reductionism. No one of

23

these methodological approaches would do justice to the object of our reflections because it is a social, a historical, and a theological phenomenon.[1]

I understand ecclesiology to be the theological self-understanding of the Christian community. For a complete ecclesiology, several levels of explanation are necessary and appropriate. An experience of church like the Second Vatican Council can be understood in different ways: for example, as "a power struggle between conservatives and progressives" and the sociological "laws" of power and conflict may be employed; or it can be understood as the "action of the Holy Spirit" and the theological categories of grace and providence and the discernment of spirits may be used; or, finally, the council can be understood as a historical event and the categories of reformation or revolution or paradigm shift may be invoked to understand it.

In contrast to the study of natural phenomena, the study of human phenomena, whether individuals or social groups, includes the data of conscious human agents. Social realities such as the church are not the products of impersonal evolutionary forces like the geological formation of mountains and volcanoes. Social groups are the results of conscious decisions by self-conscious agents. Hence, we have included the term "self-understanding" in our definition of ecclesiology. In attempting to understand the church, we must include the self-understanding of that group itself. The church is what it is today, in part, because of Paul's understanding that the Gospel was to be extended to the Gentile world and not confined to the Jews of Palestine or the diaspora. It was a conscious decision on his part based on his own understanding which has forever after determined the self-understanding of the Christian community as having a universal mission. Further, this decision of Paul's, with which the group of disciples concurred after some discussion, was not based on a shrewd instinct for the sociological survival of a group depending on its ability to adapt to its environment but on a theological understanding of the message of Jesus. Hence, I have said that it is the theological self-understanding that constitutes ecclesiology. It is not merely a study in the sociology of religion.

---

1. For a fuller explanation and justification of the use of social theory in ecclesiology see Joseph A. Komonchak, "Ecclesiology and Social Theory: A Methodological Essay," *The Thomist* 45 (1981): 262–83; on the historical-critical method see Roger Haight, S.J., "Historical Ecclesiology," part 1, *Science et Esprit* 39, no. 1 (1987): 27–46, and "Historical Ecclesiology," part 2, *Science et Esprit* 39, no. 3 (1987): 345–74.

## SELF-UNDERSTANDING:
## DIFFERENTIATION, HISTORY, VISION

The self-understanding of a human grouping is analogous to the self-understanding of an individual. It is an ongoing process never achieved once and for all, but always changing and developing in response to new experiences and new situations. How do individuals come to some self-understanding? I would suggest three main constituents, although there are others and other ways of talking about these factors. First, we come to some self-understanding by differentiating ourselves over against others. This is manifested in two ways. Negatively by coming to know who we are *not:* I am American, not Asian; I am white, not black; I am English, not Italian; I am male, not female; I am Roman Catholic, not Jewish. This over-againstness is communicated by sheer naming, by stories of what it means to be American, but also by repeated actions — Catholics go to Mass on Sundays, Jews go to synagogue on Saturdays, and so on. This self-understanding is also manifested to us by the way others treat us, what Charles Cooley years ago termed the "looking-glass self." If I am black, my self-understanding will be determined by the way whites treat me — either by overt discrimination in public places or more subtle forms of nonacceptance. If I am female, my self-understanding will be determined by the expectations others have of how I should behave, how I should dress, the type of career to pursue, the places where I am not welcome. This experience of the "looking-glass self" takes place as we assume different roles. I learn what it means to be a doctor, for example, by the way nurses defer to me, by patients' expectations that I know all there is to know about sickness, and by the general public's sense of respect. I learn who I am as a mother or father by the expectations society communicates to me, by the demands of my child, by the comments of other family members, and by the changes in relationships already established — consider how a husband and wife gradually begin to refer to one another as "mom" and "dad."

The second factor contributing to one's self-understanding is one's own history, family, and ethnic background. We learn who we are by hearing stories of how our grandfather emigrated from Ireland fleeing British persecution or from Italy during the Depression. We learn what it means to be an American by hearing stories of our history, of the Revolution, the Founding Fathers, the larger-than-life figures of George Washington, Thomas Jefferson, and Abraham Lincoln. As we grow older, our own personal history with its achievements and failures, as well as family and ethnic history, become part of our self-understanding.

The third factor involved in the self-understanding of an individual, I want to suggest, is a vision, an ideal, a goal for the future. The college student who aspires to be a doctor understands herself in the light of this goal. Her actions are determined by this future vision; she stays up late studying, parties less than her non-premed classmates. The emigrant who leaves his native land to seek a better life understands himself in the light of this vision. Thus, not only the realized past but the future possibilities contribute to the self-understanding of an individual.

The self-understanding of a social group is analogous to that of an individual and the three factors mentioned above are analogously part of the process of forming a communal consciousness. Let me use the example of the process of self-understanding that took place in forming the United States as a nation. It began when the pilgrims employed biblical symbols to understand themselves over against the world from which they had come. In a sermon aboard the *Arbella* before setting foot in New England, John Winthrop used the symbol of "Covenant" to express the social compact the pilgrims had among themselves as well as the religious compact they had with God. They understood themselves to be "a city set upon a hill," a beacon of light and a model for others. They had a sense of newness, of beginning something fresh, and of innocence, which they expressed in the symbol of Adam. The American was the "New Adam." They understood themselves as having a mission expressed in the title of Perry Miller's book, *Errand into the Wilderness*. They thought themselves to be engaged in a "noble experiment" and to be doing "God's work."[2]

This self-understanding of the emerging nation was formed in contradistinction to the "old world" from which they had emigrated, yet it was based in their religious history, and it clearly involved a vision, a goal, of what they were about in this New World. These elements have remained in varying forms throughout the later history of the country. The sense of a covenant made and broken was echoed in Lincoln's second inaugural address when he tried to make sense of the scourge of the Civil War by seeing it as a "woe due to those by whom the offense came" and that this breaking of the covenant can only be mended when "every drop of blood drawn with the lash shall be paid by another drawn with the sword."[3] The sense of newness and of a mission was expressed in the later language of "Manifest Destiny" and "Making the World Safe for Democracy."

No doubt such a description needs to be further qualified and the interpretation could be disputed, but I am merely suggesting that we

---

2. For a fuller explication of this emerging American self-understanding see such works as, R. W. B. Lewis, *The American Adam* (Chicago: University of Chicago Press, 1955); Perry Miller, *Errand into the Wilderness* (New York: Harper & Row, 1956); Seymour Martin Lipset, *The First New Nation* (Garden City, N.Y.: Doubleday & Co., 1963); and Sidney E. Mead, *The Lively Experiment* (New York: Harper & Row, 1963).

3. Robert Bellah, "Civil Religion in America," *Beyond Belief: Essays on Religion in a Post-Traditional World* (New York: Harper & Row, 1970), 168–89.

can see how the self-understanding of a social group involves the same
three factors as the self-understanding of an individual: distinction over
against the other, previous background and history, and a vision or goal
for the future. We will see in the next chapter how this developed in the
actual historical formation of the community called church.

## HOW TO UNDERSTAND SELF-UNDERSTANDING

In the next four chapters we will retrieve critically and creatively the
historical unfolding of the church's self-understanding. In order to
understand and analyze that history we will employ both sociological
and theological categories. The rest of this chapter, then, will introduce
briefly some of these categories.

### Sociological Understanding

Just as the community called church is a human social reality, so is it also
a product of human activity. Like everything else in society and culture,
the church is socially constructed. That does not mean to suggest that it
is artificial, but merely that it is not a product of nature; it depends upon
human activity. There are three moments in the social construction of
a social reality: (1) *externalization,* which is the outpouring of human
physical and mental activity, of human values and meanings; (2) *objec-
tivation,* in which the products of this human activity attain the status
of facticity external to and other than the human producers themselves;
and (3) *internalization,* in which these same objectivized products are
reappropriated into subjective consciousness.[4]
   We are all born into an already constructed social world, but this
world is continually produced and reproduced when parents communicate to children the structure of their world. For example, as soon as
a mother designates another child as one's "cousin" and another lady
as one's "aunt" and another man as one's "uncle," the social reality of
family is constructed for a person. This may be elaborated as instructions are given not to fight with your cousin or that you cannot marry
your cousin and that there is some special relationship between you
and your uncle. As the child grows up the designation of "cousin" takes
on an aura of facticity — she *really is* my cousin; it is not perceived as
something arbitrarily produced by one's parents. "Cousinhood" is an
*objective* reality. And insofar as I perceive myself as *really and truly* a

---

   4. In this section I am relying heavily on Peter L. Berger and Thomas Luckmann, *The
Social Construction of Reality* (Garden City, N.Y.: Doubleday & Co., 1966), and Peter L.
Berger, *The Sacred Canopy: Elements of a Sociological Theory of Religion* (Garden City,
N.Y.: Doubleday & Co., 1969).

cousin, I have internalized this social reality. Now I *really am* a cousin; I am not pretending to be one. This process of subjective appropriation, or internalization, is called *socialization*.

Not only is the social world humanly constructed; it must be socially maintained. The growing child may begin to question why she cannot marry her cousin, and then various reasons will be given, perhaps, in very simple maxims or proverbs at first, but later on there will be more theoretical explanations involving, for example, genetic theory. These explanations for maintaining the social world are called *legitimation*. The social reality cannot be maintained merely by verbal explanations no matter how theoretically sophisticated. There must also be an on-going acceptance and lived experience of these social realities. Others must recognize and act like cousins too. The other families we know must also have cousins, aunts, and uncles. This ongoing lived experience is called a *plausibility structure,* or the social base for maintaining reality. Should one move into another society where marriage between cousins is not only not forbidden but positively mandated, the plausibility of our world of "cousinhood" may be called into question; it may lose its plausibility or credibility. We may see that there is another way to organize family relationships and our own world of "cousinhood" will appear less "real" and more arbitrary. Living in a pluralistic situation entails a challenge to the plausibility of any one social world, as we saw in chapter 1.

Threats to the plausibility of our socially constructed world may come not only from alternative and competing "realities," but also from anomalies even within our experienced world. To pursue the example above, we may know of someone within our social group who in fact did marry her cousin without any ill effects. This may be passed off as an exception so rare it need not trouble us, or it may appear as a counterinstance that does call the reality of our social world into question. Because of the constant possibility of such counter-evidence, the socially constructed world is precarious. Hence, there is always a need to protect the plausibility structure and to reinforce the legitimations.

As mentioned above, there are various levels of legitimation, ranging from the simple designation in language, through maxims, proverbs, and folktales, to sophisticated theoretical explanations that may be categorized as "science." The final legitimation is on the level of ultimacy: nature itself, the natural law, the will of the gods, God's will, *jus divinum,* or divine order.

The applicability of these sociological categories to the understanding of the church as a social reality should be fairly obvious, and we will be using them throughout the rest of the book. At this point, let us briefly illustrate their application to the church.

Like any other social reality, the church, being a subsociety, is socially constructed. The meanings, values, and understandings of those who had an immediate experience of Jesus of Nazareth were externalized into the world in forms of behavior and modes of action and speech. The records we have tell us that their lives took on the mode we now call "discipleship" and "apostleship"; they became followers of Jesus and continued to preach what he had preached. They must have perceived themselves as a community, for they stayed together and worked together and celebrated a communal meal together. They apparently continued to perform actions that Jesus had exemplified, e.g., "baptism." These externalized meanings, values, and understandings became routinized and institutionalized over time. They gradually became objectivated and took on a reality of their own. Others became socialized into this early group and internalized these meanings, values, and understandings as their own. They too became disciples and apostles. They became "Christians." These Christians eventually had to explain themselves to others, their peers who did not perceive Jesus in the same way, and to themselves as well. They legitimated themselves by appealing to the Hebrew Scriptures as foretelling the events surrounding Jesus of Nazareth, as did the disciples on the road to Emmaus, and by seeing themselves in continuity with their Jewish ancestors, Abraham, Isaac, and Jacob. As these communities spread and multiplied they provided a plausibility structure, a social base, which made this communal life credible and acceptable both to themselves and to others. The ultimate legitimation was to understand themselves and their mission as the work of God, continued through the Holy Spirit.

These sociological processes posed some particular difficulties for the early Christian community, however. As the originating experience of Jesus and his followers became institutionalized, the fervor and self-sacrificing response of the early Christians became mixed with other more self-interested motivations such as power, prestige, and security. As prayer and worship became ritualized, the symbolic mediations became routinized and somewhat distanced from the interior feelings and dispositions of the believers. As the organization developed, it became more elaborate and complex and tended toward legalism. As the Christian community became part of the establishment at the time of Constantine, for example, the call to personal conversion became enmeshed in various forms of social and political pressure. In short, the "routinization of charisma," to use Max Weber's phrase, entails a series of tensions that we will see throughout the history of the church: between spirit and structure, between freedom and authority, between unity and diversity, between withdrawing from the world and action within the world. Such tensions are inevitable in a social group that claims a relationship to the transcendent.[5]

As mentioned above, the community called church can be understood on several levels and the sociological is only one. The use of sociological categories does not prejudice understanding the church on other levels. Indeed, to confine our analysis to the sociological level would be reductionistic. The full understanding requires theological categories as well. As Edward Schillebeeckx has said, "What is described in human experiential terms and sociologically analysed must ultimately also be expressed in the language of faith. This means that the religious language of faith becomes empty and meaningless unless it contains a recognizable reference to real human experiences and the autonomous structures implied in them."[6]

## Theological Understanding

To speak of theological "categories" is not quite accurate. Theological understanding takes place in and through *images and symbols*. Thus, in the example of the Pilgrims' self-understanding cited above, they used the biblical symbols of "covenant" and "Adam" to express their new situation. In the example of the first disciples of Jesus, they employed Hebrew scriptural symbols such as "Messiah" and "Son of Man" to understand their experience of Jesus. Later, when reflecting on who they were as a group, they appealed to the symbols of "People of God" and "Body of Christ," to mention just two.

But talking about images and symbols as the media of theological understanding in a culture whose dominant forms of knowledge are scientific, technological, objective, and empirical can be a source of confusion and misunderstanding. Much has been written in recent years about symbols, metaphor, and symbolic mediation in theology. A brief summary of how symbols function in theology may be helpful.[7]

Paul Tillich argued that symbolic language alone could speak about the ultimate or the transcendent, for symbols point beyond themselves to something else, yet they also participate in the reality to which they

5. For further discussion of these dilemmas see Thomas F. O'Dea, *Sociology and the Study of Religion* (New York: Basic Books, 1970), chap. 13, "Five Dilemmas in the Institutionalization of Religion," 240–55.

6. Edward Schillebeeckx, *Church: The Human Story of God* (New York: Crossroad, 1990), 210–13.

7. From the vast literature on the subject, I am relying most on Paul Tillich, *Systematic Theology*, vol. 1 (Chicago: University of Chicago Press, 1951); Paul Tillich, *Dynamics of Faith* (New York: Harper & Row, 1957), chap. 3; Karl Rahner, "The Theology of the Symbol," *Theological Investigations*, vol. 4 (Baltimore: Helicon Press, 1966); Avery Dulles, S.J., *Models of the Church* (Garden City, N.Y.: Doubleday & Co., 1974); Avery Dulles, S.J. *Models of Revelation* (Garden City, N.Y.: Doubleday & Co., 1983), esp. chap. 9; Thomas Fawcett, *The Symbolic Language of Religion* (Minneapolis: Augsburg, 1971).

point. Symbols open up that level of reality which is otherwise inacces-
sible to us. Both Tillich and Avery Dulles contend that symbols speak
to humans "existentially and find an echo in the inarticulate depths of
his psyche." "Symbols transform the horizons of man's life, integrate
his perception of reality, alter his scale of values, reorient his loyalties,
attachments, and aspirations in a manner far exceeding the powers of
abstract conceptual thought."[8] Symbols cannot just be invented arbitrarily. They must arise from or at least be accepted by the collective
unconscious of the group in which they appear. They must be rooted
in the corporate experience of the social group.

In the religious sphere, we can distinguish various kinds of symbols: (1) cosmic or natural symbols such as the sun, sacred mountains,
water; (2) personal or historical symbols such as Israel or the Davidic
monarchy; (3) artistic symbols such as temples, statues, and icons;
(4) literary symbols or figures of speech such as creation or the fall;
and (5) symbolic actions such as rituals and sacraments. I would add
that all theological language, even what is referred to as "second order"
language such as that regarding justification or transubstantiation, is
symbolic language.

Religious symbolic language expresses the experience of the group
but also evokes a response in the individual member with whose personal experience it must resonate to be effective. Symbols can loose this
relationship to experience and then they cease to function religiously.
They can, as Tillich used to say, die or lie dormant for a time. Symbols are
also polyvalent, or capable of bearing more than one meaning. Hence,
they are rich in layers of meaning, but not very clear, concise, or univocal. Symbols do not exist in isolation but normally are part of a symbol
system whose totality is required for their interpretation. We can therefore, speak of the Christian symbol system or symbolic deposit, which
includes not only the cross, death, and resurrection but a whole host
of related symbols.

Because symbols are polyvalent, or many-layered in meaning, they
require interpretation and invite further reflection. In Paul Ricoeur's
famous phrase, "Symbols give rise to thought." It is the function of theologians to critically reflect on and interpret the religious symbols of
their tradition and relate them to the experience of the community at
a given time. In the case of the theology of the church, or, as I prefer,
the theological self-understanding of the Christian community, there are
many images and symbols that have been employed to illuminate the
experience of that community. Paul Minear has pointed out that, depending on how you count various Greek words, there are more than

---

8. Dulles, *Models of the Church,* 24.

eighty images that refer to the church in the New Testament.[9] In an attempt to bring some order to this plethora of images and to reflect on them critically, Avery Dulles did ecclesiology a real service in his minor classic, *Models of the Church*.

"When an image is employed reflectively and critically to deepen one's theoretical understanding of a reality it becomes what is today called a 'model,'" Dulles says.[10] He then brings together the major images that have played a part in the Christian community's self-understanding under five models or types of church.

The first he calls the "Church as Institution," although I would prefer to call it the "Juridical Model." The basic image underlying this model is that of a political society. In the post-Reformation attempts to defend the visibility of the church, the Counter-Reformation theologian Robert Bellarmine compared the church to the Kingdom of France or the Republic of Venice. Such an analogy stresses the visible and structural elements of the church with the use of the juridical categories of rights and obligations. Such a model emphasizes the hierarchical structure and is clear as to the duties and obligations of both members and ministers. The primary mission of this type of church is to preserve the deposit of faith and protect the members from falling away from the truth thus guarded. This model of church is the one most familiar to Roman Catholics prior to Vatican II; it is epitomized in the teachings of Vatican I and is found in the neo-scholastic textbooks of the nineteenth and early twentieth centuries.

The second model, which Dulles calls the "Church as Mystical Communion," is based on the biblical images of the Body of Christ and the People of God. The primary analogy in this model is organic rather than political. The members of the church are seen as organically interrelated and interdependent (Eph. 4:15) with the head being Christ. The bond of union is the invisible grace of Christ and includes not only the living members on earth, the church militant, but also the saints in heaven, the church triumphant, and those in "purgatory," the church suffering. Thus it is an invisible communion of saints. This organic typology of the church has a long history, beginning with Paul, through Augustine, and right into the nineteenth and twentieth centuries. In 1943 Pius XII published an encyclical, *Mystici Corporis*, which defined the church as the Mystical Body of Christ and identified this with the Roman Catholic church. This imagery, however, has been used by many Protestant theologians, such as Emil Brunner and Dietrich Bonhoeffer, as well. It is

---

9. Paul Minear, *Images of the Church in the New Testament* (Philadelphia: Westminster Press, 1960), 28 and the Appendix, 268–69.
10. Dulles, *Models of the Church*, 27.

found in the documents of Vatican II as expressed in the image of the People of God.

Dulles's third model is the "Church as Sacrament." This model unifies the visibility emphasized in the institutional model and the invisible spiritual quality stressed in the Mystical Communion model. In the Roman Catholic understanding a sacrament is a visible sign of God's grace that makes that grace a present reality. Thus it unites the human and divine elements in the church just as Jesus as the Christ is both human and divine. The church is understood as the continuation of the Incarnation and the continuation in history of Christ's salvific work. "The Church therefore is in the first instance a sign. It must signify in a historically tangible form the redeeming grace of Christ."[11] It is a social or communal sign, not just an individualistic one. Such a model stresses the witnessing activity of Christians and hence requires active participation by the members. This model is found in a number of recent Roman Catholic theologians such as Karl Rahner, Edward Schillebeeckx, Yves Congar, and Latin American liberation theologians, as well as in the documents of Vatican II.

If the sacramental model is predominantly Roman Catholic, Dulles's fourth model, the "Church as Herald," is predominantly Protestant. This model makes the "word" primary and the "sacrament" secondary. It emphasizes faith and proclamation over structure or mystical communion. It is to be found in the theology of Karl Barth, Rudolf Bultmann, and the writings of the World Council of Churches. In this model the church is actually constituted, comes into being, by the word being proclaimed and faithfully accepted. This, of course, gives great emphasis to the local church, where this proclamation and acceptance takes place. The church exists wherever there is a community that believes in Jesus as the Christ. It does not depend on worldwide structures for its existence.

The final group of images that give rise to a way of being church centers on what Dulles terms the "Church as Servant." Stressing the notion of Christ as the Suffering Servant and as the "man for others," this model of church is oriented toward healing, reconciling, and binding up wounds, not only for its own members but for all humanity. The Good Samaritan is a prevailing image for the church. Such an ecclesiology is represented in the writings of Dietrich Bonhoeffer, Pierre Teilhard de Chardin, Harvey Cox, John A. T. Robinson, and Richard McBrien, as well as Vatican II's document on the Church and the Modern World and statements from the World Council of Churches. If the Herald model of being church carries out the injunction to "go forth and preach the gospel to all nations," the Servant model embodies the

---

11. Ibid., 72.

command to feed the hungry, clothe the naked, shelter the homeless, and care for the least of the brethren in order to enter the kingdom of God. This model has been expressed in the churches' concern for social justice and active cooperation with secular organizations for this purpose. Dulles terms this a "secular-dialogic" approach to church-world relationships.[12]

Dulles correctly argues that no one of these various typologies exists in pure form nor is any one adequate to a full understanding of the Christian community. Any actually existing community is more than likely to combine aspects from a number of these models. Nor does he suggest that these are historically sequential — that actual communities went through various stages corresponding to these models. His study is merely helpful in sorting out and organizing the multiplicity of images for the church and their implications for the lived experience of the church.

In a later essay (1980) he suggested a sixth model, which he felt was more appropriate than any of the above for "Imaging the Church for the 1980s" and which he titled "The Church as Community of Disciples."[13] Dulles favors this image for the 1980s, especially in the United States, because it has a firm scriptural basis and corresponds with the contemporary experience of being a minority group in a secular, pluralistic world, much like the experience of the early church. The image of discipleship suggests a response to a call that is both personal and demanding. It implies that faithfulness to the call may require a countercultural stance in a consumer-oriented and self-centered society. Further, the image of discipleship is a "common factor uniting all Christians with one another," and at the same time stresses equality in the church for it "undercuts the illusion that some in the Church are lords and masters."[14] We are all followers of the one Lord and we are all learners as well as teachers.

Dulles does what a good theologian should do — he critically evaluates the use to which these images have been put in the self-understanding of the Christian community and points out the consequences for the life of the church entailed by their adoption. It is to this relationship between the theology and the actual life of the community that we will now turn.

---

12. Ibid., 98.
13. Avery Dulles, *A Church to Believe In* (New York: Crossroad, 1982), chap. 1, 1–18.
14. Ibid., 12.

# RELATIONSHIP OF THEOLOGY
# TO LIVED EXPERIENCE

It should be obvious from our brief summary of Dulles's various models that a community that understands itself primarily, even though not exclusively, as a Herald will put its energies into preaching or proclaiming the Gospel to others. For example, the Church of the Latter-Day Saints, the Mormons, requires its young men to spend two years as missionary preachers. This is seen as essential to what it means to be church. A community that understands itself primarily on the Servant model will engage in activities that directly serve the needs of the homeless, the hungry, and the sick, as do many of the basic ecclesial communities in Latin America or the Catholic Worker movement in the United States. The theology, even if it is not explicit, does have direct consequences for action.

But I want to argue that this is not a one-way street. If you think like a Renaissance prince, you will live like a Renaissance prince. The reverse is also true: if you live like a Renaissance prince you will think like a Renaissance prince. The lived experience of an individual or of a community has an effect on how that community conceives of itself. There is, in other words, a *dialectical* relationship between theology and lived experience. It is as true to say that the theology affects how we behave as it is to say how we behave affects our theology. We said above that human beings externalize their meanings, values, and understandings and produce a social world that takes on an aura of objectivity. This objectivated social world in turn forms the human beings living in it. The relationship is a dialectical one.

Karl Marx argued that the infrastructure, the social base, which for him was almost exclusively conceived in economic terms, produces or determines the superstructure, the level of thinking, or ideation. By now it is generally accepted that the level of ideation also affects the social base. I have deliberately used the vague word "affects" because it is very difficult if not impossible to demonstrate a strictly causal relationship. Many factors contribute to a developing theory or theology besides the lived experience of the one theologizing, and, conversely, there are many other ingredients forming a social structure besides the theology that undergirds it. We will see that in the history of the Christian community its self-understanding was shaped to a great extent by events outside the community itself such as wars, strong political personalities, or economic factors.

This dialectical relationship between theology and its social base in the actual lived experience of a community requires both the sociological and the theological approaches to ecclesiology. There have been attempts in the not too distant past to study the church on a purely theological level, and this has led to an "idealist" ecclesiology — an understanding of what the church should be ideally. But this bore little resemblance to the actual church as we have experienced it in history. Our historically conscious age as well as our proclivity for "facts" make such an idealist ecclesiology unacceptable. Hence, a complete study of the church requires the sociological, the historical-critical, and the theological methods mentioned above. In the next four chapters we will critically survey the historical development of the self-understanding of the Christian community as a necessary component in a complete ecclesiology.

## RECOMMENDED READINGS

Berger, Peter L. *The Sacred Canopy: Elements of a Sociological Theory of Religion*. Garden City, N.Y.: Doubleday & Co., 1969.
Dulles, Avery. *Models of the Church*. Garden City, N.Y.: Doubleday & Co., 1974.

# PART II

# Recalling Our Story

# Chapter 3

# From Kingdom of God to City of God: Jesus to Augustine

The self-understanding of the Christian community includes as one of its constitutive factors its own history or background. Where we come from is part of our self-definition whether consciously appropriated or not. Christianity began in a particular time and a particular place with a particular person, Jesus of Nazareth. All the developments of the Christian community since then have contributed to our present situation and to our present self-understanding.

Our present experience of the community we call church may appear quite different from that of a Galilean peasant of first-century Palestine. This seeming disparity was captured in the early part of this century by Alfred Loisy in his famous, though usually truncated, phrase, "Jesus preached the kingdom, but what came was the church."[1] Loisy was writing to refute the claim of Adolf Harnack that there was little if any relationship between the preaching and expectations of Jesus and the church as it had developed through the ages. This was the view of many persons in the late nineteenth and early twentieth centuries, and even today some would say, "Jesus, yes; the church, no!" How did we get from Jesus to the church we now experience?

In this chapter, then, we will trace the development of the church from Jesus' preaching of the kingdom of God to its emergence as an organized religion and a dominant cultural force in the Roman empire. We will note the gradual development of the community's self-understanding to include the so-called marks of the church, unity,

---

1. Alfred Loisy, *The Gospel and the Church* (Philadelphia: Fortress, 1976), 166.

holiness, catholicity, and apostolicity, and the tensions that these entailed, tensions that persist until today.

## JESUS' PREACHING

Although there is difficulty in determining exactly what sayings in the Gospels may be legitimately attributed to Jesus himself, most New Testament scholars would agree that Mark 1:15 reflects an authentic saying of Jesus: "The time is fulfilled and the kingdom of God is at hand; repent and believe in the gospel." Determining exactly what is meant by the "kingdom of God" is somewhat more difficult. The symbol "kingdom of God" was common in the Jewish theology of that time; it was not exclusive to Jesus. As Norman Perrin said, it was "a symbol with deep roots in the Jewish consciousness of themselves as the people of God . . . within the context of the myth of God active in history on behalf of his people; indeed by the time of Jesus it had come to represent particularly the expectation of a final, eschatological act of God on behalf of his people."[2]

For Jesus, the kingdom of God is not only a future event; it is also already happening. It "is present now even if only in a small way [mustard seed, leaven; Matt. 13:31–33] but for those who perceive its presence the kingdom demands a total commitment [hidden treasure, pearl; Matt. 13:44–46]."[3] Repentance is required because it is not enough just to be born an Israelite to participate in the kingdom; one must also be righteous. The manifestation of the kingdom will involve a judgment in which the righteous will be separated from the others (dragnet, wheat, and chaff: Matt. 13:41–50). Jesus proclaims that the kingdom is inaugurated in his own words and deeds. There is a tension between the "already" and the "not yet" qualities of the kingdom. But for Jesus himself it seems that this tension was to be of very short duration. There are sayings like "Truly, I say to you, there are some standing here who will not taste death before they see the kingdom of God come with power" (Mark 9:1) and others (Luke 21:32; Matt. 10:23) placed on the lips of Jesus by the early church that, as Daniel J. Harrington says, make the conclusion inescapable "that Jesus spoke about the kingdom as coming soon."[4]

---

2. Norman Perrin, *Jesus and the Language of the Kingdom: Symbol and Metaphor in New Testament Interpretation* (Philadelphia: Fortress Press, 1976), 32, and Daniel J. Harrington, S.J., *God's People in Christ: New Testament Perspectives on the Church and Judaism* (Philadelphia: Fortress Press, 1980), 17.

3. Harrington, *God's People,* 24.

4. Ibid., 25.

One might think that Jesus' expectation of the imminent appearance of the kingdom of God would argue against the formation of any kind of organization or institution to perpetuate his preaching. New Testament scholars suggest, however, that "for Jesus the idea of the reign of God automatically implied the gathering of Israel. A people of God simply must belong to the kingdom of God."[5] And Joachim Jeremias has said, "Precisely if Jesus thought the end was near, then he must have wanted to gather the people of God of the salvific age. For the people of God belong to the emissary of God, just as the crowd of disciples belong to the prophet."[6] Gerhard Lohfink argues that Jesus' appointment of the twelve disciples was a symbolic prophetic action indicating the awakening of Israel and exemplifying the gathering of Israel that was already beginning. This symbol of the eschatological gathering of Israel is not, however, the same as founding a new community, a church. How, then, are we to understand the transition from Jesus' preaching of the kingdom of God and his symbolic and prophetic action of the eschatological gathering of Israel to the community we have come to call church?

## RECEPTION AND RESPONSE TO JESUS

In addition to the twelve whom Jesus appointed, there were many others who followed him in his travels and accepted his preaching. Harrington says:

> By accepting the teaching of Jesus these disciples were already different from other Jews of their time. Instead of abandoning these teachings after Jesus' death, the disciples treasured and proclaimed them. Also, there was a continuity in personnel between Jesus' disciples before his death and those who bore witness to him after the resurrection. In both cases the Twelve and the women were the central characters. There were even continuities in practice. The church's common meals commemorating Jesus' death and resurrection had their origin in Jesus' table fellowship with his disciples (1 Cor. 11:23–26) as well as with tax collectors and sinners. The church's free attitude toward the Law and the Pharisaic tradition can be traced back to Jesus' own example. Even baptism "in the name of Jesus" surely had its root in the eschatological ritual of moral purification practiced by John the Baptist.[7]

---

5. Gerhard Lohfink, *Jesus and Community: The Social Dimension of Christian Faith,* trans. John P. Galvin (Philadelphia: Fortress Press, 1984), 26.

6. Cited in ibid.

7. Harrington, *God's People,* 28–29.

These continuities of belief, personnel, and practice are the basis for discerning a direct continuity between Jesus and the gradually
developed institutional structure we call the church. Jesus was the
charismatic prophet whose teaching and activity provided the initial
impulse that led to the "routinization" of this charisma. Hence, it is not
accurate to say that Jesus consciously intended to found an organized institution to continue his preaching. But neither is it accurate to say that
the community called church had no basis in Jesus' preaching and activity and that it was all a later construct. The reception of Jesus' preaching
and the recognition of him as at least a prophet from God, and much
more than that later, were necessary and constitutive elements in the
formation of the Christian community.

It is important to recall that Jesus and those who accepted his teaching were Jews, and there is no evidence that they ever repudiated
Judaism as their religious tradition. Further, it does not seem that they
belonged to one of the sects existing within Judaism at that time: Phar-
isees, Sadducees, Essenes, or Zealots. Neither does it appear that Jesus
expected those he called to follow him to separate themselves from their
everyday world and form a distinct group or community by themselves
during his lifetime.

Only after Jesus' death and resurrection does a sense of community
develop. His followers did not disperse nor forget his teaching. Hans
Küng is theologically correct when he says, "As soon as men gathered
together in faith in the resurrection of the crucified Jesus of Nazareth
and in expectation of the coming consummation of the reign of God and
the return of the risen Christ in glory, the Church came into existence."[8]
The church is a post-Easter phenomenon based on the faith of the disciples in the risen Jesus. As Kenan Osborne remarks, "It is the Christian
belief in the risen Jesus as Kyrios or Lord that is at the very heart of the
Church. The resurrection is an essential element for the very meaning
and structure of the Church. Prior to the resurrection and the resurrection faith of the followers of Jesus, it appears difficult to speak about
a Church."[9]

We said in chapter 2 that the self-understanding of a group emerges
only gradually and involves distinguishing themselves over against
others. This process, however, involves both continuity and disconti-
nuity with the heritage and history from which it emerges. In the case
of the followers of Jesus of Nazareth, this was the tradition of Judaism.
Just as the symbolic action of appointing the Twelve depended for its
significance on its continuity with the meanings in Jewish tradition

---

8. Hans Küng, *The Church* (New York: Sheed & Ward, 1967), 75.

9. Kenan B. Osborne, O.F.M., *Priesthood: A History of Ordained Ministry in the
Roman Catholic Church* (New York: Paulist Press, 1988), 37.

(the twelve tribes, the twelve judges, etc.), so the emerging Christian self-understanding depended on continuity with Israel.[10] This Jewish heritage was reflected in the early community's prayer as they continued to pray at the temple (Acts 2:46; 3:1; 5:12, 21), in the breaking of bread together, which was new but which seems to have reflected the Jewish Passover celebration, in the teaching of the apostles, which depended on the Law and the Prophets and on Jesus' modification of them, and in the sharing of common goods, which was also practiced by the community at Qumran, another eschatologically minded Jewish community of Jesus' time.

The symbols employed by the early followers of Jesus to understand him and themselves were also taken from the symbolic deposit of the Jewish Scriptures and traditions. They gradually took to themselves titles that had referred to Israel: "a chosen race, a royal priesthood, a holy nation, God's own people." For their understanding of Jesus himself they adopted (and adapted) symbols such as Messiah, Son of Man, and Son of God. These were all available in the symbolic deposit of Judaism of the first century.

Distinguishing themselves from their Jewish heritage was a process that took time. The first reported conflicts within the nascent community were about the administration of common goods and whether or not they must continue temple worship, with the Hellenists rejecting it and the Hebrews remaining faithful to this tradition (Acts 6).[11] Then they had to deal with the issue of requiring circumcision and Jewish dietary laws for Gentile converts (Acts 15). As we know, the disputes were settled in favor of a pluralism of practice within the one community. The distinguishing process was furthered along by the gradual expulsion of the followers of Jesus from the synagogues (c. 85 C.E.) and by the increasingly larger percentage of Gentile Christians. "The religious institutions of Israel were regarded as finished (in themselves and for Christians)."[12] Christianity began to appear as a new religion itself.

## PLURALISM AND UNITY IN THE NEW TESTAMENT

The early Christians were not preoccupied with understanding themselves. They were primarily concerned with Jesus — who he was and

---

10. I am relying here and in the following discussion on the article, "Early Church," in *The New Jerome Biblical Commentary*, ed. Raymond E. Brown, Joseph A. Fitzmyer, and Roland E. Murphy (Englewood Cliffs, N.J.: Prentice-Hall, 1990), 1338–53; and Paul D. Hanson, *The People Called: The Growth of Community in the Bible* (San Francisco: Harper & Row, 1987); Wayne A. Meeks, *The First Urban Christians: The Social World of the Apostle Paul* (New Haven: Yale University Press, 1983).

11. *New Jerome Biblical Commentary*, par. 15, 1341.

12. *New Jerome Biblical Commentary*, par. 24, 1344.

what the significance of his life, death, and resurrection was for them.
Nonetheless, the earliest writings of the community, what later came to
be called the "New Testament," do contain a great deal of information
about their own self-understanding as a community.

There are many images and symbols that refer to the community in
the New Testament. As we noted earlier, Paul Minear says that "conser-
vatively estimated, there are more than eighty of them," and he would
divide them into major and minor images.[13] Some major images are
the familiar ones of Body of Christ, People of God, Temple of the Holy
Spirit, the New Creation, and the Community of Saints. One of the earliest terms and one that became most commonly used to refer to the
community was *ekklēsia* (church). Paul uses it in the first letter to the
Thessalonians (1:1), the earliest extant Christian document (c. 50 C.E.).
*Ekklēsia*, according to Eric G. Jay, is used in the Greek version of the
Old Testament to translate *qahal YHWH*, which means the "gathered
people of God," "a people, called into being by God, who from time to
time are gathered together for such solemn religious occasions as the
receiving of the Law (Deut. 5:22)."[14] The term hearkens back to the first
Exodus, when Israel came into being as the people of God, and hence
connotes the gathering of Israel again in an eschatological community,
that is, a community of the end times. *Ekklēsia* also had a secular usage,
referring to the assembly of the citizens of a town or village.

Paul uses *ekklēsia* to refer to gatherings of Christians in a particular
place, such as a private home (Philem. 2; Col. 4:15), the so-called house
churches. He also uses it to refer to gatherings of Christians in a particular city or region (1 Thess. 1:1; 2:14; Gal. 1:2; Rom. 16:5, 14, 15). Later
on, in Acts for example, *ekklēsia* is used to refer to the whole church
or the universal church scattered over wide geographical areas (Acts
5:11; 9:31; and 1 Cor. 12:28).[15] In the New Testament then, *ekklēsia*,
or church, refers to gatherings of Christians in particular places such as
houses, to gatherings in particular cities or regions, and to the whole
church dispersed geographically. It is an analogous term.

We can already see merely from the variety of meanings for the word
*ekklēsia* that the New Testament is not a uniform or homogeneous
book. It is a collection of writings of various genres, written at different times and places. It should not surprise us that there is a plurality
of communal self-understandings in its various documents, depending
on the concerns of the communities from which the writing emerges
or to which it is directed. Let us now turn to a brief description of the

---

13. Paul S. Minear, *Images of the Church in the New Testament* (Philadelphia: Westminster Press, 1960), 28.

14. Eric G. Jay, *The Church: Its Changing Image through Twenty Centuries* (Atlanta:
John Knox Press, 1980), 6.

15. *New Jerome Biblical Commentary*, par. 29, 1345; and Jay, *The Church*, 7–9.

communal self-understandings (ecclesiologies) of various though not all of the New Testament writings.

## Paul and His Heritage

The letters of Paul provide the earliest glimpses of the emerging Christian communities. The community at *Thessalonica* seems to have been troubled by the delay of Jesus' return or "second coming," indicating this expectation was still alive around 50 C.E. Though a local community, they were in contact with the communities in Macedonia and Achaia and Judea, and were models for them as well as imitators of them. Paul exhorts them on moral matters of chastity and charity, indicating that the daily life of Christians was expected to be different from those who do not know God. Paul also affirms the belief in the resurrection of the dead and Christian hope. He refers to some form of leadership in the community though mentions no specific functions or titles.[16]

A few years later, in the middle to late 50s, Paul's letters to the churches of *Galatia* and to *Rome* give a picture of the communities struggling to understand their relationship to Judaism. Some felt that for Gentiles to become Christians they must also become Jews, i.e., be circumcised and follow the Jewish dietary laws. Others felt that baptism was enough to incorporate one into the Christian community. Paul's answer is that even for Abraham faith in God's promises was the basis for the covenant and for the formation of the people of God, Israel; circumcision came later and merely confirmed the covenant. Hence, circumcision and strict observance of the Mosaic law are unnecessary. "Paul maintained that incorporation into Christ in baptism, and not circumcision and observance of the Law, allows the believer to be part of 'the Israel of God' (Gal 6:16)."[17] Faith makes us children of Abraham, not physical descent. The church, composed of both Jews and Gentiles, is the bearer of God's promise to Abraham and, hence, is the true Israel of God. Paul's complex argument in Romans 9–11 reminds the Gentile Christians of their spiritual roots in Judaism, yet also affirms that somehow or other all of Israel will eventually be saved by God. God still has not rejected his chosen people.[18]

Paul's position won out and the early Christian communities understood themselves to be both in continuity with Judaism and heirs to the promises to Abraham, but at the same time distinct from their Jew-

---

16. For this brief sketch and those following I am relying on the articles in the *New Jerome Biblical Commentary*; Raymond E. Brown, *The Churches the Apostles Left Behind* (New York: Paulist, 1984); Harrington, *God's People*; Frederick J. Cwiekowski, *The Beginnings of the Church* (New York: Paulist, 1988).

17. Harrington, *God's People*, 54.

18. Ibid., 61–66.

ish roots by faith in Jesus as the Messiah. Baptism was the mode of incorporation into this distinct community.

From Paul's first letter to the church at *Corinth* we learn of the divisions and dissensions already existing in that community in the middle 50s. There were groups who identified with Paul himself; others identified themselves with Apollos, with Cephas, or with Christ. There were apparently divisions along class and economic lines as well, and members of the same community were suing one another in the law courts (1 Cor. 6:1–11). They could not agree on how to deal with the pagan environment of Corinth. Could they eat meat that had been sacrificed to idols? They were divided even when they met as a church for liturgical purposes over such issues as covering the head when praying (women should, men should not) and some eating while others went hungry (1 Cor. 11). They were divided over the various spiritual gifts such as speaking in tongues and prophecy. In short, we see a community racked with dissension. Not a very edifying picture at all!

In addressing the situation at Corinth Paul asserts his authority and gives instructions for church order. He uses the famous image of the body to argue for unity even with a diversity of gifts. Each gift has its appropriate function and all should contribute to building up the community, which is the Body of Christ (chap. 12). This theology of the church as the Body of Christ has remained one of the most influential self-understandings in the history of the Christian community.

Two other letters in the Pauline tradition, though very probably not authored by Paul himself, *Colossians* and *Ephesians*, emphasize the image of the church as the Body of Christ. Christians are called to be members of one body of which Christ is the head (Col. 1:18, 24; Eph. 1:22–23; 5:23). The image of the body connotes not only the interdependence of its members but also the vitality and dynamism of a living organism. "For Colossians/Ephesians the church is a growing entity, living with the life of Christ himself," and hence there is a need to maintain the connection of the members with the head as the source of this vitality.[19] The relationship of Christ to the church is compared to that of husband and wife (Eph. 5:21–32) and hence the themes of love and holiness are characteristics of the church in these letters. Finally, in these letters the word *ekklēsia*, church, is used to refer not to the local communities but to the universal church (Col. 1:18, 24; 2:19; 3:15).

Another group of letters in the Pauline tradition, the so-called *Pastorals* (1 Tim., 2 Tim., and Titus), probably written toward the end of the first century, furnish a picture of a more institutionalized and ordered church.[20] The church is called the "household of God" (1 Tim. 3:15) and

---

19. Brown, *The Churches*, 50.
20. *New Jerome Biblical Commentary*, 892–93; Harrington, *God's People*, 75.

is depicted as having problems with false teachers, possibly an early form of Gnosticism (Harrington refers to them as "Jewish-Christian-Gnostic teachers"). Hence, the concern in these letters is to have official teachers, presbyter-bishops, who will teach sound doctrine and refute new teaching or silly myths (Titus 1:9-2:1; 1 Tim. 4:1–11; 5:17), and act as fathers or heads of households toward their communities. The analogy is appropriate since the church did meet in private houses. These letters also display a concern for respectability both in the qualities required for the presbyter-bishops and in the manner Christians should relate to the civil society. As one commentator put it, the author of the Pastorals was urging "church leaders to value and maintain ecclesial and societal structure and order. For him true (i.e., Pauline) Christianity was no countercultural movement akin to early Cynicism."[21] This theology of the church has been appealed to throughout history by those who favored what Dulles has described as the "institutional church."

## Luke/Acts

Although Raymond E. Brown considers Luke/Acts a form of the Pauline heritage, he admits that, "the author of Acts has not written a work of Pauline theology; he has written a story in which Paul plays a decisive role as a missionary witness, not as a doctrinal authority."[22] The author of these two pieces, written in the 80s, traces the development from a small band of followers in Jerusalem to a church with a mission to the entire world, "even to the ends of the earth." There is a strong sense of continuity with the history of Israel and with Jesus himself, but it is the presence of the Spirit at Pentecost that marks the real birth of the community with a sense of mission to preach the resurrected Jesus and not only the coming of the kingdom. Brown says, "Indeed, the distinguishing feature of Lucan ecclesiology is the overshadowing presence of the Spirit. The 70 times that *pneuma*, 'spirit,' occurs in Acts constitute almost one-fifth of the total NT usages of that word."[23] It is the Spirit with which the apostles are baptized and enabled to speak (Acts 1:5, 8; 2:33; 4:8, 31). The Spirit directed missionaries to promising areas (8:29, 39) and directed Peter, Paul, and Barnabas to convert the Gentiles (Acts 10:44–47; 11:12, 15; 13:2–4).

In summary, Brown says, "Thus every essential step in this story of how witness was borne to Christ from Jerusalem to the ends of the earth is guided by the Spirit, whose presence becomes obvious at great moments where the human agents would otherwise be hesi-

---

21. Robert A. Wild, S.J., "The Pastoral Letters," *New Jerome Biblical Commentary*, 893.
22. Brown, *The Churches*, 61.
23. Ibid., 65.

tant or choose wrongly."[24] This portrait of a community guided by the
Spirit in Luke/Acts is the origin of the church's confidence that the Spirit
continues to guide it throughout history. This self-understanding set
the community called church apart from other human communities as
mentioned above.

## The Matthean Heritage

The picture of the Christian community at Antioch gleaned from Matthew's Gospel, which was written between 80 and 90, is that of a
community in transition from a predominantly Jewish-Christian past
to an increasingly Gentile-Christian present and future. It seems to be
facing two crises: a crisis of identity and of moral authority. With the destruction of Jerusalem (70 C.E.), temple-oriented Judaism was no longer
possible nor was the close tie with the mother church of Christianity
available. How was the community to understand itself over against
both Judaism and Gentile paganism? Further, gradual separation from
the synagogue and the death of the authoritative apostles Peter and Paul
left them without a basis for authoritative teaching about morals. What
was the theological basis and justification for moral teaching?[25]

The Matthean solution is to see the death and resurrection of Jesus
as the turning point in salvation history. After the resurrection, "The
Kingdom of God will be taken from you and will be given to a people
that will produce its fruit" (Matt. 21:43). The church is to be understood
as the new people of God and Jesus is the new teaching authority: "All
power in heaven and on earth has been given to me. Go, therefore, and
make disciples of all nations, baptizing them in the name of the Father,
and of the Son, and of the holy Spirit, teaching them to observe all that
I have commanded you" (Matt. 28:18–20). The identity of the community is in terms of a universal mission, now no longer confined to their
originating Jewish community, and the identifying initiation rite is baptism, not circumcision. "Just as God has transferred the Kingdom from
Israel to a people bearing its fruits (21:43), so too He has transferred
the teaching function from the synagogue to the church."[26]

It is not surprising that a community that is experiencing the twin
crises of identity and authority would begin to develop institutional
structures of its own. Matthew's is the only Gospel to use the word
*ekklēsia,* church, as a self-designation. It is used three times, once of the
universal church (16:18) and twice of the local church (18:17). As Meier

---

24. Ibid., 68.

25. Raymond E. Brown and John P. Meier, *Antioch and Rome: New Testament Cradles
of Catholic Christianity* (New York: Paulist, 1983), 57ff.; Brown, *The Churches,* 126–35;
Harrington, *God's People,* 96–101; Cwiekowski, *Beginnings,* 154–59.

26. Brown and Meier, *Antioch and Rome,* 65.

remarks, "The term *ekklēsia* certainly means for Matthew the church as a visible structure and society, having authoritative officials and authoritative functions."[27] The first use (16:18), so important for the Roman Catholic Church's later argument for the Petrine primacy, really stresses Peter's teaching authority, which extends to the whole church. Peter is seen as the chief rabbi for the new community, but it would be anachronistic to think that Matthew was legitimating either a monoepiscopal structure (one bishop per see) or what later developed into the papacy.

The second use of *ekklēsia* (18:17) shows a local community in the process of disciplining a sinner. In this scene, it is not one local leader who makes the decision, but the church decides as a group. Matthew also has warnings against church leaders using marks of distinctive clothing or seeking places of honor (23:5) or employing titles: "As for you, do not be called Rabbi. You have but one teacher, and you are all brothers. Call no one on earth your father; you have but one Father in heaven. Do not be called Master; you have but one Master, the Messiah. The greatest among you must be your servant" (23:8–11). Such a warning suggests that there may have been a nascent "clericalism" in the community at Antioch. All of these concerns have made Matthew's Gospel a primary source for later institutional developments in the church.

## The Johannine Tradition

In contrast to the concerns of Matthew's Gospel, the Johannine tradition shows little interest in church offices or structures. Although written about the same time (c. 90 C.E.) and faced with problems similar to Matthew's community, i.e., distinguishing themselves over against Judaism and relations within the community itself, the Fourth Gospel emphasizes the relationship of the individual believer to Jesus and the dwelling of the Paraclete-Spirit in the believer.[28] It invokes the images of vine and shepherd to depict the relation of Jesus and individual Christians. Brown says that "the core of the ecclesiology is a personal, ongoing relation to the life-giver come down from God." Jesus is the animating principle still operative as the Spirit in the life of the community.

John's Gospel also displays a lack of distinction based on charisms or offices within the community. There is a pervasive egalitarianism. Not even "apostles" are mentioned; the term does not appear in the Gospel or Letters of John. Rather the emphasis is on discipleship, and the "Beloved Disciple" is the model Christian. This egalitarianism extends

---

27. Ibid., 66.
28. Brown, *The Churches*, 85; and Harrington, *God's People*, 102–3.

to the women in the Gospel in a way distinct from the other Gospels. "Martha serves as the spokeswoman of a confession of faith (11:27: 'You are the Christ, the Son of God') that is placed on Peter's lips in Matt 16:16–17 . . . " and it is Mary Magdalene, not Peter, who is the first to see the risen Jesus in John 20:14.[29] The Samaritan woman in chapter 4 is also depicted as coming close to recognizing Jesus as Messiah.[30]

It is the Paraclete-Spirit who continues Jesus' presence on earth and who is the authoritative teacher now and for the future (16:6ff.). As Brown says, "The Paraclete will receive everything he has to say from Jesus; but, dwelling in the heart of each Christian, he will contemporize it in each period and in each place, thus enabling Christians to face the things to come."[31] The Christian community, then, saw itself as led by the Spirit after Jesus' departure. The Spirit is the ultimate authority for settling disputes within the community because the Spirit teaches what Jesus taught. This contrasts with the Matthean picture of Peter the Apostle as the chief teacher for the church.

The self-understanding of the church in the Johannine tradition provides a basis for later developments that emphasize the role of the Spirit rather than of offices and structures and for the model of church that Dulles called "the community of disciples."

This brief survey of the major traditions within the New Testament demonstrates the variety and diversity of the communities' self-understandings. I have stressed this because too often the church is presumed to be a homogeneous and monolithic organization from the moment after Pentecost. But underlying this plurality and diversity, there was a basic unity. We have already seen how Paul used the term *ekklēsia* to refer not only to local churches but to the universal church (1 Cor. 10:32), thereby indicating some sense of unity among these smaller groups. These communities were united by circulating letters and by messengers. Wayne Meeks notes that "the letters themselves, the messengers who brought them, and the repeated visits to the local assemblies by Paul and his associates all emphasized this interrelatedness."[32] In addition, traveling Christians could expect hospitality in foreign cities from the local community, and we know that alms were sent from one community to another (1 Cor. 16:1–4; 2 Cor. 8–9; Rom. 15:25–28).

Perhaps the most important expression of this unity was in the fundamentals of the early Christian proclamation, the *kerygma*. Although in the actual act of proclamation no two verbal expressions would have

---

29. Brown, *The Churches*, 94–95.
30. Raymond E. Brown, *The Community of the Beloved Disciple* (New York: Paulist, 1979), 187–89.
31. Ibid., 108.
32. Meeks, *First Urban Christians*, 109.

been exactly the same, there was a *core* or common kerygma in Acts, John, and Paul. James D. G. Dunn summarizes the three components of this core:

> First, the proclamation of the risen, exalted Jesus — expressed by the Acts sermons' emphasis on the resurrection of Jesus as such, by Paul's emphasis on the present Lordship and representative significance of Jesus, and by John's presentation of the historical Jesus in the full illumination of Easter faith.
>
> Second, the call for faith, for acceptance of the proclamation and commitment to the Jesus proclaimed. This is the most consistent feature in all three cases. . . .
>
> Third, the promise held out to faith — whether it be put in terms of Spirit, or of its various aspects (forgiveness, salvation, life) or of a continuing relation thus established between exalted Christ and believer (union with Christ, mutual indwelling).[33]

Unity of the early Christian communities was also manifested in their common rituals of baptism and the Lord's Supper. The epistle to the Ephesians, that great letter on the unity of the church, lists the basis for the church's unity as "striving to preserve the unity of the spirit through the bond of peace; one body and one Spirit, as you were called to the one hope of your call; one Lord, one faith, one baptism; one God and Father of all, who is over all and through all and in all" (Eph. 4:3–6). But this whole letter is encouraging Christians "to celebrate their unity by appropriate conduct," indicating that it was by no means a fully realized fact.[34]

On the basis of this survey, we can draw several conclusions. First, within the New Testament itself we find a plurality of images and a plurality of self-understandings, which at the same time maintains communion, *koinōnia,* among the churches. We find both unity and pluralism in ecclesiology even then.

The diversity of self-understandings arose from the diverse circumstances of the various communities and the different problems each faced. Nonetheless, there was great concern to preserve the faith as it had been handed down from the apostles; the apostolic tradition was the bond of unity.

Second, from the earliest writings to the latest there is a gradual development, not uniform among the various communities nor continuous in any one community. Offices and structures emerged earlier in some places than in others, and there were different offices existing in

---

33. James D. G. Dunn, *Unity and Diversity in the New Testament: An Inquiry into the Character of Earliest Christianity* (Philadelphia: Westminster Press, 1977), 30.

34. Paul J. Kobelski, "Introduction" to "The Letter to the Ephesians," *New Jerome Biblical Commentary,* 885.

different communities at the same time. The developments were gradual and were influenced by events outside the control of the Christian
community itself, such as the fall of Jerusalem and the expulsion from
the synagogues. Such events pushed the early communities to clarify
their relationship to Judaism and to the pagan world.

Third, as it gradually became clear that the kingdom Jesus had
preached was not coming as soon as had been expected, the community
had to figure out its relationship to the kingdom. Not the kingdom itself, but its inauguration in the resurrected Jesus became the focal point
of their preaching. They became the community proclaiming Jesus, his
memory, and his teaching. They were not the kingdom, but the bearers
of the good news about its initiation.

Finally, the communities portrayed in the New Testament were preoccupied with who Jesus was, with Christology, not with ecclesiology.
The process of self-definition was an ongoing one that continued beyond the writing of the New Testament. We turn now to that continuation.

## DEVELOPMENTS IN THE SECOND
## AND THIRD CENTURIES

As we retrace the chronological development of the self-understanding
of the early Christians, it is important to remember that the division of
time into centuries dating from the birth of Christ was a later development and not a form of periodization used by the early communities
themselves. So also is the division of early Christian writings into the
New Testament and other noncanonical writings. The "canon" of the
New Testament as we now know it developed only gradually. The earliest list we have is found in the Muratorian Fragment, in the late second
century, and there were other writings that were regarded with some
authority but that were not finally included in the canonical writings.
Some of these other documents, however, are sources for our knowledge of the emerging self-consciousness of the early church. We will
deal with a representative selection of these sources and not attempt a
complete history of the church.

In the First Letter of Clement from Rome to the church at Corinth
(c. 94–96 C.E.), we find the New Testament images of the church as the
Body of Christ and the New Israel, but also the church is referred to
as Christ's army (xxxvii). There is also mention of the appointment of
presbyter/bishops (the Greek words *presbyteros* and *episkopos* are used
interchangeably) by the apostles, thus introducing the notion of apostolic succession. It is not clear from the texts (xlii and xliv) whether this
is a succession of the presbyteral body as a whole or a succession of

individuals. Clement does compare the order of ministry in the Christian communities to the divinely ordered Jewish levitical structure that had existed until the destruction of the temple at Jerusalem.[35] Although Clement writes from Rome, he does not write as the bishop of that city, and there is no real evidence of a single bishop, or monoepiscopate, at Rome until the middle of the second century. Finally, this letter does distinguish between the responsibilities assigned to priests in the book of Leviticus and those of the layperson (*laikos*).

Slightly later (c. 108–17?) we find in a series of letters from Ignatius of Antioch clear affirmation of the threefold ministry of bishop, priest, and deacon with which we are familiar. He speaks of one bishop, a group or council of presbyters, and a group of deacons. The bishop is the chief teacher of the church and no baptism and no Eucharist should be conducted without reference to the bishop to whom obedience and respect are due. This emphasis on structured ministry may have been caused by threats to doctrine from within and from intermittent persecution from outside the church.[36] The images of the church found in these letters are the Body of Christ and God's building.

This image of the church as God's building also appears in the *Shepherd of Hermas* (c. 150), but this writing introduces a nonbiblical notion of the church as God's creation. The central concern of Hermas, as Jay points out, is "the moral purity of its members, and he advocates a rigorous exercise of discipline."[37] He also speaks of *presbyteroi* and *episkopoi* in the plural, but some find hints of a monoepiscopate at Rome in this writing, although this is not clear.[38]

Another source from about the middle of the second century is the *Epistle to Diognetus,* which does not use the word "church" but speaks of Christians as the soul of the world, analogous to the Platonic understanding of the relation of the soul to body. He sees Christians as confined in the world the way the soul is shut up in the body. Christians dwell in the world, but are not of the world. They are a new race who only pass their time on earth but whose true home is in heaven.[39] This view was later reflected in the monastic tradition and various forms of Christian spirituality.

An outstanding example of the community's self-understanding developing in the face of a threat may be found in the case of Irenaeus, bishop of Lyons in Gaul, c. 177 C.E. His *Adversus Haereses (Against Heresies)* is a polemical refutation of the Gnostic teachings of Marcion and Valentinus. The Gnostics claimed to have secret knowledge (*gno-*

---

35. Jay, *The Church,* 32–33, and Cwiekowski, *The Beginnings,* 182–83.
36. Ibid., 190–91; Jay, *The Church,* 35–38.
37. Ibid., 38–39.
38. Ibid., 40; Brown and Meier, *Antioch and Rome,* 204.
39. Jay, *The Church,* 41.

*sis*) that was necessary for salvation and that they had from the apostles by way of a secret tradition. Against this, Irenaeus argued that the teaching of the apostles was publicly available to all and was found both in the written tradition, Scripture, and in the oral tradition handed on through the successors of the apostles. This true apostolic tradition is summarized in what he calls the "canon of truth" as follows:

> The Church, though dispersed throughout the whole world, even to the ends of the earth, has received from the apostles and their disciples this faith: (She believes) in one God, the Father Almighty, Maker of heaven, and earth, and the sea, and all things that are in them; and in one Christ Jesus, the Son of God, who became incarnate for our salvation; and in the Holy Spirit, who proclaimed through the prophets the dispensations of God, and the advents, and the birth from a virgin, and the passion and resurrection from the dead, and the ascension into heaven in the flesh of the beloved Christ Jesus, our Lord, and His (future) manifestation from heaven in the glory of the Father "to gather all things in one" (Eph. 1.10) and to raise up anew all flesh of the whole human race. (*Adv. Haer.* I, x.l)

Irenaeus argues that this canon of truth is uniform and universal, i.e., may be found in Spain, Gaul, Egypt, Libya, and elsewhere in this form. Indeed, his claim seems to have been true since we find his contemporary, Tertullian from Carthage, and slightly later Origen of Alexandria, giving almost identical summaries of faith. That this canon of faith is substantially identical with the teaching of the apostles is guaranteed by the unbroken succession of official teachers in the various sees. Had there been hidden or secret teaching, as the Gnostics claimed, it would surely have been handed down through this line of teachers. Irenaeus gives a list of the bishops of Rome as an example, and says he could do the same for Antioch or other churches. The list is of those who succeeded one another in the teaching chair (*kathedra*) of the see, not a list of who laid hands on whom. These were the guardians of the canon of truth, but they were assisted by the guidance of the Holy Spirit.

Irenaeus has been accused of subordinating Scripture to this oral tradition, but J. N. D. Kelly says that for Irenaeus the canon of truth, "far from being something distinct from Scripture, was simply a condensation of the message contained in it.... The whole point of his teaching was, in fact, that Scripture and the Church's unwritten tradition are identical in content, both being vehicles of the revelation."[40] The dis-

---

40. J. N. D. Kelly, *Early Christian Doctrines,* 2d ed. (New York: Harper & Brothers, 1960), 39. See also, Jay, *The Church,* 43–49; Chadwick, *The Early Church,* 80–83; and Johannes Quasten, *Patrology* (Westminster, Md.: Newman Press, 1950), 1:299–302.

tinction and sometimes separation of Scripture and tradition were later developments.

In Irenaeus we find a picture of a church threatened by the Gnostic teaching, which forces it to clarify its self-understanding as a community guarding the Gospel message handed down from the apostles, with official teachers, the bishops, who are primarily responsible for its preservation. The uniformity and universality of this teaching is guaranteed by succession in the teaching chairs of the churches and by the assistance of the Holy Spirit. The message is to be found both in written form, Scripture, and in other forms of teaching in the church. This is the source for the notion of succession in the apostolic teaching office, the magisterium in the church.

A younger contemporary of Irenaeus, *Tertullian* of Carthage, trained as a lawyer, held a view of the church very similar to that of Irenaeus. He also held that there was a *regula fidei*, his term for the canon of truth, which enabled the church to interpret Scripture correctly and was the source of the unity of the church. Tertullian, writing in Carthage, a church not founded by an apostle, bases the notion of apostolicity not on a list of successors from an apostle, but on the teaching itself. As Jay says, "If they hold the same faith as the churches founded by the apostles they are to be accounted no less apostolic than they."[41] This apostolic tradition is what maintains the church in unity.

In his later years (c. 207), Tertullian began to lean toward Montanism, a sect that emphasized the charismatic element of Christianity, the speaking in tongues, a rigorist and ascetic discipline, and no forgiveness of postbaptismal sin. Under the Montanist influence, Tertullian emphasized the ministry of inspired prophets over that of the bishops, presbyters, and deacons. He taught that the church was a "society of the Spirit, and its true members are spiritual men."[42] He distinguished this "spiritual" church from the "organizational" church, which did not include the bishops. However, as Jay says, he was "protesting not so much against the idea of ministerial order as such as against the failure of bishops, whether by laxity or by officialism, to be what they should have been."[43] There apparently was some laxity creeping into the church and Tertullian and the Montanists express their concern for the holiness of the church. They are only the beginning of a long tradition of such concern.

A similar awareness of the church as an organized community with the need for a structured ministry and at the same time a recognition of its failures and defects can be found in the writings of Origen in the

---

41. Jay, *The Church*, 51.
42. Ibid., 54.
43. Ibid., 55.

first half of the third century (c. 185–255). As Kelly says, he sees the "Church as an organized community, describing it as 'the congregation of Christian people' or 'the assembly of believers'; and he has a high opinion of the office and responsibilities of its ministers, and deplores their all too frequent unworthiness."[44] He distinguishes between the empirical church and the spiritual church, which is the true church, the assembly of the saints or perfect ones. This true or heavenly church existed before the creation of the world (he cites Eph. 1:4). Although undoubtedly influenced by the Platonic notion that earthly realities are imperfect copies of their heavenly prototypes, Origen's distinction is not exactly that. Jay says, "Rather he seems to envisage the Church on earth as the historic community in which men, by participation in Christ, become fitted to be members of the heavenly Church," somewhat akin to the later medieval distinction between the church militant and the church triumphant.[45] Origen's distinction is not the same as a later one between the church of the elect and those impenitent sinners who will be damned, because Origen taught that all creatures will ultimately be saved. Somehow or another the earthly church and the heavenly church will coincide.[46]

In these early patristic writings we see the beginnings of the development of what later came to be called the "marks of the church": one, holy, catholic, and apostolic. The unity was to be found in the rule of faith, in its apostolic origin, and the truth of this apostolic teaching was evidenced in its universality (catholicity) and uniformity. Although they recognized that there were sinners within the community, nonetheless holiness was a characteristic expected in the church. They clearly recognized the need for structured offices and official teachers to preserve the unity and guard the apostolic heritage, and they affirmed the need for the Holy Spirit as well. These issues constantly resurface in the history of the community's self-understanding as we will see in the following pages.

## CYPRIAN AND AUGUSTINE

Developments in the self-understanding of the Christian community from the middle of the third century to the middle of the fifth were driven as much, if not more, by events outside the community as threats from within. By the third century Christianity was widely disseminated throughout the Roman empire both geographically and in most levels

---

44. Kelly, *Early Christian Doctrines*, 202.
45. Jay, *The Church*, 63.
46. Ibid., and Kelly, *Early Christian Doctrines*, 202–3.

of society. We have already seen that Irenaeus and Tertullian used the identity of the faith over great geographical distances as an argument for its authentic apostolicity. But this great dispersion was ambiguous in its consequences. The church took on a stature rivaling that of the official Roman pagan religious tradition and seems to have provoked something of a revival of that tradition. At the same time, "Throughout the empire the church had been accepting a large number of nominal converts as well as committed individuals such as Cyprian."[47] Thus, when the first general persecution of Christians throughout the empire occurred under the emperor Decius in 250, the church was growing in numbers but not necessarily in strength of commitment.

It is not our purpose to trace the entire history of the church in these chapters, but merely the major developments in its self-understanding. Two figures stand out as providing the most significant thought on the nature of the church during this period and their contributions dominated ecclesiology in the West throughout the Middle Ages: Cyprian and Augustine.

Although a recent convert and trained as a lawyer, Cyprian was elected bishop of Carthage in 248. During the ten years of his episcopate, until he was martyred in the persecution of Valerian in 258, the church in North Africa experienced severe crises. The issues had to do with the unity of the church and the holiness of the church. During the brief but severe persecution under Decius (250–51), literally thousands of Christians either offered incense before the Roman idols or statues of the emperor, or they bribed commissioners for the official documents (*libelli*) that testified that they had done so. W. H. C. Frend says, "When confronted with the choice of empire or Christian church in 250, the great majority of Christians played safe and sacrificed."[48] When it was all over, the church was faced with the issue of forgiving the fallen (*lapsi*) or not. There was a longstanding tradition that three sins could not be forgiven on earth: murder, adultery, and apostasy. A second issue was, if apostasy could indeed be forgiven, who could forgive? Could those who had remained steadfast and not sacrificed, called *confessors*, presumed to be endowed with the Holy Spirit in a special way and therefore possessing the power of the keys, forgive the *lapsi* themselves, or was forgiveness reserved to the bishop alone? The issue of the holiness of the church quickly evolved into an issue of authority in the church and, subsequently, into an issue of the unity of the church.

---

47. Frend, *The Rise of Christianity*, 322. In addition to this, I am drawing on Chadwick, *The Early Church*, 116–24; Jay, *The Church*, 65–74; W. H. C. Frend, *The Early Church* (London: Hodder and Stoughton, 1965), 107–18; and Kelly, *Early Christian Doctrines*, 203–7.

48. Frend, *The Rise of Christianity*, 322.

There were deep divisions at Carthage and at Rome over these issues. Rival bishops were elected in both sees. Cyprian called a council
of bishops of North Africa to resolve the crisis and they decided that
the *lapsi* could be forgiven on a case-by-case basis, but by the bishop
alone. Cyprian communicated this resolution of the issue to Cornelius,
the bishop of Rome. There, however, the stricter position, that apostasy could not be forgiven on earth, was represented by Novatian, who
was elected by a minority as bishop at the same time the majority had
elected Cornelius. There was a schism within the church, but not based
on disagreement about the "rule of faith." This could no longer serve
as the touchstone of unity all by itself. It was a necessary but insufficient criterion of unity. Cyprian argued that the episcopate was the
principle of unity in the church. In an individual diocese there can be
only one bishop, the one who succeeds to the vacant see. In the case
of Novatian in Rome, and Cyprian's rival in Carthage, they were not
elected to a vacant see and hence were not legitimate successors in that
see. In the case of the church universal, the unity of the church was
manifested in the communion among the college of bishops. He wrote,
"Episcopatus unus est, cuius a singulis in solidum pars tenetur" ("The
episcopate is a unity of which a part is held by each in solidarity).[49] For
Cyprian, although each bishop is autonomous in his own see, he exercises the whole authority of the episcopate and is responsible for the
whole episcopate.[50] Thus was born the notion of episcopal collegiality,
a notion restored to its rightful place in Roman Catholic ecclesiology by
Vatican II, as we will see in chapter 6.

Cyprian's emphasis on the bishop as the focal point and criterion
of unity in the church led him so far as to say, no bishop, no church.
"You ought to know that the bishop is in the Church, and the Church in
the bishop; and if anyone be not with the bishop, then he is not in the
Church."[51] Likewise, he could say that you could not have God for your
Father, if you did not have the church for your mother, and consequently
his famous dictum, *Extra ecclesiam, nulla salus* (Outside the church,
there is no salvation), a saying that has been forever after interpreted,
reinterpreted, and misinterpreted.

Although Cyprian founds the unity of the church on the episcopate,
he cites the texts (Matt. 16:18–19 and John 20:20–23) that were later
used to support the claim that the papacy was the basis of the church's
unity. He wrote in *De unitate:*

> The Lord speaks to Peter, saying, "I say unto thee, that thou art
> Peter; and upon this rock I will build my Church...." And al-

---

49. Cyprian, *De unitate ecclesiae*, 5.
50. Jay, *The Church*, 70.
51. Cyprian, Ep. lxviii, 8.

though to all the apostles, after his resurrection, He gives an
equal power, and says, "As the Father hath sent me, even so send
I you ... "; yet, that he might set fourth unity, He arranged by
His authority the origin of that unity, as beginning from one. As-
suredly the rest of the apostles were also the same as was Peter,
endowed with a like partnership both of honour and power; but
the beginning proceeds from unity. ... " (4)

This text seems to acknowledge Peter as a point of unity without suggesting any superiority of authority or power over the other apostles.
There is another version of this chapter, however, the so-called papal
text, which "asserts that the 'primacy is given to Peter,'" that Christ set
up 'one throne,' and asks whether 'he who deserts the throne of Peter,
on which the Church is founded' is confident that he is in the Church."[52]
Because of the varying claims of Protestants and Roman Catholics about
the papacy, this text has been much disputed. A number of historians
have suggested that the so-called papal text was an earlier version from
Cyprian's own hand, which was later revised after a disagreement with
Stephen over the validity of Novatian baptism a few years later. In any
case, the ambiguity of either version about the respective importance
of the episcopacy and the papacy reflects the stage of development of
ecclesiology at that time. Only later does the papacy enlarge its claims
and attempt to realize them.

Cyprian provides us with a few other insights about the bishops in
the middle of the third century. First, they were apparently "elected";
but Jay suggests that this may have meant that they were chosen by other
bishops with some input from the presbyters, "but that the people had
a definite power of veto."[53] Cyprian also refers to the bishop as *sac-
erdos* (priest), indicating a tendency to compare the Christian ministry
with the Aaronic priesthood and its sacrificial functions. At this time, the
primary function of the bishop was teaching and preaching, hence, the
frequent mention of the *kathedra,* but there is a foreshadowing of the
later cultic emphasis. In summary, I think Jay is correct when he says,
"It is true to say that Cyprian's hierarchical and sacerdotal view of the
Church was to dominate western Christianity for centuries."[54]

Before discussing Augustine's contributions to the development
of the Christian community's self-understanding a few other factors
should be noted briefly.

There were other general persecutions, most notably that of Dio-
cletian in 303–5. It was only fifty-five years after Cyprian's death that
Constantine and Licinius issued the Edict of Milan in 313 granting

---

52. Jay, *The Church*, 70.
53. Ibid., 71.
54. Ibid., 73.

religious liberty to all and restoring property taken from individual
Christians and from the churches as corporations. The church moved
from being the object of persecution to a position of prestige and power
with Constantine's conversion and involvement in the life of the church.
The church came to be modeled on the administrative structure of
the Roman empire, and its ecclesiastical regions coincided with the
civil provinces. The five patriarchial sees, Jerusalem, Alexandria, Antioch, Rome, and Constantinople, developed with special jurisdictional
powers, and a hierarchical administrative system replaced the collegial
episcopate so stoutly proposed by Cyprian.[55] Just as the era of persecution had stimulated reflection on the community's self-understanding,
its new-found position as an accepted and even established pillar of the
empire posed new questions.

Although there was some theological reflection on the church in the
East, as J. N. D. Kelly remarks, "their expressly stated ecclesiology was
neither original nor profound, the reason being that the subject was not
a vital issue in the East."[56] It was Augustine in the West who made the
major contribution to ecclesiology, and indeed, to many other areas of
theology. Of Augustine, Roy W. Battenhouse concludes: "The civilization
of medieval Christendom was to owe more to him than to any other of
the Church Fathers. Gregory the Great turned to him for scriptural commentary and theology, Charlemagne for political theory, Bonaventura
for mysticism, and Aquinas for elements of scholastic philosophy. Later,
with the coming of the Reformation, Luther and Calvin became his disciples and, after them, Pascal — each gathering from the bishop of Hippo
fresh stimulus for revitalizing Christian piety."[57] Granted his immense
theological and philosophical influence, we are interested here only in
his ecclesiology.

Like Cyprian, Augustine's concerns about the church were occasioned by the results of the great persecution and the Donatist schism
that resulted. By the time Augustine became bishop of Hippo in 396,
the Donatist schism had racked the church in North Africa for eighty-five
years. Basically, the Donatists were a rigorist group who believed that
the Catholics had become contaminated because one of the consecra-
tors of the Catholic bishop of Carthage, Caecilian, had handed over the
Scriptures to the authorities. Just as sacrifice before the idols was taken
for apostasy, so too, surrendering the sacred books was considered
apostasy in North Africa. Those who did were called *traditores*. A church
that tolerated and consorted with the apostate *traditores* could not be
the true church of Christ. As J. N. D. Kelly says, "The Donatists took the

---

55. Ibid., 75–76.
56. Kelly, *Early Christian Doctrines*, 403.
57. Roy W. Battenhouse, *A Companion to the Study of St. Augustine* (New York: Oxford
University Press, 1955), 54.

line of rigorism; the validity of the sacraments, they taught, depended on the worthiness of the minister, and the Church ceased to be holy and forfeited its claim to be Christ's body when it tolerated unworthy bishops and other officers."[58] As with Cyprian, the question of the holiness of the church soon evolved into an issue about its unity when the rigorists elected another bishop in Carthage, Majorinus, whose successor was Donatus, from whom the schismatic group took its name.

Augustine's main images for the church are the mystical body of Christ and the fellowship of the Holy Spirit. The mystical body image stresses the unity of the church with Christ its head. Christ and his members form one person, an organic unity, and just as the human body is animated by the soul, so the mystical body is animated by the Holy Spirit, which is its life-principle. "But since the Holy Spirit is love personified, the product of the mutual love of the Father and the Son, the life-principle of the Church can be equally well described as love."[59] Thus, his second image, the fellowship of the Holy Spirit, is also the fellowship of love. Those who do not love God and their fellow Christians, who sever the bond of love, put themselves outside the church. As Jay puts it, "For Augustine true unity and charity are synonymous, and consequently schism and lack of charity are closely linked. The schismatic actions of the Donatists . . . betray their failure in charity. And since the Holy Spirit is the giver of charity he [Augustine] concludes that the Donatists do not have the Holy Spirit."[60]

Since the Donatists accepted the apostolic rule of faith and the Scriptures, and since they also had validly ordained bishops, Augustine appealed to another criterion to show that the Donatist church was not the true church of Christ, namely, catholicity. The Donatist church could not be the true church because it was confined to North Africa and not "catholic" in the geographical sense, nor was it in communion with the other apostolic sees, especially Rome. Further he argued, citing the parable of the wheat and the tares, that the church was a *corpus permixtum* including both the saints and evildoers. The judgment as to who was saved was God's alone and would not be made plain in the time of Donatus but only at the end of time. Augustine drew a "distinction between the essential Church, composed of those who genuinely belong to Christ, and the outward or empirical Church."[61]

Augustine's doctrine of predestination led him to refine this distinction between a visible and an invisible church. As Kelly points out, "In the last resort, he came to see, the only true members of the Church . . . could be 'the fixed number of the elect.' . . . Augustine never

---

58. Kelly, *Early Christian Doctrines*, 410.
59. Ibid., 414.
60. Jay, *The Church*, 86.
61. Kelly, *Early Christian Doctrines*, 414–17; Jay, *The Church*, 88.

attempted to harmonize his two conceptions, that distinguishing the
Church as a historical institution from the true Church of those really
devoted to Christ and manifesting His spirit, and that identifying Christ's
body with the fixed number of the elect known to God alone."[62] Subsequent theologians have built on both notions and the Reformers'
stress on the spiritual character of the church led Roman Catholics to
emphasize its visible quality.

As mentioned above, Augustine's argument from the catholicity of
the church that the Donatist church could not be the true church
of Christ included the notion of communion with other apostolic
churches, especially with Rome. At this period, it does seem that he "attributed to the Pope a pastoral and teaching authority extending over
the whole Church, and found a basis for it in Scripture. At the same time
there is no evidence that he was prepared to ascribe to the bishop of
Rome, in his capacity as successor of St. Peter, a sovereign and infallible
doctrinal magisterium. . . . The truth is that the doctrine of the Roman
primacy played only a minor role in his ecclesiology."[63]

Another major contribution of Augustine to ecclesiology derived
from his battle with the Donatists, namely, his theology of the relations of church and state. It was to set the tone for the medieval church
and provide a basis for Luther's later appeal to the German nobility. As
Frend puts it, "What Augustine was to do in his letters and discussion
between 399 and 412 was to justify the state's intervention in the religious lives of its subjects so that persecution became accepted as part of
its role."[64] Although he never doubted the right to call upon the authorities for help against schismatics and heretics, "the actual invocation of
repressive measures against his opponents was accepted by Augustine
reluctantly."[65] His reasoning assumed that the state had originated after the Fall and was God's means of restraining sinful humanity. Now
it had the additional function of protecting the liberty of the church to
pursue its mission and protect it against its enemies. Further, Augustine
appealed to Luke 14:23, "Go out to the highways and hedgerows and
make people come in that my home may be filled," as a justification for
persecution. Frend comments, "Seldom have Gospel words been given
so unexpected a meaning."

Finally, the sack of the city of Rome by Alaric in 410 caused a major crisis in the self-understanding of the Roman world of that time.
Some contended that the calamity was due to abandoning the ancient
Roman gods in favor of Christianity. To respond to this charge, Augustine wrote his famous *City of God*. It amounts to an interpretation of

62. Kelly, *Early Christian Doctrines*, 416.
63. Ibid., 419.
64. Frend, *The Rise of Christianity*, 670.
65. Ibid., 671.

world history from a Christian perspective in which history is seen as "the intermingling, sometimes the co-operation, sometimes the enmity and always the tension between these two cities, the earthly and the heavenly, both constituted by love, the former 'by the love of self even to the contempt of God, the heavenly by the love of God, even to the contempt of self.' "[66] Augustine identifies the heavenly city, the City of God, with the church. It is not clear, however, which concept of the church he means here, but Jay suggests that it is probably the invisible church, the congregation of saints, those on earth and those in heaven, including the angels. Augustine's notion of the tension between the two cities has had great influence on later Christian thinking about the relationship of the church and the "world." This tension between the "two swords," the spiritual and the temporal, will dominate the story of the development of the Christian community through the next one thousand years.

## SUMMARY

In this chapter we have traced the developments from the preaching of the kingdom of God by a charismatic Galilean carpenter to the formation of Christianity as a worldwide religion integrated with the Roman empire. In the process we have seen that the Christian community did come to some self-understanding by differentiating itself from Judaism, as well as from Gnosticism, Novatianism, Donatism, etc. At the same time, it tried to maintain continuity with its apostolic origins and was concerned with preserving the apostolic faith it had inherited. This apostolic faith was to be the bond of unity, although gradually other criteria of unity emerged. The wide geographical dissemination of the faith, its catholicity, became one sign of the unity. The community was always concerned with the holiness of its members, but what the criterion of holiness should be varied from time to time and place to place.

In tension with the desired unity there was a plurality of self-understandings we saw within the New Testament itself. In tension with the desire to preserve its apostolic origins was the need to confront new situations and answer new questions, the need to adapt to new circumstances as the community moved into the Gentile world of the Roman empire. In tension with the claim of catholicity was the tendency to form smaller groups of pure, uncontaminated Christians unconcerned with the rest of the church and the rest of the world — the sectarian tendency. In tension with the claim of holiness was the awareness of the failures of its members and the need for continuing forgiveness. The church was also a "school for sinners."

---

66. Jay, *The Church*, 91.

As the community perdured over time and the "second coming" was obviously delayed, various forms of institutionalization developed. The need for order in the community and the need to preserve the apostolic teaching called forth some forms of leadership, or "overseership." These emerged only gradually and not in the same order in all churches. These ecclesial structures were influenced by those in civil society but were adapted to the needs of the churches in different times and different locations. During this period, the elements of future developments in church organization emerge: the tripartite division of ministry into bishops, presbyters, and deacons, some form of primacy of the Roman church, episcopal collegiality, the emergence of patriarchates, and the regular use of synods and councils on all levels.

Finally, we have noted that the self-understanding of the Christian community was frequently influenced by world events over which the church had no control: the fall of Jerusalem, expulsion from the synagogues, Constantine's conversion, and the fall of Rome. We will see in the following chapters that such events have sometimes pushed the church in directions conflicting with the Good News it tries to proclaim. It seems that the emergence of the Christian church is rather understandable from a sociological perspective and from a historical point of view. At the same time, the community understood that these developments were the work of God, in and through the Holy Spirit.

## RECOMMENDED READINGS

Brown, Raymond E. *The Churches the Apostles Left Behind*. New York: Paulist, 1984.

Chadwick, Henry. *The Early Church*. London: Penguin, 1967.

Cwiekowski, Frederick J. *The Beginnings of the Church*. New York: Paulist, 1988.

Frend, W. H. C. *The Rise of Christianity*. Philadelphia: Fortress, 1984.

Harrington, Daniel J. *God's People in Christ: New Testament Perspectives on the Church and Judaism*. Philadelphia: Fortress, 1980.

Chapter 4

# Christendom:
# Church and Society
# in Tensive Unity

In the life stories of individuals, great or ordinary, some periods are more formative, more significant than others. There are times when life seems to go on placidly and without major crises, and then there are times when one is forced to reorient one's life, to come to a new self-understanding. This is also true in the life of a community. The early years are especially formative and set the lines of development for the future. We have spent some time discussing the formative period of the Christian community, especially the New Testament period, in the previous chapter.

By the middle of the fifth century, as represented by Augustine, the main outline of the self-understanding of the Christian community was set. Its basic characteristics, that it is one, holy, catholic, and apostolic, had been elaborated in the face of various challenges from within and from without. It had institutionalized certain structures to preserve these characteristics, especially unity and apostolicity, and had established a worldwide organization patterned on the structure of the Roman empire. It had gained acceptance and prestige as *the* religion of the empire, but at the same time watered down the harsher demands of the Gospel. It had become a church of the "masses." Patterns of life and governance were rather firmly set, and some of them were further delineated in the succeeding centuries. But the next thousand years are not as significant in developing the *self-understanding* of the Christian community as was the previous period, although there are many important events in the *lived experience* of the church. For ecclesiology, especially from a Roman Catholic perspective, the first 450 years and the last 450 years are the most determinative for our contemporary reflections on the church.

In this chapter we will continue to retrieve our communal history in broad strokes from the end of the fifth century to the beginning of the sixteenth century, a period usually designated the Middle Ages.[1] Two themes in the development of ecclesiology dominate this period: the rise and decline of the monarchical (even, imperial) papacy, and the tension between the spiritual and temporal, or secular, powers. Again, it is necessary to remind ourselves that we are not tracing the complete history of the church in this period, but only those aspects significant for the self-understanding of the Christian community.

## THE GROWTH OF THE PAPACY

R. W. Southern points out that there are various periods in the Middle Ages each with distinctive characteristics: the Primitive Age, c. 700 – c. 1050; the Age of Growth, c. 1050 – c. 1300; and the Age of Unrest, c. 1300 – c. 1550. Nevertheless I believe he is correct in stating:

> For the whole of this period — from the age of Bede to that of Luther, from the effective replacement of imperial by papal authority in the West in the eighth century to the fragmentation of that authority in the sixteenth, from the cutting of the political ties between eastern and western Europe to Europe's breaking out into the wider western world beyond the seas — the papacy is the dominant institution in western Europe.
>
> The commanding position of the papacy give the Middle Ages its unity.[2]

Of course, the position of the papacy varied considerably throughout this period, and there was always a discrepancy between its claims and its actual practice. Further, the varying strength of the papacy was closely intertwined with the second theme mentioned above, the struggle between the church and the secular powers. This story is another example of the dialectical relationship between the lived experience of the community and its theorizing, or theologizing, but the theology of the papacy is not as important as the historical factors.

---

1. For the sake of continuity in telling the story, I am consciously extending the designation backward to include late antiquity. The term "Middle Ages" usually includes the period from 700 C.E. to 1550 C.E., but in the extended sense used here, following Southern, it means the "period from the collapse of the Roman Empire to the collapse of the western church-state." See R. W. Southern, *Western Society and the Church in the Middle Ages,* Pelican History of the Church, vol. 2 (London: Penguin Books, 1970), 24.

2. Ibid., 26.

We have seen that in the early church, the see of Rome, believed to be the place of martyrdom of Peter and Paul, had been accorded some kind of primacy. Cyprian and Augustine argued that communion with Rome was a criterion for the true church. But, as J. N. D. Kelly remarks, "The real framers and promoters of the theory of the Roman primacy were the popes themselves."[3] Popes like Damasus (366–84), Siricius (384–99), and Innocent (402–17) advanced the claims to primacy on both the theoretical and practical planes, but it was Pope Leo I, the Great (440–61), whose famous *Tome of Leo* was accepted at the Council of Chalcedon (451), who summarized the doctrine of papal primacy. In this and many other writings, Leo claims that (1) Christ chose Peter and gave him precedence over the other apostles; (2) the Matthean text 16:18 ("upon this rock") refers to Peter himself and not his faith; (3) Peter was actually bishop of Rome and his authority is perpetuated in his successors; (4) the authority of the other apostles came through Peter, and that of the bishops is derived not immediately from Christ but through the bishop of Rome, who is a kind of *Petrus redivivus;* and therefore (5) the bishop of Rome has a plenitude of power, *plenitudo potestatis,* over the whole church, whereas the other bishops only share in this responsibility, *pars sollicitudinis.*[4]

Succeeding popes, such as Gelasius (492–96) and Gregory I, the Great (590–604), made similar claims. But Gregory made such claims credible by his energetic pastoral activity, defending Rome from the invading Lombards, fighting famine and plague, and promoting missions for the conversion of the barbarians, and by exercising his authority with humility and a deep spirituality. It was not just the *claims* of the popes that gave rise to the papal monarchy but its "prestige was enhanced by the character and energy of the popes themselves."[5]

In addition to the personal character of the popes, there were other factors contributing to the growth of papal authority. In popular piety, for example, there was great devotion to St. Peter and to relics, and so Southern contends that the pope "in practice owed most of his authority to the fact that he was the guardian of the body of St. Peter."[6] Another factor contributing to the increase in papal prestige was that the rise of Islam from 650 to 750 gradually cut off parts of the Eastern church from contact with Rome. The three ancient patriarchates of Alexandria, Antioch, and Jerusalem were isolated and ceased to have

---

3. J. N. D. Kelly, *Early Christian Doctrines,* 2d ed. (New York: Harper & Brothers, 1960), 419.

4. Sermon iv and Letter xiv, as cited in Eric G. Jay, *The Church: Its Changing Image through Twenty Centuries* (Atlanta: John Knox Press, 1980), 97–98, and Kelly, *Early Christian Doctrines,* 420–21.

5. Jay, *The Church,* 99; and Yves Congar, *L'Eglise de saint Augustin a l'epoque moderne* (Paris: Editions du Cerf, 1970), 34–35.

6. Southern, *Church in the Middle Ages,* 30.

influence in the church as a whole, with the consequent growth in importance of Rome. The pope ruled Rome as the secular deputy of the emperor in Constantinople, although the influence of Constantinople was felt through Greek speech and customs (a number of the popes themselves were Greek-speaking).

Papal claims to temporal authority in the West were also articulated in a famous forged document dating from the latter part of the eighth century, the *Donation of Constantine*. It purports to be a letter from the Emperor Constantine to Pope Silvester I written on March 30, 315. It lists the gifts of the emperor to the pope in gratitude for being cured of leprosy through the pope's intercession: "the grant of pre-eminence over the patriarchal sees of Antioch, Alexandria, Jerusalem, and Constantinople, and all other churches; the gift of the imperial insignia, together with the Lateran palace in Rome; and finally the transfer to the pope of the imperial power in Rome, Italy, and all the provinces of the West."[7] This claim to temporal power in the West, though without a basis in historical fact, gained wide acceptance and culminated in the crowning of Charlemagne as emperor of the Romans by Pope Leo III on Christmas Day of the year 800. Such a combination of symbolic acts and documentary legitimation, however, was still not enough to make the claim effective. That would be the work of centuries.[8] Southern remarks that it was a mistake for the pope to think that he had asserted his temporal authority by crowning an emperor, "because in creating an emperor the pope created not a deputy, but a rival or even a master." Thus, the second theme of the struggle between the spiritual and temporal powers during the medieval period was produced by the first, the attempt to establish papal supremacy. It is also true, however, that the tension between secular rulers and the church forced the church to clarify the position of the pope in order to preserve the independence of the church.

The temporal powers were represented not only by the emperor but also by local feudal lords, who were constantly warring among themselves and who gained control over bishops and abbots by gifts of land and church buildings. Bishops and abbots, indeed the church as a whole, became part of the feudal system in which each person, from the lowest serf up to the emperor, stood in vassalage to the next person up on the hierarchical scale. So, as Eric Jay says, "the bishops and abbots, were overlords in respect of those who worked in their service, and vassals in respect of the dukes and kings from whom the Church received gifts of land."[9] The spiritual and temporal functions were in-

---

7. Ibid., 93.
8. Jay, *The Church*, 101.
9. Ibid.

extricably interwoven. The notion of the separation of church and state had no meaning at all in this situation.

From the end of the eighth century through the ninth and tenth centuries another development took place in the life of the church that had a lasting effect on its self-understanding, and that was the increasing distinction between the clergy and the laity.[10] Yves Congar says:

> During this period the faithful no longer understood Latin. From the end of the eighth century the Canon of the Mass was said in a low voice, the priest celebrated with his back to the people, the faithful no longer brought their offerings to the altar, solitary masses multiplied in the monasteries.... From this period one could begin to make a list of passages in which the Church consists principally of the clergy.[11]

Although the image of the Body of Christ and of the *congregatio fidelium* remain in use, the laity become mere passive spectators and the active life of the church is carried on by the clergy. By the twelfth and thirteenth centuries, as Southern says, the ideal church "was a society of disciplined and organized clergy directing the thoughts and activities of an obedient and receptive laity — kings, magnates, and peasants alike."[12] The clergy were the only ones educated and this gave them "a monopoly of all those disciplines which not only determined the theoretical structure of society but provided the instruments of government."

But this was not the whole story. Secular rulers made use of the hierarchy and clergy for their own ends. Although crowned in St. Peter's on February 2, 962, with Pope John XII presiding, Otto the Great (d. 973) "regarded the bishops as his most suitable collaborators by reason of their education and their lack of children.... Unmarried bishops could not pass duchies or counties on to their sons."[13] Hence, Otto and others made bishops secular rulers so as to be free to appoint their successors and maintain control over the territory. Otto made his own brother, Bruno, who was the archbishop of Cologne, Duke of Lotharingia. The papal claims to temporal authority were ignored by Otto and his successors, and popes were required to take an oath of allegiance to the emperor. Bishops were nominated by the temporal power and were employed as officials of the crown. "The old canon law that required that

---

10. Although the term "lay" came into use as early as the third century, the laity were quite active participants in the life and governance of the church. It was only at this period that they became passive spectators. See Alexandre Faivre, *The Emergence of the Laity in the Early Church*, trans. David Smith (New York: Paulist Press, 1990).

11. Congar, *L'Eglise*, 57.

12. Southern, *Church in the Middle Ages*, 38.

13. Thomas Bokenkotter, *A Concise History of the Catholic Church* (New York: Doubleday & Co., 1979), 121–23.

a bishop be elected by clergy and people was completely forgotten. Actual control over the appointment was seized by the King and his great vassals. A ceremony called lay investiture reflected this fact."[14] Further, the episcopal nominee usually paid a substantial fee for his appointment. Thus, simony, the buying and selling of spiritual goods, became common throughout the whole church. It was in reaction to this secular dominance and corruption of the church that the Gregorian Reform of the eleventh century was directed.[15]

This reform, although named after Pope Gregory VII (1073–85), actually began under Pope Leo IX (1049–54) and those around him, including two monks, Hildebrand and Humbert. The latter wrote a treatise, *Libri adversus simonaicos*, attacking the "proprietary Church system and lay investiture as twin manifestations of the same evil: perversion of proper order." Right order in the church required that laymen obey the clergy, that bishops should be elected by the clergy and confirmed by the people and should not be invested by laymen but consecrated by the metropolitan and neighboring bishops. He argued, further, that laypersons must obey the clergy not only inside the church but outside, in the temporal order as well. His basic premise was "the unitary nature of society. Since Church and State actually form one body, Christendom — whose animating principle is the faith — it can be directed to its final goal, eternal salvation, only by the priesthood. Therefore, whenever the spiritual and temporal come into conflict — as often they must — the spiritual authority must have the final word."[16] This view of the relationship of the spiritual and temporal orders prevailed in the church throughout this period, and indeed, in some quarters right up until the twentieth century.

To make good on such a claim, the reformers had to liberate the papacy from control by the emperor and Roman nobles. A major reform with continuing significance for ecclesiology was decreed in 1059 by Pope Nicholas II (d. 1061): it excluded the emperor and the nobles from papal elections and stipulated that from that time on only the cardinals were to elect the pope, although some form of confirmation by the emperor was allowed.

It was the other monk mentioned above, Hildebrand, who became Pope Gregory VII in 1073 and who claimed and established, at least for a while, the absolute supremacy of the pope over the temporal order. Although the reformers appealed to the *Donation of Constantine* and

---

14. Ibid., 123.

15. I am grateful to my colleague, Professor Louis Pascoe, S.J., of Fordham University, who, after reading this section, commented that there really were two competing ecclesiologies, imperial and papal, both of which implied the views of their beneficiaries as the proper ecclesiology for Christendom.

16. Bokenkotter, *A Concise History*, 124.

incorporated it into canon law, this document portrayed the emperor as *giving* the imperial power to the pope. But, as Southern remarks, "It was not thus that Gregory VII saw his position. For him and for all his successors, the primacy was the gift of Christ himself, and the papal authority over kings and emperors came from no human transference of imperial authority but from God alone."[17] Gregory's view of the papacy is expressed in the famous *Dictatus papae*, sayings of the pope, contained in a collection of his letters. Among the statements we find:

> the pope can be judged by no one;
>
> the Roman church has never erred and never will err till the end of time;
>
> the Roman church was founded by Christ alone;
>
> the pope alone can depose and restore bishops;
>
> he alone can call general councils and authorize canon law;
>
> he alone can use the imperial insignia;
>
> he can depose emperors;
>
> all princes should kiss his feet;
>
> a duly ordained pope is undoubtedly made a saint by the merits St. Peter.[18]

Although some of these claims seem extravagant, he was able to actualize at least one when he excommunicated and deposed Emperor Henry IV and forced him to stand penitentially in the snow outside a castle at Canossa in 1077. But this did not terminate secular control over the church. Lay investiture was dealt with in various countries with various forms of compromise, the German version of which was included in the Concordat of Worms (1122). From this time, the papacy was able to exercise its jurisdiction in everyday affairs of European life, and the pope would be a dominant force both spiritually and temporally for centuries. Jay argues that the high point of the papacy was reached with Pope Innocent III (1198–1216) who was able to excommunicate King John of England in 1209 and make him a papal vassal. It was Innocent who also asserted that he was not the vicar of Peter, but the vicar of Jesus Christ himself.[19]

---

17. Southern, *Church in the Middle Ages*, 101.

18. Ibid., 102, quoting from *Gregorii VII Registrum, M.G.H. Epistolae Selectae, ii*, ed. E. Caspar, 201–8. These were actually chapter headings for a collection of canon law that Gregory intended to draw up but never did.

19. Jay, *The Church*, 109.

Finally in recounting the growth of the papal monarchy, we must
mention Pope Boniface VIII (1294–1303), whose bull *Unam Sanctam*
(1302) gave classical expression to the theory of the supremacy of the
spiritual over the temporal in the image of *the two swords*. Citing Luke
22:38, he argues that "both swords, therefore, the spiritual and the temporal, are in the power of the church. The former is to be used by the
church, the latter for the church; the one by the hand of the priest, the
other by the hand of kings and knights, but at the command and permission of the priest."[20] We can see adumbrations of this doctrine as far
back as Augustine and remnants of it in Luther's "Open Letter to the
Christian Nobility" in 1520.

## OPPOSITION TO THE PAPACY: ANOTHER VIEW

The growth of the papal monarchy and its struggle for independence
from, if not domination of, the temporal power is the unifying thread in
the story of the church's self-understanding in the Middle Ages. But, as
usual in history, there were countercurrents, submerged eddies running
against the tide that eventually surface.

Although there were a variety of movements in opposition to the
power and wealth of the papal church, such as the Albigensians (or
Pure Ones) and the Waldensians (also called the Poor Ones of Lyons) in
the late twelfth and early thirteenth centuries in southern France, the
main countercurrent that surfaced in the medieval period had its origins much earlier, and that is the synodal or conciliar tradition. From the
point of view of ecclesiological developments this was another strand
in the Christian self-understanding that runs throughout its history but
was obscured in the West, though not in the East, by the growth of the
papal monarchy.

As far back as the second century we have evidence of the bishops
meeting in local synods to deal with threats to church order and discipline concerning such issues as the dating of Easter.[21] Such gatherings
of bishops became "a regular and indispensable feature of church life,
the ordinary institutional expression of the cohesion of local Eucharistic communities in a universal body." Over four hundred synods and
meetings of bishops are known to have been held between the middle of the second century and the pontificate of Gregory the Great.[22]

---

20. Quoted in Jay, *The Church*, 111.
21. Brian E. Daley, S.J., "Structures of Charity: Bishops' Gatherings and the See of Rome
in the Early Church," in Thomas J. Reese, S.J., ed., *Episcopal Conferences: Historical,
Canonical, and Theological Studies* (Washington, D.C.: Georgetown University Press,
1989), 27.
22. Ibid., 28.

These meetings were an important means of preserving ecclesial and political unity. We saw in the previous chapter that Cyprian, though he strongly emphasized the position of the bishop as the touchstone of church unity, also relied on councils in North Africa to deal with threats to the church in a unified manner. He also communicated the results of these councils to the pope at Rome. For Cyprian, it was the unity of the episcopal college as well as communion with the bishop of Rome that guaranteed the unity of the church universal.

Augustine, too, had participated in many councils in North Africa and had to argue, against the Donatists, that conciliar decrees did not have the same authority as Scripture itself. The Donatists regarded decisions of earlier councils as divinely inspired and permanently binding. Augustine replied that "only Scripture is infallible, and conciliar statements must be judged by its standard."[23]

The experience of the conciliar form of governance existed on several levels, general, regional, and local. The general or ecumenical Council of Nicaea (325) decreed that the bishops "of each civil province should gather in synod twice a year," and popes like Leo and Gregory often encouraged "bishops to observe the canonical requirement of regular provincial and regional meetings."[24] Such provincial or regional synods also received or confirmed decisions of general councils. For example, following the Council of Chalcedon, Emperor Leo I, in 458, "specifically asked provincial synods throughout the Eastern Empire to meet and consider whether or not they still wished to adhere to the Chalcedonian Christological formula."[25]

The relationship of these various councils and synods to the bishop of Rome varied over time. Brian Daley says that until the middle of the fifth century there was no claim that the decisions of such gatherings required the approval, formal or informal, of the bishop of Rome, but by the time of Gregory the Great he could claim that papal consent was needed for the decisions of local synods to have force. But Gregory's style, as mentioned above, led him to recognize the rights of all bishops, "even if they limited his own exercise of power," and he was the one to assume the title of *servus servorum Dei* (the servant of the servants of God). Nonetheless, we have seen the growth of papal claims throughout the Middle Ages, and this was bound to come into conflict with the long-standing *experience* of conciliar and synodal governance in the church. The development of the *theory* or *theology* of conciliarism, however, came to the fore only in the period we are describing, the thirteenth and fourteenth centuries.

---

23. Ibid., 49.
24. Ibid., 45.
25. Ibid., 31.

The occasion for the growth of conciliar theory and for the so-called conciliar epoch was the papacy itself. The struggle between Boniface VIII and Philip the Fair, king of France, over the exemption of the clergy from taxation or prosecution issuing from Boniface's bull *Clericos Laicos* (1298) was eventually resolved in favor of the French king. In order to deal with the dominance of the French, as well as unsettled political conditions in Rome, Pope Clement V, elected two years after Boniface's death, moved the papal residence to Avignon in 1309. There, for the next seventy years, despite the competence and personally devout character of most of the Avignon popes, the papal court lived in isolation and luxury. It developed an efficient administrative and financial system and greatly extended papal taxation in a ruthless manner. This, combined with

> the spectacle of a rich, luxurious and powerful sovereign and his bureaucracy, living in their palace-fortress completely out of touch with the imperial city of the apostles, which had always been the center of the faith, was of itself a permanent scandal, and it is certain that during its prolonged stay the papacy and its court compromised with worldly standards and aims in an organic fashion which was more detrimental to the Church than previous excesses of individuals.[26]

The scandal of the Avignon papacy was minor, however, compared to what followed. Shortly after Pope Gregory XI returned the papacy to Rome in 1377, he died. When the college of cardinals, sixteen in all, assembled on April 7, 1378, in Rome to elect a successor, they were under some pressure from the Roman populace, although how much is disputed, to elect an Italian. They quickly elected the archbishop of Bari, who took the name Pope Urban VI. He soon showed himself to be a tyrant of the worst sort. As one historian describes the situation, "Seizing any and every occasion, he upbraided them [the cardinals] publicly and privately — often in paroxysms of rage — for their vices, their treachery, their luxury, their simony. The personality change was so radical that contemporaries as well as later historians feel that Urban may have been mentally unhinged by his sudden and unexpected election or perhaps by illness."[27] By September, after abandoning Rome, this same college of cardinals declared the election of Urban VI invalid, claiming they were under duress, and elected a new pope, Clement VII. Thus began what has come to be called the "Great Schism" (or sometimes, the "Great Western Schism" to distinguish it from the break between the Eastern and Western churches of 1054).

---

26. David Knowles and Dimitri Obolensky, *The Middle Ages (The Christian Centuries)* (London: Darton, Longman, and Todd, 1969), 2:406.

27. Bokenkotter, *Concise History,* 194.

Neither pope would admit that he was not legitimately elected, and each gained the allegiance of various civil governments, splitting Western Christendom into two camps. "The Holy Roman Emperor, England, the Netherlands, Castille, Hungary, Poland, and Portugal stood behind Urban, while France rallied to Clement VII, who returned to Avignon in 1379 and was soon joined by Scotland, Luxembourg, and Austria."[28] Each pope also maintained the loyalty of his own group of cardinals who, when these two died, elected successors: Urban VI at Rome was followed by Boniface IX (1389–1404), Innocent VII (1404–6), and Gregory XII (1406–15); while Clement VII at Avignon was followed by Benedict XIII (1394–1417). Before the Great Schism was finally resolved, yet another pope was elected by the Council of Pisa in 1409, Pope Alexander V (1409–10), and his successor, John XXIII (1410–15), thereby providing a third contestant for the papal throne!

Two major ways of breaking the impasse were advocated and attempted: the *via concessionis,* inducing one or both claimants to resign, which is what the Council of Pisa thought they had accomplished and why they elected a new pope; and the *via concilii,* superseding the rivals by a general council.[29] It was this situation, then, that occasioned the other major current in the Christian community's self-understanding, its corporate or collegial aspect, to surface and come to some degree of maturity. David Knowles and Dimitri Obolensky are correct in their assessment that many modern historians have generally assumed that between 1076 and 1378 the only alternative to the orthodoxy of the papal monarchy was the imperialistic position. "In fact, however, the social and ecclesiastical background during this period, and canonist reflection, had given birth to a theory parallel to the monarchic, of the Church as a corporation, or rather a hierarchy of corporations, of which the lowest was the body of the faithful and the highest the college of cardinals."[30]

## Conciliar Theory

In addition to the experience of synods and councils, the images of the Body of Christ, People of God, and *congregatio fidelium* had never disappeared from the church's self-understanding. *Congregatio fidelium,* for example, is the image most frequently used by Thomas Aquinas. When it was clear that the papacy was not the unifying force it claimed to be, the other expression or manifestation of church unity, the collegial or corporate nature of the church, was emphasized. The earliest articu-

---

28. Ibid., 195.
29. Knowles and Obolensky, *The Middle Ages,* 417.
30. Ibid., 417–18.

lations of what later came to be known as "strict conciliarist theory" are traced to the twelfth- and early thirteenth-century commentators on the *Decretum* of Gratian, such as Joannes Teutonicus (d. 1246), who argued that a general council must be above the pope in matters of faith for a pope could lapse into heresy. If he did so, some commentators thought that the college of cardinals could depose him while others held this right belonged to a general council. Another source seems to have been found in the commentators on the *Decretales* of Gregory IX, who applied the Roman law of corporations to both the local churches and to the universal church. They maintained that "the key to that church's unity lay in the corporate association of its members."[31]

Another source seems to be in two proponents of imperial superiority, William of Ockham and Marsilius of Padua, who argued that the church is not to be defined as a clerical body but as the whole body of the faithful. Further, Marsilius argued that although the priesthood was divinely established, the hierarchic structure of bishops, archbishops, and pope is simply a human contrivance and must be grounded in the consent of the faithful. This consent is to be expressed by direct election of bishops and "head bishop" and by an elected general council. This general council can speak infallibly on matters of faith because Christ promised infallibility only to the universal church.[32]

With such affirmations in the air, it did not take long after the double election of 1378 for such figures as Conrad of Gelnhausen and Henry of Langenstein to offer a coherent statement of a "strict conciliar theory." Although there were variations among the conciliarists, the theory contains three basic strands: (1) the demand for reform in head and members of the church; (2) the application of corporation theory to the church with the college of cardinals and a general council having a constitutional role in the government of the church, making it a "mixed government"; (3) the assertion that ultimate authority rests in the church as a whole, defined as the *congregatio fidelium*, which could be exercised through its representatives in general council, even, in certain critical cases, against the wishes of the pope, and which could if necessary depose him, thus asserting the superiority of general council over pope.[33] The most prominent of those who held some form of this theory, generally called "conciliarists," were Francis Zabarella (1360–1417), Dietrich of Niem (c. 1340–1418), Pierre d'Ailly (1350–1420), Jean Gerson (1363–1429), and Nicholas of Cusa (c. 1400–1464).

---

31. Francis Oakley, "Conciliar Theory," *Dictionary of the Middle Ages*, 3:516. See also Brian Tierney, *Foundations of the Conciliar Theory: The Contribution of the Medieval Canonists from Gratian to the Great Schism* (Cambridge: Cambridge University Press, 1955).

32. Oakley, "Conciliar Theory," 515.

33. Ibid., 511–12.

## The Conciliar Epoch

This theology of the church, evoked by the schism, fueled the efforts to heal it in a series of councils over the next forty years. We have already mentioned the Council of Pisa, 1409, which had been convoked by cardinals from both allegiances and which summoned both claimants to attend. They did not show up and the council deposed them both and elected Alexander V, as mentioned above. But Alexander V died a year later and John XXIII was elected, among whose cardinals were Zabarella and Pierre d'Ailly. Hence, Pisa resolved nothing. John XXIII called another general council at Rome, but hardly anyone showed up and it was suspended for lack of participants. Because the schism was splitting the empire, the recently elected Holy Roman Emperor, Sigismund of Luxembourg, with John XXIII's agreement, summoned a council to begin November 1, 1414, at Constance.

Some papalists later wanted to dispute the legitimacy of this council, but virtually "the whole of Western Christendom was represented including five patriarchs, twenty-nine cardinals, thirty-three archbishops, more than five hundred bishops, a hundred abbots, three hundred doctors of sacred science, and eighteen thousand other clerics."[34] John XXIII abandoned the council and was tried and deposed. The council declared in a famous decree, *Sacrosancta*, April 6, 1415, that its authority was directly from Christ and claimed the obedience of all, including the pope, in matters of faith and reform. Gregory XII, of the Roman line, resigned, but Benedict XIII, of the Avignon line, held out until he was deposed in 1417. The council was divided as to whether to elect a pope right away or proceed with the reform of the church first. A compromise was reached, and the council issued another famous decree, *Frequens*, on October 9, 1417, obliging all future popes to call councils first after five years, then after seven years, and every ten years thereafter. They then proceeded to elect a new pope, Martin V, and the thirty-nine-year schism was ended.[35] Among the leaders of the Council of Constance were some of the outstanding conciliarists mentioned above, d'Ailly, Gerson, Zabarella, and Dietrich of Niem, and their influence is reflected in the decrees mentioned.

Although the Great Schism was ended, the struggle between popes and councils was not. Martin V reasserted papal supremacy but observed the decrees of Constance and called a council in 1423, which met first at Pavia and then at Siena. It lasted only a year and did little by way of reform. Another council was summoned to meet in Basle in 1431, but the new pope, Eugenius IV, tried to dissolve it. The council

---

34. Bokenkotter, *Concise History*, 198.
35. Ibid., 201, and Knowles and Obolensky, *The Middle Ages*, 420–21.

refused to be dissolved and declared itself superior to the pope insisting that it could not be adjourned or transferred even by the pope. At the request of the Greek Orthodox the council was transferred to Ferrara, then to Florence (1438–45), but only a minority from Basle went. The Council of Basle remained in session off and on, and in 1439 deposed Eugenius IV as a heretic and elected Pope Felix V. The great powers, however, gradually withdrew their support of the Council of Basle, and, after agreement with the German princes, the Holy Roman Emperor Frederick ordered its members to leave. The council dissolved, and Felix resigned in 1449. Bokenkotter summarizes:

> The papacy had triumphed over conciliarism, but it failed to re-establish its moral and spiritual leadership over Christendom. In many ways the real victor of the crisis was the modern state, which exploited the quarrel between Pope and council in order to expand its authority over the church. In England, France, and Spain, at least, national Churches were rapidly arising.[36]

We have discussed the conciliar experience and theory at some length because it is an important strand in the development of the Christian community's self-understanding that is frequently ignored in favor of tracing the monarchical papacy and its struggle with the temporal powers. But even more important is the fact that the corporate understanding of the church existed along side of and interacted with papal theory throughout this period, and perdured long after. It was the immediate background for Luther's call for a "free and open council" and for reform of the church in "head and members." Conciliarist principles were advocated by Gallican writers as exemplified by the *Declaration of the Gallican Clergy* (1682) and later by the Febronians in Germany. The Dogmatic Constitution *Pastor Aeternus* of Vatican I (1870) proclaims papal infallibility and condemns conciliarist principles in language taken from the Gallican declaration. Finally, some of the remnants of the corporate understanding of the church reappear in Vatican II's affirmation of episcopal collegiality and encouragement of national episcopal conferences, as we shall see. The rise of the papal monarchy in the Middle Ages did not destroy it. This corporate understanding of the church, expressed in episcopal collegiality, in synods and councils, regional and general, has a long history and the story is not over yet.

---

36. Bokenkotter, *Concise History,* 206.

## REFORM IN HEAD AND MEMBERS

Each of the councils in the fifteenth century, Pisa, Constance, Basle, and Florence, had listed and decried various abuses in the church and called for reform. None succeeded in achieving it. The decree *Frequens,* which required that councils be held at regular intervals, was intended to guarantee that reform would take place by conciliar action even if the pope did lead the way himself. There were some popes who were interested in reform. Pius II (1458–64), for example, drew up a bull, *Pastor Aeternus,* initiating reform, but he died before it could be issued. Other popes, the so-called Renaissance popes, Sixtus IV (d. 1484), Innocent VIII (d. 1492), and Alexander VI (d. 1503), for example, "wallowed in corruption unparalleled since the tenth century," completely subordinating the religious functions of their office to unworthy temporal gains.[37] Finally, Pope Julius II convoked the Fifth Lateran Council (1512–17), which proposed a whole range of reforms, but the pope at the end of the council, Leo X (d. 1521), did nothing to implement them. It could rightly be said that at the beginning of the sixteenth century the whole world, including some curial cardinals, cried out for reform. They were not prepared, however, for it to come from an obscure Augustinian monk in Germany!

Once again, we will not attempt to recount the entire history of the Reformation but only its contribution to the development of the church's self-understanding. The issues that sparked Luther's protest initially were in areas of theology other than ecclesiology, though with implications for ecclesiology. The rallying cry of the Reformation, *sola gratia, sola fide, sola scriptura,* summarize his concerns. His fundamental insight was that justification comes only from God by grace through faith. All the works of humans — prayers, pilgrimages, acts of charity, etc. — cannot bring about justification.

The preaching of indulgences by the Dominican friar Johann Tetzel seemed to Luther to be a direct contradiction of this fundamental insight, for, at least as the teaching was popularly understood, it said that by the payment of money someone could be freed from the temporal punishment due to sin in this life or in the next, in purgatory.[38] What is more, at least some of this money went to the pope in Rome to pay for his building projects. Luther's reaction was to draw up ninety-five theses (summary statements of theological positions) and offer to debate them publicly. As the story goes, he posted these theses on the door of the castle church in Wittenberg on October 31, 1517. Though the

---

37. Ibid., 211.
38. A more theological understanding of indulgences was based in the belief that the lives and deeds of the saints accumulated "merit" in heaven, and the church on earth could draw upon this "spiritual treasury" to remit the temporal punishment due to sin.

theses themselves were rather technical, theologically speaking, copies were printed and, unknown to Luther, widely circulated in Germany within a few weeks. Jay says, "They gained wide support, and gradually he found himself cast in the role of leader in a revolt against papal supremacy over the church."[39] What we now call the Reformation had been launched.

Within a very short time, the issue shifted from the theology of indulgences to other abuses in the church — the corruption of the Roman curia, papal taxation, the unwillingness of the pope to institute reform or call a council to do so — and the very hierarchical structure of the church itself. Only those things that could be found in Scripture could be justified and, hence, his other fundamental principle, *sola scriptura*.

Luther's understanding of the church flowed directly from his basic theological position of justification by grace through faith, for those who had this justifying faith were the *congregatio fidelium*, or the congregation of saints. This free gift, grace, of God was given in the life, death, and resurrection of his Son, Jesus Christ, who had redeemed humankind. But it continues to be offered through the preaching of the Gospel and in the administration of the sacraments. Hence, Luther defined the church as the "congregation of saints in which the Gospel is rightly taught and the sacraments are rightly administered."[40] He fills out this definition later in *On the Councils and the Church* (1539) by adding the "office of the keys, the presence of ministers and offices in the church, prayer, the public praise of God, and finally... inner temptation and outward persecution as characteristics."[41]

Since the church is the congregation of those who have faith and since faith is invisible, the true church is invisible. The church we see is a community *permixtum,* as was held by Augustine. Hence, Luther says: "We shall call the two churches by two distinct names. The first, which is natural, basic, essential, and true, we shall call 'spiritual internal Christendom.' The second, which is man-made and external, we shall call 'physical, external Christendom.' "[42] For Luther, however, it is one and the same church that is both visible and invisible in different dimensions. Internal Christendom is to external Christendom as the soul is to the body.

In asserting that the visible, external church is "man-made" Luther denied that ecclesiastical institutions, hierarchy, and papacy are divinely ordained; they are of human origin and, therefore, fallible and changeable. There is some dispute as to whether or not Luther himself thought

39. Jay, *The Church,* 162.

40. Augsburg Confession, art. 7.

41. Paul Althaus, *The Theology of Martin Luther,* trans. Robert C. Schultz (Philadelphia: Fortress Press, 1966), 289.

42. Luther, *On the Papacy at Rome, Luther's Works* 39:69–70.

that the office of preaching was of divine origin, but later Lutheran writings, the Augsburg Confession (art. 5), for example, seem to indicate that the public ministry is of divine institution.[43] At the same time, Luther insisted on the priesthood of all believers in that all are called to preach the Gospel, to edify the neighbor, to forgive, and to reconcile. Some in the community, however, should be chosen for the special ministry of preaching in public and administering the sacraments. These are called pastors. Luther wanted to repudiate the difference in rank or status between clergy and laity that had developed in the medieval church, but not to deny the need for some order within the Christian community.

On the issue that so dominated the period, the relationship of the spiritual to the temporal power, Luther appeals to Augustine's understanding of the City of God and the City of Man, but for Luther these are "two kingdoms." This language is used to describe not only the two realms of church and state, but also the more general relationship between the spiritual and the temporal spheres and the activities of individual Christians on their own behalf and in behalf of others.[44] If the world were made up only of real Christians, of true believers, there would be no need for the coercive force of the secular powers. Unfortunately that is not the case. The Christian prince, or temporal ruler, because he is a Christian and shares in the priesthood of all believers, has the obligation to use his office for the good of the church when this is necessary, although he cannot interfere in the realm of conscience. Luther called on the German nobility insofar as they were Christian princes to supervise the reform of the church and, if necessary, call a council, because those who had the responsibility for doing so, the priests, the spiritual power, had failed to do so.[45] Like Augustine, Luther saw that there was sometimes need for the temporal power to intervene in spiritual affairs for the good of the church. But political events and the opportunism of the German nobility (and others) found in this doctrine justification for much more interference than Luther envisioned. Jay says that in the end "the Lutheran churches were to exist under something akin to State absolutism in things spiritual as well as temporal. . . . For Lutheranism the authority of pope and bishops had passed to the Christian prince."[46]

---

43. Jay, *The Church*, 165–67; and the discussion of recent scholarship on this topic in John Reumann, "Ordained Ministry and Laymen in Lutheranism," in Paul C. Empie and T. Austin Murphy, eds. *Eucharist and Ministry, Lutherans and Catholics in Dialogue IV* (Minneapolis: Augsburg, 1979), 227–82.

44. Heinrich Borknamm, *Luther's Doctrine of the Two Kingdoms in the Context of His Theology* trans. Karl H. Hertz (Philadelphia: Fortress Press, 1966), 8 and 16.

45. Luther, "An Open Letter to the Christian Nobility" (1520), in *Three Treatises* (Philadelphia: Fortress Press, 1960).

46. Jay, *The Church*, 169.

The Reform movement initiated by Luther spread rapidly to other areas, and by 1522 Huldrych Zwingli was leading it in Zurich, by 1523 Martin Bucer in Strasbourg, by 1530 Guillaume Farel in Neuchâtel. In 1535, Farel went to Geneva, where he involved John Calvin in the work there. Both Calvin and Farel were temporarily banished but in 1541 returned to Geneva, where Calvin remained for the rest of his life. Like Luther, Calvin too perceived the church as both invisible, all the elect known only to God, and visible, all on earth who profess to worship one God and Christ. Like Luther and Augustine, this latter is a *corpus permixtum:*

> in this church are mingled many hypocrites who have nothing of Christ but the name and outward appearance. . . . Just as we must believe, therefore, that the former church, invisible to us, is visible to the eyes of God alone, so we are commanded to revere and keep communion with the latter, which is called "church" in respect to men.[47]

Mixed though it is, this visible church is the means ordained by God to bring the elect to their predestined salvation. Like Cyprian and Augustine, Calvin holds that there is no salvation apart from this church.[48]

Although Calvin referred to the pope in Rome as the "Antichrist," he believed that the fourfold ministry of pastors, teachers, elders, and deacons was of divine ordinance. It is this "order by which the Lord willed his church to be governed."[49] But only Christ may be called the head of the church. The papal model tends to replace Christ and usurp this role for a human in his stead. Ministers in the church, chosen by Christ, do "serve as his ambassadors in the world, to be interpreters of his secret will, and, in short, to represent his person."[50] In summary, Calvin has a lofty view of the ministry and a "high ecclesiology" in general, in contrast to some of the more radical reformers, as we will see below. His rejection of bishops, however, was a major break with the tradition.

Although Calvin is sometimes portrayed as running Geneva as a theocracy, his position on the relationship of church and state, or of the spiritual and temporal powers, is more nuanced than is sometimes supposed. For Calvin, there is a sharp distinction between ecclesiastical and civil power:

> For the church does not have the right of the sword to punish or compel, not the authority to force; not imprisonment, nor the

---

47. John Calvin, *Institutes of the Christian Religion,* trans. Ford L. Battles, Library of Christian Classics 21, ed. John T. McNeill (Philadelphia: Westminster Press, 1960), Bk. 4, I, 7, 1021–22.

48. Ibid., 1016.

49. Ibid., 1053ff.

50. Ibid.

other punishments which the magistrate commonly inflicts. . . .
The church does not assume what is proper to the magistrate; nor
can the magistrate execute what is carried out by the church.[51]

In practice, however, such a clear distinction was not always maintained. Calvin had a horror of disorder, which he saw represented in the
radical reformers, but at the same time he shared their desire for a pure
church, a church of the saints, uncontaminated by heresy. As Bouwsma
says, "This impulse . . . explains his effort to convert Geneva into a visible
community of saints. . . . Toleration of the least impurity would lead to
the infection of the whole."[52] His ultimate device for maintaining such
purity was excommunication. Although the clergy had the primary responsibility for admonishing and correcting others, Calvin established
a "consistory" of elders in Geneva to maintain discipline in that community. Bouwsma remarks that this consistory of elders "in fact assumed a
major responsibility that had previously belonged to the council" of the
city. This fusion (or confusion) of the responsibility for order in the community was also based on Calvin's identification of the church with the
local community, such as Geneva. Again Bouwsma suggests that "the
coincidence of church membership with residence in the town made
the Genevan church a 'mixture' of righteous and wicked, a situation
that, . . . aroused his [Calvin's] deepest anxieties and drove him toward
clerical supremacy."[53] Calvin repeatedly affirmed the authority of clergy
over the laity, and their duty to censure the vices of all, including kings
and queens. Calvin did not share Luther's doctrine of the priesthood
of all believers. It is not surprising then, that he has been charged with
establishing a theocracy!

We mentioned above that Calvin's understanding of the church
differed from the so-called radical reformers, the left wing of the Reformation, sometimes also called "Separatists" or, more frequently, "Anabaptists." Although the names covered a wide variety of opinions and
they did not necessarily hold to a coherent system of doctrine, a fair
summary of their ecclesiological principles can be found in the Anabaptist Confession of Schleitheim (1527). This document, Chadwick
says, is the

nearest to a confession agreed by the early Anabaptists. [It] proclaimed adult baptism and separation from the world, including
everything popish, and from attendance at parish churches and

---

51. *Institutes*, Bk. 4, XI, 3, 1215.
52. William J. Bouwsma, *John Calvin: A Sixteenth-Century Portrait* (New York: Oxford
University Press, 1988), 217–18.
53. Ibid., 217.

taverns. It condemned the use of force or going to law, or becoming a magistrate, or the taking of oaths.[54]

The Anabaptists expressed the sectarian tendencies we have seen earlier in the Montanists, Novatianists, and Donatists. They tended to form small separate groups, each being autonomous, with no responsibility to or supervision by a larger body. They embraced the "voluntary principle," in opposition to both Protestant and Catholic attempts to impose their religious tradition with the help of the secular power. They were concerned with the personal holiness of their members and believed that this could be achieved only by separating themselves from worldly enticements and involvement in worldly affairs — the characteristics Troelstch would later use to define a "sect."[55] They placed great emphasis on the personal guidance of the Spirit, and hence some were referred to as "Pentecostals." There were some extremists among them, such as Thomas Munzer, who lead the "Peasants Revolt" of 1524–25, which so horrified Luther, and John of Leyden, who instigated a bloody revolt in the city of Munster in 1534–35, which gave the whole Anabaptist movement a bad name. Some Separatists from the Leyden congregation brought this ecclesiological tradition to the New World aboard the *Mayflower* in 1620.[56]

Before concluding this broad survey of the developments in the self-understanding of the Christian community in this period, we must say something, briefly, about the ecclesiology of Eastern Orthodoxy from which the Western church had been isolated even before the formal excommunications of 1054. Before this time, as Jay says, "divisive influences were at work: the difference in language; a growing diversity in ecclesiastical customs; and a mounting contempt, in the West for the effete and dilettante Byzantines, and in the East for the barbarian westerner."[57] Although there were some doctrinal differences (the use of the *filioque* in the creed, for example) there was little difference in ecclesiology. Jay, citing Congar, points out that the church was more "a fact that is lived" than a dogma or a theological treatise.[58]

In contrasting the ecclesiology of the Orthodox with that of Western Christianity, Ware summarizes:

> Unlike Protestantism, Orthodoxy insists upon the hierarchical structure of the Church, upon the Apostolic Succession, the episcopate, and the priesthood; it prays to the saints and intercedes for the departed. Thus far Rome and Orthodoxy agree — but where

---

54. Owen Chadwick, *The Reformation* (Baltimore: Penguin Books, 1964), 189.
55. Jay, *The Church*, 177–80.
56. Chadwick, *The Reformation*, 208.
57. Jay, *The Church*, 143.
58. Ibid., 148.

Rome thinks in terms of the supremacy and the universal jurisdiction of the Pope, Orthodoxy thinks in terms of the college of
bishops and of the Ecumenical Council; where Rome stresses Papal infallibility, Orthodoxy stresses the infallibility of the Church
as a whole.[59]

As mentioned above, the Orthodox church has preserved the collegial, synodal, or conciliar tradition, which was submerged in the
Western church.[60] Each local church is the full expression of the catholic church and the bishop has the fullness of episcopal authority in it.
But, as Jay put it, "the bishops together form a collegial body of which
each member exercises the totality of episcopal authority within his
own sphere. In this collegiate body none has an inherent juridical right
over others."[61] Orthodoxy has always recognized that the ancient patriarchial sees have more authority than others and has accorded Rome a
primacy of honor, but it has denied that any see has jurisdiction over
any other. Each local church is relatively autonomous, with bishops
being appointed by the Governing Synod of each autocephalous (self-
heading) church.[62] The unity of the church universal is constituted by
the communion of the heads of the local churches.

The outward structure of the church, however, is secondary to its
sacramental character. The church is basically a "Eucharistic society, a
sacramental organism which exists . . . wherever the Eucharist is celebrated." The term "Body of Christ" refers to both the church and the
sacrament.[63] This image, Body of Christ, is a dominant theme in Orthodox ecclesiology, as is the notion of the church as an "earthly heaven
wherein the heavenly God dwells and walks," a place where the invisible and the visible cosmos are united. There is no clear distinction in
Orthodoxy between the church and the world, the sacred and the secular, the church and the state. As Jay says, "This is why the Eastern Church,
from the time of Constantine and throughout the Byzantine period, conceived of Church and State (under a Christian ruler) as a single society,
governed by two hierarchies, ecclesiastical and imperial, each autonomous, but acting in 'symphony.' "[64] This tradition of close identification
of church with the secular society of a particular region has continued
into the present in eastern Europe.

The importance of the Orthodox church in the total history of the
church is not represented by this brief treatment of its ecclesiology, but

---

59. Timothy Ware, *The Orthodox Church* (Baltimore: Penguin Books, 1963), 243.
60. Michael A. Fahey, "Eastern Synodal Traditions: Pertinence for Western Collegial
Institutions," in Reese, *Episcopal Conferences*, 253–56.
61. Jay, *The Church*, 156.
62. Ibid., 299.
63. Ware, *The Orthodox Church*, 246.
64. Jay, *The Church*, 152, and Ware, *The Orthodox Church*, 49.

for our purposes it will suffice. We will deal with the various attempts at reunion between East and West in the later chapter on ecumenism.

## SUMMARY

In this chapter we have considered the developments in the self-understanding of the Christian community over the millennium we have loosely termed the Middle Ages, from Late Antiquity on one end to the Protestant Reformation on the other. We have seen that the dominant themes in this period have been (1) the rise and decline of the papacy, understanding the church primarily as a monarchy with descending orders of power on the feudal model; and (2) the struggle between the spiritual authority of the church and the temporal or secular powers, represented by the emperor, Frankish kings, local dukes and nobles, and, toward the end of the period, by the emerging nation-states. As a countercurrent to these dominant story lines, the corporate understanding of the community, represented by the conciliar movement and conciliar theory remained alive and surfaced for a time.

It should be clear that the community's self-understanding, the theology of the church, was not articulated in a vacuum. Such non-theological factors as the waning of Constantinople, the barbarian invasions in the West and the Islamic onslaught in the East, the personal character and energy of individual popes, and the development of the feudal structure of society in the Middle Ages all contributed to this self-understanding. Further, the fact that most of this "theologizing" was done by lawyers — from Tertullian through the papalists, commentators on the Decrees of Gratian and papal decretals, and the conciliarists — contributed to casting the theology of the church in a juridical framework of rights, powers, and obligations.

Through it all, however, the images of the church developed in the New Testament — Body of Christ, Temple of the Holy Spirit, *congregatio fidelium*, People of God — were not lost but were appealed to right down to Luther and Calvin. The theologizing also included principles from Roman law and corporation theory. Neither were the earlier concerns for the unity of the church, the holiness of its members, its catholicity, and its continuity with the apostolic tradition forgotten. But scandals in the church, especially those of the Avignon papacy and the Great Schism, forced these questions to be framed in new ways. The scandals, both individual and institutional, led to the frequent and insistent cry for reform in head and members and a realization that the ancient formula *ecclesia semper reformanda* would be an ongoing necessity. Attempts at reform were frequently thwarted by those in power, not only in the church but also by secular rulers who manipulated both popes and councils for their own ends.

Despite the relatively unified society that we call Christendom, there was constant tension and conflict, a see-sawing back and forth between the spiritual and the temporal powers, between the authority of the church and the authority of the secular rulers. By the time of the Reformation, this tension was not resolved either in theory or practice. Developments in Lutheranism favored the dominance of secular rulers, while Calvinism leaned in the opposite direction, and Catholicism maintained claims to the supremacy of the spiritual as embodied primarily in the Roman papacy. Emerging national consciousness in Europe only exacerbated this tension and continued it into the seventeenth, eighteenth, and nineteenth centuries, as we will see in the next chapter.

## RECOMMENDED READINGS

Chadwick, Owen. *The Reformation*. Baltimore: Penguin Books, 1964.

Knowles, David, and Dimitri Obolensky. *The Middle Ages*. London: Darton, Longman, and Todd, 1969.

Luther, Martin. "An Open Letter to the Christian Nobility" (1520), in *Three Treatises*. Philadelphia: Fortress Press, 1960.

Southern, R. W. *Western Society and the Church in the Middle Ages*. London: Penguin Books, 1970.

# Chapter 5

# Catholic Reform and Reaction

The Protestant Reformation was the background against which all further developments in the Christian community's self-understanding took place right up until the Second Vatican Council. Both sides defined themselves over against the other, and, in a polemical tone, emphasized those aspects of the church that the other found questionable. This chapter will focus on the Roman Catholic developments, with only passing reference to the Protestant side, during the period from the Reformation to Vatican II.

## CATHOLIC REFORM

Though Luther had been excommunicated in 1520, his protest only gradually developed into a full-blown schism. Moderates expected that a reform council would occur and that there would be a reconciliation between opposing theological viewpoints. Subsequent popes, remembering the Councils of Basle and Constance, feared a general council and found excuses for delay in summoning one. Some popes felt that they could reform the church by papal decree. The secular powers were divided; some of them wanted a council and some did not. There were attempts at reconciliation short of a general council, such as the Colloquy of Ratisbon in 1541, where moderates from both sides actually did agree on a formulation of the doctrine of justification by faith, but the conservatives on both sides were suspicious and objected to the concessions.[1] In the end, it was the conservatives who triumphed.

---

1. Owen Chadwick, *The Reformation* (Baltimore: Penguin Books, 1964), 267–69.

Under prodding from Emperor Charles V, Pope Paul III (1534–49) finally faced the inevitable and summoned a general council, which convened at Trent in northern Italy on December 13, 1545, with less than thirty bishops in attendance.[2] It is surprising, as Congar remarks, that "this council which was supposed to respond to the Reformation did not treat the ecclesiological problem" explicitly.[3] It did reiterate that the hierarchical nature of the church is by divine institution (sess. 23, can. 6), that there is a visible and external priesthood in the New Testament (sess. 23, can. 1), and that the church has the right to judge and interpret Scripture (sess. 4).[4] In discussing other theological issues, such as the sacraments and justification, the council seems to presuppose the hierarchical understanding of the church. There is no discussion of papal primacy but the council did seek the approval of the pope for its decrees.

On the practical side, the Council of Trent issued decrees aimed at reforming many of the abuses of which Luther and others had complained, such as requiring bishops to reside in their dioceses (sess. 6, chap. 1; sess. 23, chap. 1). The reform decree that many regard as most important for the life of the post-Tridentine church was that requiring bishops to establish seminaries in their dioceses (sess. 23, chap. 18). The form of clerical training that this initiated perdured until Vatican II.

A fuller treatment of Trent's understanding of the Catholic Christian community is to be found in the *Catechism* it authorized, which was largely written by Charles Borromeo and published by Pope Pius V in 1566. Frequently citing St. Augustine, the *Catechism* defines the church as "the Christian Commonwealth" and the "congregations of the faithful" or "the faithful dispersed throughout the world" (chap. X, q. ii).[5] It then notes the various images used to designate the Christian commonwealth in the New Testament: the house and edifice of God, the flock of Christ, the spouse of Christ, and the body of Christ (q. iii). Though the church is one, there are two component parts, "the one called the Church triumphant, the other, the militant." The church triumphant are those "who have triumphed over the world, the flesh, and

---

2. The number went up to seventy in 1547. For details on the council, see Hubert Jedin in Erwin Iserloh, Joseph Glazik, and Hubert Jedin, *History of the Church*, vol. 5: *Reformation and Counter Reformation*, trans. Anselm Biggs and Peter W. Becker (New York: Seabury Press, 1980), 466–98; and Hubert Jedin, *A History of the Council of Trent*, trans. E. Graf, 2 vols. (London: Thomas Nelson & Sons, 1961).

3. Yves Congar, *L'Eglise de saint Augustin a l'epoque moderne* (Paris: Editions du Cerf, 1970), 364. Jedin suggests that this was due to the "opposition of the Gallicans and 'episcopalists'" in *Reformation and Counter Reformation*, 540.

4. For these and the following references see *Canons and Decrees of the Council of Trent*, original text with English trans. H. J. Schroeder (St. Louis: B. Herder Book Co., 1950).

5. *The Catechism of the Council of Trent*, trans. Theodore Alois Buckley (London: George Routledge and Co., 1852), 93.

the devil, and who...enjoy everlasting bliss." The church militant are
those who are still waging war against the world, the flesh, and the devil
on earth, including both good and bad Christians.[6] The *Catechism* mentions the visibility of the church composed of good and bad, but does
not speak of an invisible church. Only infidels, heretics and schismatics, and the excommunicated are excluded from the church (qq. vii and
viii). It acknowledges that the word "church" refers not only to the "Universal Church," but also to local churches such as Corinth, Galatia, and
Laodicea, and to house churches. It also is used sometimes to refer to
"the prelates and pastors of the Church" and to the place where the
faithful assemble, but is used especially "to signify the multitude of the
good and the bad; and not only the governing, but also the governed"
(q. ix).

The *Catechism* then gives a brief and traditional exposition of the
"peculiar properties" of the church, its unity, holiness, catholicity, and
apostolicity (qq. x–xv). What is significant, however, is that the only mention of the papacy, the Roman Pontiff, is under the question on the unity
of the church. Citing the Fathers from Jerome through Ambrose, the argument is simply that "a visible Church requires a visible head," and
that Christ "appointed Peter head and pastor of all the faithful...when
he committed to his care the feeding of his sheep" (John 21:15; q. xi).[7]
We will see that this concern with the unity of the church is the basis for Vatican I's decree on papal infallibility. The *Catechism* has no
other discussion of papal primacy or of the hierarchical structure of the
church.

The position of the Roman pontiff was stressed, however, by the
theologian many consider the most illustrious defender of the Roman
Catholic position in post-Reformation controversies, the Jesuit and later
cardinal Robert Bellarmine (1542–1621). Bellarmine introduced the
pope into the very definition of the church, for which he was rebuked
by the Gallicans. In his famous *Controversies,* he defined the church
as the "assembly of humans bound together by the profession of the
same faith and the communion of the same sacraments under the governance of legitimate pastors especially under the one vicar of Christ
on earth, the Roman pontiff."[8] Just as strongly did he defend the visibility of the church saying, "The Church is a congregation of men which
is as visible and palpable as are the assembly of the people of Rome,
of the Kingdom of Gaul, or the republic of Venice." It was Bellarmine's
understanding of the church that Dulles used as the paradigm for his

---

6. Ibid., 95.
7. Ibid., 99–101.
8. Quoted in Congar, *L'Eglise,* 372 (translation mine).

"institutional model" (see chap. 2) and that was most determinative for Roman Catholic ecclesiology until Vatican II.

Congar, in summarizing post-Tridentine theology, describes it as a "system, Catholic and Roman, dynamic and conquering outwardly, but closed in on itself, in a perceived state of siege."[9] The ecclesiology that legitimated this system was that of a society organized like a state, having at the summit of the pyramid the pope assisted by the Roman congregations made up of the cardinals and the bureaucracy. The church was seen and defined not as an organism animated by the Holy Spirit but as a society organized by Christ with the Spirit as guarantor of its authority. The notion of the church as the *congregatio fidelium*, which we saw in the *Catechism* of the Council of Trent, faded, and more and more the "church" was seen as a juridical institution with the means and regulations necessary for salvation whose application was the privilege of the hierarchy. It was defined as a *societas perfecta*, a perfect society, which contained in itself all the means necessary to achieve its end.[10] This self-understanding of the Roman Catholic community is the one found in the "manuals," the textbooks of theology in use right up until the beginning of Vatican II.

The Protestants during this period clarified and reinforced their understanding of the Christian community over against Rome and one another in a series of confessional statements such as that issued by the Reformed Church of France (1559), the Scottish Confession of Faith (1560), the Belgic Confession of Faith (1561), the Westminster Confession (1647), and the Savoy Declaration (1658). These confessions reiterate the two characteristics of the correct preaching of the Gospel and the administration of the sacraments but add the note of church discipline.

In summary, Jay points out that during the later sixteenth and seventeenth centuries there was a tendency for both Catholics and Protestants to define their respective ecclesiologies very closely and rigidly. He describes it as a "hardening process."[11] New orthodoxies developed and remained in place through the eighteenth and most of the nineteenth centuries.

## THE AGE OF REASON

The Reformation spawned a series of "religious wars" that ravaged Europe off and on until the conclusion of the Thirty Years War at the Peace

---

9. Ibid., 381.

10. Ibid., 383–85 (translation and paraphrasing mine).

11. Eric G. Jay, *The Church: Its Changing Image through Twenty Centuries* (Atlanta: John Knox Press, 1980), 216.

of Westphalia in 1648. All sides realized that religious disputes were not
going to be settled by war, and, tired, devastated, and depleted, they
sought to live and let live. The principle *cujus regio, eius religio* (the
religion of the ruler is the religion of the territory), first enunciated at
Augsburg in 1555, was extended to all the territories of the Holy Roman
Empire at Westphalia (1648). Europe was occupied with other things
than religious disputes.

The New World had been discovered twenty-five years before Luther
had posted his theses, and its development, colonization, and new-
found wealth seemed more important than theological questions. Further, a whole new worldview was developing independently of religious
thought and of religious authority. When Galileo looked through his
telescope in 1609, he initiated a whole new way of viewing the cosmos
and the place of humans in it, as well as new views of society, morals,
and all forms of human knowledge. Empirical evidence and human reason replaced the Bible and church authority. This period, roughly 1648
to 1789, is generally called the "Age of Reason," or the "Enlightenment."

The great confidence in human reason actually had its origins before 1648 with René Descartes (1596–1650), whose method of critical
doubt was influential throughout the period, but he was soon followed
by Baruch Spinoza (1632–77) and Gottfried Leibniz (1646–1716). The
expectations of what human reason could achieve were reinforced by
the remarkable discoveries in the late sixteenth and seventeenth centuries in the natural sciences. In addition to Copernicus, Kepler, and
Galileo, Isaac Newton (1643–1727) in physics, Robert Boyle (1627–91)
in chemistry, and John Ray (1627–1705) in botany revolutionized the
understanding of the physical universe. These scientific results led to
greater emphasis on sense experience as a source of knowledge and
led to the empiricism of John Locke (1632–1704), George Berkeley
(1685–1753), and David Hume (1711–76).

All of these movements, rationalism, scientific discoveries, and empiricism, posed threats to the authority of the church and of the Bible.
As Gerald R. Cragg remarks, "The role of reason was magnified, that of
revelation was depressed."[12] Tradition came to be viewed as inherited
prejudice, and critical reason and empirical science were to replace it.
Early attempts to harmonize reason and science with the Bible alarmed
church authorities. For example, the French priest Richard Simon wrote
his *Critical History of the Old Testament* (1678), in which he ap-
proached the Bible like any other historical document and "questioned
many of the traditional assumptions regarding the authorship and historical character of the Bible." He was subsequently expelled from his

---

12. Gerald R. Cragg, *The Church and the Age of Reason: 1648–1789* (London: Penguin
Books, 1960), 13.

order.[13] Such attempts were only the beginning of the problems posed by the emerging modern consciousness for the church, some of which persist even to the present.

The rationalism, empiricism, and scientism of the Age of Reason did not evoke any new treatises on ecclesiology, or new self-understandings within either Protestant or Catholic communities. They did, however, according to Jay, "engender certain new ideas about the Church which . . . have been very influential. These are the idea of the Church as an ethical society, and the concepts of toleration and the 'denomination.' "[14] John Locke, in his essay *The Reasonableness of Christianity*, sees the church as primarily a society of those who voluntarily obey the law and will of Christ, for which they will receive reward or punishment in another world. The church is primarily an institution for the improvement of moral standards, a view that has persisted in some quarters to the present.[15]

Locke's reasonableness was also reflected in *A Letter Concerning Toleration* (1689), in which he argues against fanaticism and for mutual toleration, as well as against the intervention of civil magistrates to compel religious positions.[16] Though religious toleration had been granted in many European countries, such as France with the Edict of Nantes (1598), it was not an established fact and there were numerous attempts to revoke it in the latter part of the seventeenth century. Nonetheless, the idea of religious toleration gradually came to prevail. Concomitant with the notion of toleration of religious differences was the idea that membership in the various separated Christian communities was a matter of personal choice and they were all equally acceptable options. This has come to be called "denominationalism." Jay remarks: "That Christendom was divided into denominations came to be regarded as a natural, even desirable state of affairs. . . . Concern for the unity of the body of Christ drops into the background."[17] Thus, while such attitudes as toleration and denominationalism were not, strictly speaking, redefinitions of the church, they certainly affected how Christians thought about and behaved toward one another. The roots of the gradual privatization of religion lie here.

---

13. Ibid., 48, and, Thomas Bokenkotter *A Concise History of the Catholic Church* (New York: Doubleday & Co., 1979), 269.

14. Jay, *The Church*, 221.

15. Ibid., 221–22.

16. Ibid., 223–24.

17. Ibid., 225.

## REACTION

If the Age of Reason did not stimulate any new theological treatises on the church, any new self-understanding *within* the Christian community, it did significantly alter its relationship to the culture surrounding it. From the time of Constantine to the Reformation, Christianity and the culture of the known world had been integrated in the synthesis we have come to call "Christendom." With the Age of Reason, the culture began to develop independently of and even in opposition to Christianity. The church viewed this developing culture as hostile and threatening. It adopted a defensive posture and even a siege mentality, which, for Catholic Christianity, did not end until Vatican II. Condemnation of scientific discoveries, of philosophical movements, and of new forms of political life became the characteristic mode of ecclesial behavior.

The disintegration of Christendom was accompanied by a rising nationalism. This manifested itself with regard to the church as Gallicanism in France, Febronianism in Germany, and Josephinism in Austria. In France a certain spirit of Gallican independence had appeared as far back as Philip the Fair against Boniface VIII and later at the University of Paris. In the latter part of the seventeenth century, as Cragg remarks, an infallible papacy faced an absolute monarchy.[18] Conflict was inevitable. Drawing on the ecclesiology of Cyprian and with frequent references to the conciliarist theory of Gerson and d'Ailly, Gallicanism can be summarized in the Four Gallican Articles drawn up by Bossuet, bishop of Meaux, and adopted by an assembly of the French clergy in 1682. They claimed that (1) the pope has no power in temporal matters; (2) general councils are superior to the pope in spiritual affairs; (3) the generally accepted laws of the French church are inviolable, and the papacy must conform to them; (4) in matters of faith, the pope's decisions become irreversible only when ratified by a general council.[19] It should be clear that Gallicanism stands in the conciliar tradition described in chapter 4. The king ordered that these articles be taught in the universities and all seminaries, and, even though they were officially revoked in 1693, they continued to be influential in France and in the United States through the French Sulpicians, who taught in the seminaries until the middle of the nineteenth century.[20] We will see that Vatican I was still concerned with the threat of Gallicanism in the decree on papal infallibility in 1870.

A similar movement occurred in Germany and in Austria in the latter part of the eighteenth century. In Germany, the bishop of Trier, Johann von Hontheim (1701–90), wrote a book, *On the Present State of the*

---

18. Cragg, *Age of Reason,* 23.
19. Ibid., 24; Jay, *The Church,* 225–26; Congar, *L'Eglise,* 398–99.
20. Ibid., 401–2.

*Church and the Legitimate Power of the Roman Pontiff,* in 1763, under the pseudonym Febronius, which expressed the Gallican articles in German form, recalling Cyprian's notion of the corporate episcopacy and allowing the pope only a primacy of honor.[21] A movement of reform in Austria known as Josephinism, introduced by the Emperor Joseph II (emperor 1765–90), made similar claims for supremacy of the civil ruler over the pope, and again, even though the movement died with the emperor, the ideas remained influential. The tensions between the spiritual and the temporal powers, and between the church as papal monarchy and a corporate or conciliar body, which we saw in the previous chapter, continued during this period in the forms of Gallicanism, Febronianism, and Josephinism.

The rationalism, empiricism, and scientism mentioned above infected the churches themselves. Both theology and church life became overly formal and sterile. Cragg says,

> The intellect was in the ascendant, and in a particularly arid form, while vast and intricate dogmatic systems fortified the rival positions of Lutheran and Calvinist theologians.... Strict orthodoxy became an obsession. Logic, pedantry, and the parade of learning had sometimes usurped the central place even in worship.[22]

The same could be said of Roman Catholic theology and church life.

In reaction several movements arose: Pietism, Methodism, and among Catholics Jansenism. Pietism had its origin in Germany with Philip Spener (1635–1705), who in 1675 published his *Pia desideria,* which called for a revival of a personal religion more devotional in character and more evangelical in its preaching.[23] Other leaders of the movement were August Francke (1663–1727) and in Bohemia Count Nikolaus von Zinzendorf (1700–1760), who gave refuge to a group of Moravian exiles at his estate at Herrnhut. His group has come to be known as the Moravian Brethren or, in North America, as the Church of the Brethren.[24]

A similar evangelical movement in England was initiated by John Wesley (1703–91), his brother Charles (1707–88), and George Whitefield (1714–70). This movement eventually split from the Church of England and was established as the Methodist Church in the United States in 1784.

Jansenism was somewhat different but shared the stress on personal conversion and a concern for the holiness of members of the church. It

---

21. Jay, *The Church,* 231.
22. Cragg, *Age of Reason,* 99.
23. Ibid., 101.
24. Jay, *The Church,* 226–27.

originated with Cornelius Jansen (1585–1638), bishop of Ypres, but perdured through most of the eighteenth century with such able leadership
as that of Blaise Pascal, whose *Provincial Letters* (1656–57) brilliantly
attacked the main opponents of the Jansenists, the Jesuits. The main
theological concerns of Jansenism were not with ecclesiology, but with
a belief in the radical corruption of human nature and the consequent
inability of humans to observe moral rectitude on a natural level. All
human actions were seen to be "wicked and even [human beings'] pre-
tended virtues were vices. Grace was only given to the predestined;
others were inexorably doomed to eternal punishment for their sins
through no fault of their own, since they simply did not receive the
necessary grace."[25] This led to a very rigorist morality and, eventually,
to a split with Rome, which condemned Jansenism in the bull *Unigeni-
tus* in 1713. This was the origin of what came to be known as the "Old
Catholic Church."

Jay is correct in saying that "these new churches developed no
unique ecclesiologies."[26] They did, however, raise the ancient concern
for the holiness of the church and the tension that creates with the desire to maintain the unity of the church. Even with the rise of toleration
and denominationalism, the church-sect tension remained.

Finally, in reaction to the Age of Reason another more general
cultural movement, Romanticism, should be mentioned. The Romantic movement was the protest in many fields "against the inference
that common sense was preferable to emotion or that correct and
formal values could compensate for the loss of freshness and joy.
Mystery and wonder, beauty and spontaneity asserted their right to a
place in any adequate conception of a satisfying life."[27] Its chief representatives were the Swiss-French Jean-Jacques Rousseau (1712–78)
and, in Germany, J. W. Goethe (1749–1832), J. C. F. Schiller (1759–
1805), and F. von Schelling (1775–1854). Congar says that "the most
common and most certain trait of this complex reality [Romanti-
cism] was the idea that life was a total movement uniting diversity
in unity."[28] Although Romanticism did not produce a theology itself, it was influential on nineteenth-century theology, especially the
Tübingen school and Newman, just as Pietism was for Schleiermacher's
theology.

---

25. Cragg, *Age of Reason*, 277–78.
26. Jay, *The Church*, 227.
27. Cragg, *Age of Reason*, 283.
28. Congar, *L'Eglise*, 418.

## THE REVOLUTION AND THE NINETEENTH CENTURY

Divisions of history are always somewhat arbitrary, and significant epochs do not always coincide with the divisions of the Western calendar into centuries. Most historians would agree that the Age of Reason ends with the French Revolution. Indeed, Cragg says, "The champions of Enlightenment began by advocating stability; they ended by ushering in the French Revolution."[29] It was in many ways the climax of the Age of Reason. But the Revolution spilled over beyond 1789 into the nineteenth century. Some historians call the period from 1789 to 1815 the period of Revolution; others list the age of Revolution to be from 1789 to 1848.[30] For our purposes, we are treating the years 1789–1848 as one period.

As with the seventeenth and eighteenth centuries, the events of world history or, more accurately, European history, are the major determinants for any developments in the self-understanding of the Christian community. External factors are more important than ones internal to the life of the church. Again, we are not attempting a complete history of the church during this period, but merely recalling the story of the church's self-understanding, its ecclesiology. Understanding the church's reaction to the events of the revolution and the rest of the nineteenth century is most important for understanding the developments in ecclesiology, especially in the Roman Catholic Church, right up until Vatican II.

The French Revolution began when King Louis XVI convened the Estates-General, which had not met since 1614, to consider moderate reforms and solve financial problems. But the Third Estate, the commoners, sought a more radical reform abolishing the *ancien régime*, the privileges due to birth, and replacing the arbitrary government of the monarchy with one representing the rising middle class. They were joined by the First Estate, the clergy, and by the oath on the Tennis Court, June 20, 1789, they forced the king to allow them to meet as the National Assembly.

At first, there was no real conflict between the Revolution and the Roman Catholic church. But the church was such an integral part of the old system — controlling education and care for the sick, with power of censorship over publications, its parish priests the official registrars of births, marriages, and deaths — that some reform of the ecclesiastical

---

29. Ibid., 13.
30. For the first see Kenneth Scott Latourette, *The Nineteenth Century in Europe: Background and the Roman Catholic Phase* (New York: Harper & Bros., 1958), 202; for the second see E. J. Hobsbawm, *The Age of Revolution: 1789–1848* (New York: Mentor Books, 1962).

system was inevitable.[31] A committee of the National Assembly, with a bishop as president, was appointed to recommend reforms. Its proposals became law in July 1790, under the title of the Civil Constitution of the Clergy. Fifty-seven dioceses were suppressed; archbishoprics were abolished; cathedral chapters and other dignities were abolished and were replaced by elected diocesan councils; bishops and pastors were to be elected by the civil electorates. The bishop of Rome ceased to have any juridical authority over the Gallican church and was accorded a primacy of honor only. Vidler comments, "The Civil Constitution should not be regarded as a reckless or revolutionary innovation. It implemented, in a somewhat extreme form, the pre-revolutionary Gallican principles."[32]

The real crunch came toward the end of 1790 when a law was passed requiring all bishops and clergy to take an oath to obey the Civil Constitution. The pope hesitated to approve it, and the clergy had to make a decision without knowing his will. Approximately half the clergy took the oath and half did not. "Thus the effect of the Civil Constitution, whatever its merits, was to split the French Church in two, and for ten years it remained split. Nearly all the bishops were non-jurors and most of them emigrated."[33] Finally, on March 10, 1791, the pope condemned the constitution and forbade the clergy to take the oath. By that time the damage had already been done.

At first, those who refused to take the oath were allowed to continue their priestly ministry, but in May 1792 persecution of the "nonjuring" priests began, with the result that "some thirty thousand to forty thousand priests were thereupon driven out of their native towns and hounded into hiding or exile. Later, on March 18, 1793, the death penalty was imposed on those deportees who dared to return."[34] As the Revolution took on the character of a religion itself, persecution was extended to the "constitutional" clergy as well. There was an effort to de-Christianize France altogether, and the Goddess of Reason was enthroned on the altar of Notre Dame cathedral. The Christian calendar was abolished and churches turned into "Temples of Reason." Priests were urged to marry and many did. The total number of priests who "put aside the cloth" is estimated at about twenty thousand.[35]

De-Christianization spent its force by 1794, and the following year the free exercise of religion was allowed. But with Napoleon's Italian campaign, the Revolution turned on the papacy itself. In 1797, French

---

31. Bokenkotter, *Concise History*, 287; Alec R. Vidler, *The Church in an Age of Revolution: 1789 to the Present Day* (Baltimore: Penguin Books, 1961), 13–18.
32. Ibid., 16.
33. Ibid., 17.
34. Bokenkotter, *Concise History*, 291.
35. Ibid., 294.

troops entered Rome and took Pope Pius VI prisoner. In the process of being taken to France, he died. His successor was not elected until 1800, and shortly thereafter Napoleon defeated the Austrians at the battle of Marengo and took control of Italy. Napoleon was enough of a statesman to know that religion had a certain social utility, and he was determined to bring about the unity of the French church. Accordingly, he negotiated a concordat with the pope in 1801, which became a prototype for other concordats in the nineteenth century. Its chief provisions were, according to Bokenkotter:

> All bishops, both constitutional and nonjuring, had to hand in their resignation to the Pope; the First Consul had the right to name the bishops, and the Pope had the right to institute them canonically; the Church would not seek to recover its alienated property; the clergy would derive their income from the salaries paid by the state; and the practice of the Catholic religion would be subject to whatever police regulations were required for the public order.[36] Napoleon also mandated the teaching of the Gallican articles of 1682 in all seminaries.

This concordat, however, did not end the troubles between Napoleon and the church. Pius VII refused to allow the Papal States to join Napoleon's blockade of England, and Napoleon seized them. Pius then excommunicated Napoleon. Napoleon responded by arresting the pope in 1808 and carrying him off in captivity, to France where he remained for six years. Only after Napoleon's defeat in Russia did he allow the pope's return to Rome on May 24, 1814. The Congress of Vienna (1814–15) brought peace to Europe and restored the pope as the absolute monarch of the Papal States.

The year 1815 may mark the end of the period of the French Revolution, but its effects remained. Europe would never again return to a hierarchical society with an alliance of throne and altar, and the secularization of society begun in 1794, with its concomitant anticlericalism, continued throughout the nineteenth century.

I have recalled in some detail the experience of the church in France during this period because it is impossible to underestimate the effects of this experience on the church's self-understanding, especially at Vatican I. If the Age of Reason had threatened the authority of the church in various intellectual spheres, the Age of Revolution threatened its very existence. The memory of a divided church, a captive pope, a secularized state, and a hostile populace only reinforced the siege mentality begun in the eighteenth century. The specter of Gallicanism remained alive and was hovering over Vatican I, as we shall see. The control of the

---

36. Ibid., 297.

church by the temporal power had been even greater than during similar struggles in the Middle Ages. In the minds of many, the possession
of the Papal States became an absolutely necessary means to guarantee some independence of the church from the secular rulers, whether
monarchical or republican.

In the period from 1789 to 1815, the Revolution was chiefly political and social in nature, but there was a more extended sense of the
"Revolution," as summarized by Kenneth Scott Latourette:

> The revolution had many facets and eventually affected all as-
> pects of civilization. They were in the realms of ideas, politics,
> religion, industry, transportation, agriculture, and economic the-
> ory, and in the accompanying changes in social structure. They
> included the widening of men's horizons on the age of the earth,
> on the structure of matter, and on the dimensions of the universe
> in which man finds himself. They led to a progressive emancipa-
> tion of man's mind and included a humanitarian concern for the
> welfare of man and hope for improvements in that welfare.[37]

In the economic and industrial spheres, the industrial revolution
and the increasing mastery of humans over their physical environment
caused new problems for which the church seemed ill-prepared, and
which seemed to make religion increasingly less necessary. The scientific revolution and the application to the Bible of the historico-critical
method posed threats in the realm of religion itself. Charles Lyell's
*Principles of Geology* (1830, with revised editions through 1872) and
Charles Darwin's *Origin of Species* (1859) gave rise to an increased
desire for certainty in religious matters and a concomitant despair of
human ability to achieve it. Scientific knowledge bred more doubts than
certainties in the realm of religion. Taken all together, these aspects of
the Revolution led to an increasingly hostile and defensive posture on
the part of the church and an increased concern with authority as a
guarantor of certainty throughout the nineteenth century.

Nowhere was this posture better illustrated than the way the church
dealt with liberal movements within Catholicism. Despite the conservative backlash that followed the Congress of Vienna and the death
of the moderate Pope Pius VII in 1823, there was a countercurrent
of liberal Catholicism led by the French priest Felicité de Lamennais
(d. 1854). Believing that the reactionary monarchy was doomed, he
argued for the separation of the church from it, that is, for separation of church and state. He likewise espoused freedom of education,
freedom of the press, and universal suffrage. Lamennais attracted a following of younger clergy and educated laypersons and published a

---

37. Latourette, *The Nineteenth Century in Europe*, 203.

newspaper, *L'Avenir,* to further his ideas. But Lamennais was ahead of his time and the church could not forget its recent experience. Pope Gregory XVI in an encyclical, *Mirari Vos,* condemned the principles of liberalism in 1832. "The encyclical rejected the separation of Church and state, denounced liberty of conscience as sheer madness, and referred to liberty of the press as abominable and detestable."[38] This was not just a rejection of a political and social program. Rome detected two major theological errors underlying it: a rejection of all supernatural revelation and religious indifferentism.

The liberal Catholics should not be confused, however, with the economic Liberals, the industrialists, big bankers, and traders who gave Liberalism its negative connotations. They merely wanted the church to adapt to the historical and cultural changes that they saw to be inevitable. Their opponents were called "integralists" because they espoused an integral relationship between church and state, more specifically between throne and altar. They saw the monarchical principle in both church and society as almost divine; they could see nothing good in liberalism and identified it with all the excesses of the French Revolution. "They wanted the Church to seek wherever possible a close alliance with any regime that would closely unite Church and state. These Catholics were authoritarian and intransigent in temperament."[39] Their chief representatives were a French journalist, Louis Veuillot, editor of *L'Univers,* and the Jesuits who edited *La Civiltà Cattolica* in Rome. By 1850, the church throughout Europe was divided between liberals and integralists, each group being suspicious of the other, and an atmosphere of heresy hunting began.

Before moving into the second half of the nineteenth century, we need to focus on some developments in theology in both the Catholic and Protestant communities. We have concentrated on the effects of the Revolution on the Roman Catholic church because it "suffered the most acutely from the revolution" and Protestantism suffered far less "because of the geographic location of its chief centres," mainly in Germany.[40] But it was precisely in Germany that the renewal of Protestant theology, in protest both against rationalism and the excesses of the Revolution, took place in the person of Friedrich Schleiermacher, rightly called the father of modern Protestant theology.

Schleiermacher (1768–1834) was raised in the pietist tradition of the Moravian Brethren and was influenced by the Romantic movement. For him, religion was not primarily a collection of doctrines to be accepted on faith, but a "feeling of absolute dependence" of which

---

38. Bokenkotter, *Concise History,* 308.
39. Ibid., 312.
40. Latourette, *The Nineteenth Century in Europe,* 203–4.

humans are immediately conscious; this self-consciousness becomes a God-consciousness, an intuitive contact with God. Although this is common to all religions, what was unique about Christ was his perfect God-consciousness, "a veritable existence of God in him." His redeeming work was to communicate this God-consciousness to others. This, however, is a corporate process since it is the nature of human beings to be social and to communicate what is in them.[41] Christ communicated his own God-consciousness to his disciples, and "after Christ's departure the disciples' common apprehension of Christ changes into a spontaneous prolongation of His fellowship-forming activity, and it was through this activity . . . that the Christian Church arose."[42] The church, then, is the association of those who share this God-consciousness communicated through Christ. It is the fellowship of believers animated by the Holy Spirit and is the perfect image of Christ.[43] Schleiermacher also used the image of the church as the Mystical Body of Christ.

For Schleiermacher, the church is both immutable and mutable, both invisible and visible. The "Church is ever self-identical as the *locus* of the Spirit in the human race," but "everything mutable in the Church is as such determined by the world."[44] Because the "world" exists within the church, i.e., "the activity of the flesh striving against the Spirit," it is necessary to distinguish between the visible and the invisible church: "By the Invisible Church is commonly understood the whole body of those who are regenerate and really have a place within the state of sanctification: by the Visible Church, all those besides who have heard the gospel and therefore are called, and who confess themselves outwardly members of the Church." The latter he calls the "outer circle of the Church" or "candidates for the Church."[45] More than most Protestant theologians, Schleiermacher is wary of the close relationship of church and state. In the *Speeches,* he says, "As soon as a prince declared a church to be a community with special privileges, a distinguished member of the civil world, the corruption of that church was begun and almost irrevocably decided."[46]

Schleiermacher was the most influential Protestant theologian of the nineteenth and early twentieth centuries, and because of his appeal to human experience, he is regarded as the founder of modern liberal Prot-

---

41. Friedrich Schleiermacher, *On Religion: Speeches to Its Cultured Despisers,* trans. John Oman with an introduction by Rudolf Otto (New York: Harper & Row, 1958), 148.
42. Friedrich Schleiermacher, *The Christian Faith,* ed. H. R. Mackintosh and J. S. Stewart (New York: Harper & Row, 1963), 2:568–69.
43. Ibid., 578ff.
44. Ibid., 583.
45. Ibid., 677.
46. Schleiermacher, *Speeches,* 167.

estant thought. The doctrine of the church, however, was not a major concern to most Protestant theologians during this period.

On the Catholic side, the Romantic movement was influential among a group of theologians in the beginning of the nineteenth century known as the "Tübingen School." A Catholic faculty of theology was initiated at Tübingen in 1817 and was in dialogue with Protestant theology and with other intellectual movements of their day. "They were determined to show that their faith had nothing to fear from historical criticism or philosophical discussion. The ideas of organism, in contrast to mechanism, and of development, in contrast to a fixed and closed system, were fundamental for them."[47] J. M. Sailer (1751–1832), J. S. Drey (1777–1853), and J. A. Möhler (1796–1838) were the leading representatives.

For the development of the self-understanding of the Christian community, Möhler is the most important. Influenced by the organismic philosophy of Schelling and the mystical immanentism of Schleiermacher, whom he knew personally, Möhler in his *Unity in the Church* (1825) presented the church as basically life and love, which externalizes itself in various forms of liturgy, dogma, and moral codes. Individuals are formed by the holy life spread throughout the church and make it their own by contemplation. "The identity, the unity of being, between the individual consciousness of the believer and the collective consciousness of the Church — tradition — is therefore not only the starting point of Christian life but also its goal, since it should always be developed and deepened."[48] This life (love) has priority over all the forms in which it is always expressing itself imperfectly. "Christianity does not consist in words, formulas and statements; it is an inner life, a holy power."[49] Yet he does not deny that external forms are necessary. Dogmas were developed in response to needs, attacks, and errors. Bishops, metropolitans, and the pope are images of the love active in the community. This life, this love, creates forms necessary for its continuance and development.

In a later work, *Symbolik* (*Symbolism*), 1832, Möhler understands the church more as the real presence of Christ guaranteeing the authenticity of the inner experience than an expression of a collective consciousness. There is more emphasis on the church as a visible community founded by Christ,

> in which the redemptive and sanctifying action of his earthly life continues, under the direction of his Spirit, until the end of the world.... The Church is Christ acting and manifesting himself

---

47. Vidler, *Age of Revolution*, 32.
48. Hervé Savon, *Johann Adam Möhler: The Father of Modern Theology*, trans. Charles McGrath (Glen Rock, N.J.: Paulist Press, 1966), 40.
49. Ibid., 43, quoting *Unity in the Church*, n. 13, 33.

through the ages, in a way at once symbolic and living, and so
constantly continuing, by an eternal renewal, his work of reconciliation and salvation.[50]

This continuing living presence of the Word, for Möhler, is the basis for
his understanding of "Tradition." "Tradition is the living Word remaining
in the heart of believers," and again, "This vital, spiritual force, which we
inherit from our fathers and which is perpetuated in the church, is interior tradition."[51] The Word in Scripture is interpreted by this collective
sense. Thus, Scripture and Tradition form a living unity.

In sum, the church is the continuation of the Incarnation, the Mystical Body of Christ. It is both human and divine. As Congar remarks, this
ecclesiology was influential on the Roman School, especially its early
members, and through them on the First Vatican Council.[52] Möhler's
balanced formulation of the relationship between the interior spiritual
element and the external element, the priesthood and the hierarchy in
particular, was, however, not maintained.

Möhler and the Tübingen School were a more or less unique case
of theological vitality in Catholic theology in the nineteenth century.
In the wake of the French Revolution many universities had been shut
down and the Roman schools replaced them. The Roman College re-
opened in 1824 under the direction of the Jesuits, and its theologians
formed what has come to be called the "Roman School" of theology. Beginning with Giovanni Perrone, Carlo Passaglia, and Klemens Schrader,
these theologians formulated the ecclesiology that dominated the Catholic community's self-understanding through the nineteenth century,
at Vatican I, and right up until Vatican II.[53] Perrone had read Möhler
and cited him frequently, and thus the incarnational and Mystical Body
imagery passed into this ecclesiology. But for various historical reasons
mentioned below, it focused on the juridical and hierarchical structure
and lost the vital organic aspect that the image suggests. The later representatives of this Roman ecclesiology, John Baptist Franzelin (1816–86)
and Joseph Kleutgen (1811–83), were the official theologians and putative authors of the decrees of Vatican I. Since the Roman ecclesiology
reaches its zenith in the decree on papal infallibility, *Pastor Aeternus,*
let us now turn to Vatican I.

---

50. Ibid., 95, citing *Symbolik,* I, chap. 4, n. 34, and chap. 5, n. 36.
51. Savon, *Johann Adam Möhler,* 96; Yves Congar, *Tradition and Traditions* (New
York: Macmillan, 1967), 193–95.
52. Congar, *L'Eglise,* 421.
53. I have described this ecclesiology in my *Authority in the Church: A Study in Changing Paradigms* (Missoula, Mont.: Scholars Press, 1974); see also, Gerald A. McCool,
*Catholic Theology in the Nineteenth Century* (New York: Seabury Press, 1977).

# VATICAN I

We have already mentioned some of the historical factors that led up to Vatican I: the rejection of liberal Catholics' attempts to come to terms with the modern world by Gregory XVI in 1832, the threat to the authority of Scripture and the church posed by various scientific discoveries, the domination of the church and captivity of the popes under Napoleon, and the general siege mentality that intensified during the period of the Restoration. No factor is more important, however, than the character and experience of the pope whose long reign has left a permanent imprint on Roman Catholicism, Pius IX, Pio Nono in Italian (1846–78).

When elected, Pius IX was reputed to be something of a liberal and at first lived up to his reputation. "He issued a general amnesty for political prisoners, made provision for sharing the government of the Papal States with laymen, and finally granted his subjects a constitution that set up a bicameral form of government whose lower house, the Council of Deputies, was elected by direct suffrage."[54] He also instituted a form of habeas corpus and abolished political press censorship. Personally, he was open and charming. He held garden parties in the Quirinal Palace, lighted the streets of Rome with gas, and was cheered by the Roman populace. "Probably no Pope in modern times has enjoyed so wide a popularity as that enjoyed in those first months by Pius IX."[55]

The liberal honeymoon was short lived, however. In 1848 the pope was forced to flee Rome in disguise, and Garibaldi's revolutionaries took control of the city. Within two years the French retook the city and escorted the pope back on April 12, 1850, firmly resolved to show no more leniency toward liberalism. There followed further attempts to unite Italy, including the Papal States, under a liberal Piedmontese monarchy. After a vain attempt to defend the Papal States, Pius IX lost them and refused any negotiated settlement with the Piedmontese. The pope felt it was his sacred duty not to surrender the Papal States, and thus he became the "Prisoner of the Vatican" at his own instigation, a situation that perdured until the Lateran Treaty of 1929.

In addition to his unhappy experience with liberal democracy in Italy, the Gallican bishops in France were still strong and again insisted on the right of the local dioceses to regulate their own affairs without interference from Rome. Pius IX responded by prohibiting bishops from holding national councils and established national seminaries in Rome for training the clergy, especially potential bishops. The North American

---

54. Bokenkotter, *Concise History*, 314.
55. E. E. Y. Hales, *The Catholic Church in the Modern World* (New York: Image Books, 1960), 101.

College was established in 1859. Those who favored such movement toward greater centralization in Rome were called "Ultramontanes" (those beyond the Alps from the northern European viewpoint). This movement triumphed in the proclamation of the dogma of the Immaculate Conception on December 8, 1854, when the pope "read the decree with the bishops looking on as simple spectators."[56]

The growth of Ultramontanism and the pope's personal conservatism reached a peak with his famous *Syllabus of Errors,* December 8, 1864, which listed eighty errors of the modern world, concluding with No. 80: "The Roman Pontiff can and ought to reconcile and harmonize himself with progress, with liberalism, and with modern civilization."[57] Anyone who held that (or any of the others) was *anathema.* An uproar ensued, with even the average Catholic shocked to hear such a thing. The pope was further confirmed in his perception of the hostility of the modern world, and yet he remained personally attractive and popular, holding huge public audiences in Rome and attracting pilgrims from all over Europe.

Such was the atmosphere when the pope convoked the First Vatican Council, which opened on December 8, 1869, with about seven hundred bishops in attendance. After a fair amount of preconciliar debate, it was clear by the time the council convened that it was divided: "an overwhelming majority who favored a strong statement defining papal infallibility and reaffirming the *Syllabus,* and a minority who opposed any such moves."[58] The council issued only two decrees, *Dei Filius,* on Revelation, and *Pastor Aeternus,* defining papal infallibility, both in 1870. The council intended to do a further document on the church in general and on its relationship to the state, but because of the Franco-Prussian war, the French troops guarding Rome were withdrawn and the Italian nationalist troops occupied Rome on September 20, 1870. The council was never officially concluded, but adjourned *sine die.*

Because of the importance of the decree on papal infallibility for the Roman Catholic community's self-understanding and the difficulty it poses for non-Catholics, as well as the way it is frequently misunderstood by both, I want to discuss it at some length.

The dogmatic constitution *Pastor Aeternus* consists of an introduction and four chapters with a "canon" concluding each chapter. The introduction argues that, for the saving work of redemption to continue for all time, Christ built his church so that "all who believe might be united together in the bond of one faith and one love."[59] Just as Christ sent apostles, he also "wished shepherds and teachers to be in

---

56. Ibid., 329.
57. Ibid., 324.
58. Ibid., 333.
59. This and all the following citations are from J. Neuner and J. Dupuis, eds., *The*

His Church until the consummation of the world (cf. Mt. 28:20)." In order that the episcopate itself might be one and all believers preserved in unity, "He placed St. Peter at the head of the other apostles, and established in him a perpetual principle and visible foundation of this twofold unity." But because "the gates of hell, with a hatred that grows greater every day, are rising up everywhere against the Church's divinely established foundation," it is necessary to propose for all to believe the "perpetuity and the nature of this sacred apostolic primacy."[60] It is clear that the council's concern is for the unity of the church, and that the atmosphere is perceived as very hostile and threatening.

Chapter 1 argues, citing John 1:42 and Matthew 16:16, "that the primacy of jurisdiction over the whole Church was immediately and directly promised to and conferred upon the blessed apostle Peter by Christ the Lord." The council explicitly repudiates the alternative view that "this primacy was not given immediately and directly to blessed Peter, but to the Church and through the Church to Peter as a minister of the Church," the view of the conciliarists. It further rejects the view that this was only a primacy of honor and not of jurisdiction.[61]

The second chapter argues that this primacy of jurisdiction given to Peter is "according to the institution of Christ our Lord Himself, that is, by divine law" continued perpetually in his successors in that primacy, namely, the Roman Pontiffs.[62]

Chapter 3 discusses the nature and extent of this primacy of jurisdiction, saying that it is the "full power of feeding, ruling and governing the whole church," that it is "truly episcopal" and immediate, and that it "not only pertains in matters of faith and morals, but also in matters that pertain to the discipline and government of the Church throughout the whole world." This power, however, is "far from standing in the way of the power of ordinary and immediate episcopal jurisdiction by which the bishops . . . feed and rule individually, as true shepherds, the particular flock assigned to them."[63]

This chapter is important for revealing the historical positions the council was opposing. It asserts that "the Roman Pontiff has the right of freely communicating with the shepherds and flocks of the whole Church," against the remnants of the *patronato real* (royal privilege) of Spain, which forbade direct communication between Rome and the bishops or religious superiors in colonial Latin America. It condemns those "who make this communication subject to the secular power" or

---

*Christian Faith in the Doctrinal Documents of the Catholic Church*, rev. ed. (New York: Alba House, 1982), 226–34.

60. Ibid., 226–27.
61. Ibid., 228.
62. Ibid., 229.
63. Ibid., 230.

who deny its "binding force unless it is confirmed by the placet of the secular power," against Gallicanism, Febronianism, and Josephinism. Finally, it condemns "those who say that it is permitted to appeal to an ecumenical Council from the decisions of the Roman Pontiff, as to an authority superior to the Roman Pontiff," against conciliarism.[64]

The fourth and final chapter of the decree argues that "the supreme power of teaching is also included in this apostolic primacy." Citing the Fourth Council of Constantinople, the Second Council of Lyons, and "the long-standing custom of the Churches and the form of the ancient rule," it says that the Holy Spirit was promised to the successors of Peter not "that they might disclose a new doctrine by His revelation," but that "they might jealously guard and faithfully explain the revelation or deposit of faith that was handed down through the apostles," and this "for the salvation of all."[65] The paragraph defining papal infallibility reads as follows:

> It is a divinely revealed dogma that the Roman Pontiff, when he speaks *ex cathedra*, that is, when, acting in the office of shepherd and teacher of all Christians, he defines, by virtue of his supreme apostolic authority, a doctrine concerning faith or morals to be held by the universal Church, possesses through the divine assistance promised to him in the person of Blessed Peter, the infallibility with which the divine Redeemer willed His Church to be endowed in defining the doctrine concerning faith or morals; and that such definitions of the Roman Pontiff are therefore irreformable of themselves, not because of the consent of the Church [*ex sese, non autem ex consensu ecclesiae*].[66]

Although the definition may sound extravagant to many contemporaries, Küng correctly says that "it is a fact that this very definition signifies a very clear *limitation vis-à-vis* all that which frequently has been asserted about the infallibility of the pope in the Catholic Church before the Council. One could rightly view it as a victory for the council minority."[67] The definition contains four limitations: (1) the pope must be speaking *officially* in his capacity as "shepherd and teacher of all Christians," not speaking as a private theologian or even as a bishop; (2) he must appeal to his supreme apostolic authority, i.e., *ex cathedra*; (3) the object of the teaching must concern matters of faith and morals, i.e., revealed doctrines or doctrines necessary to maintain, preach, or defend the content of revelation; and (4) he must propose the teaching

---

64. Ibid., 231.
65. Ibid., 233.
66. Ibid., 234.
67. Hans Küng, *Structures of the Church*, trans. Salvator Attanasio (New York: Thomas Nelson & Sons, 1964), 366.

as something to be held by the whole church, i.e, a doctrine having universal obligatory force.[68] These limitations were explained by the official *relator* (presenter) of the document at the council, Bishop Gasser, and are not later additions. They are frequently ignored by both Catholics and others in their understanding of papal infallibility.

In addition to the above-mentioned limitations, there are other conditions made clear by the discussions of the council. Dulles lists four: a valid infallible definition (1) must be in agreement with Scripture and Tradition; (2) must be in agreement with the present faith of the church, i.e., "will find an echo in the faith of the Church and will therefore evoke assent, at least eventually";[69] (3) be in agreement with the universal episcopate, which is usually manifested by (4) sufficient investigation and consultation with the universal church, especially the bishops, cardinals, and theologians.[70]

These intrinsic limitations on and conditions for the exercise of papal infallibility are frequently ignored not only in the popular understanding of this doctrine but even by some of its ardent champions. In addition, as with all historically situated events, there were some presuppositions and categories of thought operative at Vatican I that may seem problematic to us today. Although Dulles rhetorically poses them as questions, I think we can assert that Vatican I presupposed: (1) "that revelation could be directly and adequately embodied in human propositions"; (2) that a doctrine "deemed requisite for an adequate profession of faith at any one time must always remain requisite"; (3) that the "Christian Church was fully and adequately present in Roman Catholicism"; and (4) "that faith is a collection of divinely guaranteed propositions."[71] Today, I think we have a more modest view of the ability of human language and thought categories adequately to capture revealed truth; a more historically conscious attitude toward the threats to faith at any given time; a much more ecumenical view of the relationship of the Roman Catholic church to the whole Christian church; and an understanding of faith that includes all aspects of the human person, not just an intellectual assent to propositional truths. All of these presuppositions and thought categories must be kept in mind in attempting to understand the decree on papal infallibility of Vatican I.

The First Vatican Council had originally intended to provide a full treatment of the church and of the relations of church and state, but the council never finished its business, because the day after *Pastor Aeter-*

---

68. Ibid., 368–71; and Avery Dulles, "Moderate Infallibilism: An Ecumenical Approach," in *A Church to Believe In* (New York: Crossroad, 1982), 136–38.

69. Dulles, "Moderate Infallibilism," 139.

70. Küng, *Structures of the Church*, 370, citing the official acts of the council, Mansi, 52, 1213.

71. Dulles, "Moderate Infallibilism," 143–44.

*nus* was approved on July 18, 1870, the Franco-Prussian war broke out.
Hence, it is important to keep in mind that the relationship between
the infallible teaching authority of the pope and that of the bishops
was not dealt with until Vatican II, and, in the meantime, the Roman
Catholic church lived with a very unbalanced ecclesiology. The Ultramontanes had won, and those who thought the dogma "inopportune,"
such as Cardinal Newman, remained quiet or went underground. Newman presciently believed that Vatican I would not be the last word on
the subject.

Looking back after more than a century, it would seem that the definition of papal infallibility marked the zenith of papal claims whose
trajectory we have followed throughout our historical retrieval. But we
have also noted that there were always countercurrents to those claims
that continued to manifest themselves. Many felt that Vatican I put the
final nail in the coffin of conciliarism and Gallicanism and that there
would never again be a serious challenge to papal authority or need
for another ecumenical council. But, in addition to those like Newman
who took a longer historical perspective, there was another attempt to
break out of the siege mentality and come to terms with the modern
world, the movement known as "Modernism."

## MODERNISM AND
## THE EARLY TWENTIETH CENTURY

With the death of Pius IX and the election of his successor, Leo XIII,
in 1878, an atmosphere of openness prevailed. Although Leo XIII himself could not be called a liberal Catholic, "his pontificate was one long
and somewhat successful effort to place the Church on a new footing
in regard to modern secular culture."[72] He discouraged the monarchist
leanings among French Catholics, tried to restore good relations with
Germany after Bismarck's attack on the church (the *Kulturkampf*), and
tried to update the church intellectually. In 1879, he issued an encyclical, *Aeterni Patris,* urging a restoration of Thomism as an intellectual
tradition for Catholic philosophy and theology. He opened the Vatican archives and instituted a biblical commission to foster and oversee
biblical and historical research. His famous encyclical *Rerum Novarum*
(1891) was the *magna carta* for modern Catholic social thought. All of
these together helped to "force Catholics out of their medievalism and
state of siege mentality."[73]

---

72. Bokenkotter, *Concise History,* 341.
73. Ibid., 341–42.

In such an atmosphere it was not surprising that a group of Catholic scholars would try to incorporate recent advances in biblical and historical studies into theology, with the expectation of approval from church authorities. Modernism is a complex phenomenon both in its origin and in its various representatives. There was a form of "philosophical modernism" in France, "social modernism" in Italy, and "theological modernism" in both France and England. It is not to the point here to give a complete historical survey of Modernism, but only to indicate its place in the development of the self-understanding of the Roman Catholic community.[74]

Although there were many important figures in the background, Alfred Loisy (1857–1940) and George Tyrrell (1861–1909) were generally considered the leaders of the movement and were the two against whom the encyclical *Pascendi Gregis* and the decree *Lamentabili* (1907) were primarily directed, although they were not mentioned by name. Loisy's book *The Gospel and the Church* (1902) was a reply to both of Adolf Harnack's claims in *Das Wesen des Christentums* (1900) that the essence of Christianity had been lost for eighteen hundred years and that all its various historical developments had been distortions and perversions of this original essence. Loisy, in defense of Roman Catholicism, argued that change is the natural condition for the preservation and expression of vitality of anything, including the church. In a famous passage, frequently quoted only in truncated form, Loisy says:

> Jesus foretold the kingdom, and it was the Church that came. . . . There is no institution on earth or in history whose status and value may not be questioned if the principle is established that nothing may exist except in its original form. Such a principle is contrary to the law of life, which is movement and a continual effort of adaptation to conditions always new and perpetually changing.[75]

Loisy argues that the church preserved the "fundamental ideas of Christ's teaching" though it does not realize the kingdom fully or finally but only prepares the way for its accomplishment. The identity of the

---

74. For fuller treatments of Modernism, see Gabriel Daly, *Transcendence and Immanence: A Study in Catholic Modernism and Integralism* (New York: Oxford University Press, 1980); Alec R. Vidler, *The Modernist Movement in the Roman Church* (Cambridge: The University Press, 1934), *20th Century Defenders of the Faith* (London: SCM Press, 1965); John Ratté, *Three Modernists* (New York: Sheed & Ward, 1967); Meriol Trevor, *Prophets and Guardians* (London: Hollis & Carter, 1969); Lester R. Kurtz, *The Politics of Heresy: The Modernist Crisis in Roman Catholicism* (Berkeley: University of California Press, 1986).

75. Alfred Loisy, *The Gospel and the Church*, introduction by Bernard B. Scott (Philadelphia: Fortress Press, 1976), 166.

church, like that of an individual, is not determined by immobile external forms but through the continuity of the consciousness of life. The
church has from the beginning adapted the Gospel to the needs of the
people it was addressing. His argument against Liberal Protestantism
(Harnack) and his defense of Roman Catholicism was that the adaptations and changes that have occurred in history were not all distortions
and perversions of some primitive essence that now we can and should
recover, but the necessary and legitimate developments of the Gospel,
true to Christ's teaching.

Loisy also applied his evolutionary model to the development of the
church's dogmas, cult, and authority. Of dogmas he says,

> The conceptions that the Church presents as revealed dogmas are
> not truth fallen from heaven, and preserved by religious tradition
> in the precise form in which they first appeared. . . . Though dog-
> mas may be Divine in origin and substance, they are human in
> structure and composition.[76]

He makes a distinction between the truth that alone is unchangeable
and its image in human minds.

Speaking of the church's authority, he says that some form of authority is necessary in any society and that the basically hierarchical structure
of the church was to be found in the New Testament, though not in the
same form as it existed in the Roman Catholic church of his time. Some
development in forms is necessary if the church is to live, but he did
not think that development was terminated with the highly centralized,
authoritarian, and juridical structure at present. Like Newman, Loisy believed that the declaration of the First Vatican Council was not the last
word on the subject.[77]

The other outstanding Modernist, George Tyrrell, was not as concerned with ecclesiology as Loisy. He did share the goal of a theology
more historically conscious than the scholastic theology in which he
had been trained. He was not as concerned with the facts of history as
he was with the facts of experience. The liberal theologian, he wrote,
does not "ask or care that his theology be substantially identical with
that of the past, but only that it be truer to experience than that which
it supersedes."[78] He felt that theology develops and changes, but revelation does not. They are "generically different orders of Truth and
Knowledge." Thus Tyrrell dealt with the anomalies raised by history and
experience for theology and dogmatic statements by locating change in

---

76. Ibid., 210–11.
77. Ibid., 210. For a fuller discussion, see my *Authority in the Church*, 153–58.
78. George Tyrrell, *Through Scylla and Charybdis* (London: Longmans, Green & Co.,
1907), 136.

theology, but distinguishing it from the apostolic revelation that has an "unchanging, unprogressive character."[79]

Both Loisy and Tyrrell, and the Modernists generally, were trying to come to terms with the nineteenth century's developments in historical-critical method and modern experience as a whole. They thought that they were doing Roman Catholicism a service. Rome and the Roman scholastic theologians saw it otherwise. Historical awareness, historical-critical methods, and any notions of development or evolution seemed to relativize the church's teaching (dogmas) and authority. The leading theologian of the Roman School, Cardinal Louis Billot (1846–1931) wrote a treatise, *De Immutabilitate Traditionis contra modernam haeresim evolutionismi* (1904), directed against Loisy. Billot's ideas and even his very words can be found in the two documents condemning Modernism. Billot was interested in defending the immutability of tradition, which he identified with the magisterium, because it was very closely connected to infallibility. For him, to

> admit that the sense of the ancient church about some dogma of our religion was different than the sense of the church at present and that what is preached by the church today, may be corrected tomorrow, then it follows that the ancient tradition (read magisterium) erred and that today's preaching may also err. For Billot, that is a denial of infallibility and of the promise of Christ.[80]

Underlying this argument is, of course, an ahistorical model of truth and of human knowledge. This inability to account for change "prevented the Roman theologians and the Roman congregations from solving, or even appreciating, the genuine questions with which historical science and modern philosophy confronted the Church at the time of the modernist crisis."[81] This clash between the nonhistorical epistemology, metaphysics, and theology of the Roman School and the historical consciousness and historical-critical methods of the nineteenth and twentieth centuries perdured right up to and including the Second Vatican Council, as we shall see in the next chapter.

Based on this Roman theology, Modernism was harshly condemned by Pius X in 1907 in the decree *Lamentabili*, which listed a series of propositions purportedly held by the Modernists, especially Loisy and Tyrrell, and the encyclical *Pascendi Dominici Gregis*. Loisy was excommunicated in 1908, and Tyrrell died in 1909. Others who were associated or who were considered sympathetic ran for cover and gave up any attempt to come to terms with the problems of historical criticism

---

79. Ibid., 4–5.
80. Sanks, *Authority in the Church*, 89, citing Billot, *De Immutabilitate*, 98–99.
81. McCool, *Catholic Theology*, 240.

in biblical studies and development in the history of dogma. Roman curial congregations were practically paranoid about the spread of such
pernicious ideas, and Councils of Vigilance were set up in each diocese.
In 1910, the "Oath against Modernism" was required of all clergy, pastors, confessors, preachers, and teachers of philosophy and theology. It
required internal assent to *Lamentabili* and *Pascendi* and read in part:
"I sincerely accept the doctrine of the faith as handed down to us from
the apostles through the orthodox Fathers in exactly the same meaning
and always in the same purport. Therefore, I entirely reject the heretical
theory of the evolution of the dogmas, viz., that they change from one
meaning to another, different from the one which the Church previously
held."[82] The oath was finally officially abolished by Pope Paul VI in 1967.

The consequence of this "reign of doctrinal terror," as Alec R. Vidler
called it, was to set back biblical and theological scholarship among
Roman Catholics for at least a generation. Speaking of its effects on
Catholic intellectual life in the United States, Jay Dolan says, "The fear
of heresy settled over episcopal residences, chanceries, seminaries, and
Catholic institutions of higher learning. Security, safety, conservatism
became national imperatives. Free intellectual inquiry in ecclesiastical
circles came to a virtual standstill."[83] It was against this background that
Vatican II appeared as such a dramatic reversal of course. This post-
Modernist fear of change and development also explains why there was
practically no development in Roman Catholic ecclesiology in the first
half of the twentieth century.

For many historians the real end of the nineteenth century came
in 1914. World War I shattered that century's illusions of progress, of
confidence in human reason and its products. Science and technology
were seen to be ambiguous at best, capable of bringing massive death
and destruction as well as ease and comfort to human life. This disillusionment was reflected in theology by the birth of Neo-Orthodoxy,
also referred to as Crisis Theology or Dialectical Theology, in Protestant theology. Its towering figure was Karl Barth (1886–1968) whose
*Commentary on the Epistle to the Romans* in 1919 rejected the liberal
theology that had prevailed among Protestants since Schleiermacher.
Although there were many developments in Barth's theology over his
long career, his early view of the church was rather negative, calling the
church the work of humans, not of God. Somewhat later he seems to
have regarded the church primarily as an event. When the Word of God
is proclaimed and received, the church comes into existence, and thus
could appear to lack permanent objective reality. Barth placed great em-

---

82. Neuner and Dupuis, *The Christian Faith*, nn. 143–44, 50.
83. Jay P. Dolan, *The American Catholic Experience* (Garden City, N.Y.: Doubleday &
Co., 1985), 319.

phasis on the encounter between God and humans that took place in the proclamation of the word and the response in faith. The theology of the church was not a major preoccupation of this theology.[84]

In the Roman Catholic tradition, the ecclesiology of the Roman School continued to dominate, and theological textbooks reproduced with minimal modifications the understanding of the church articulated by Billot and his successors at the Gregorian University in Rome. There was some renewed interest in the church as the Mystical Body of Christ. In the collection of Roman Catholic church documents referred to above (p. 106 footnote 59) the next entry under the rubric "church" after the condemnation of Modernism is the encyclical *Mystici Corporis* of Pius XII in 1943. Reportedly authored by Sebastian Tromp, one of Billot's successors at Rome's Gregorian University, the encyclical once again affirms the visibility of the church: "The Church is visible because she is a body," but at the same time recognizes the presence of charismatic gifts in the community.[85] The encyclical identifies the "true Church of Jesus Christ" with "the holy, catholic, apostolic, Roman Church" and calls this the mystical Body of Jesus Christ. It speaks of the bishops as "first among the members of the Lord" and as true shepherds who feed the flocks entrusted to them, and "although their jurisdiction is inherent in their office, yet they receive it directly from the same supreme Pontiff."[86] Finally, it denies that there can be a distinction between a church of charity and a juridical church: "There can, then, be no real opposition or conflict between the invisible mission of the Holy Spirit and the juridical commission of ruler and teacher received from Christ. Like body and soul in us, they complement and perfect one another, and have their source in our one Redeemer."[87]

The self-understanding of the Roman Catholic community at the time of the opening of the Second Vatican Council was that of *Mystici Corporis,* although there were some theologians in Germany and France who were quietly continuing historical and biblical research that would bear fruit in Vatican II. It is against the background of all the forces and movements from the post-Reformation period, through the Age of Reason and the Age of Revolution, through the various reactions to these, and the rejection of the modern world in the nineteenth and early twentieth centuries, that the amazing renewal and openness of Vatican II must be seen.

---

84. For a fuller discussion of Barth's ecclesiology, see Jay, *The Church,* 351–71, and Colm O'Grady, *The Church in the Theology of Karl Barth* (Washington: Corpus Books, 1968).

85. *Mystici Corporis,* in Neuner and Dupuis, *The Christian Faith,* 237.

86. Ibid., 238–39.

87. Ibid., 240.

# RECOMMENDED READINGS

Bokenkotter, Thomas. *A Concise History of the Catholic Church*. Garden City, N.Y.: Doubleday & Co., 1979.

Cragg, Gerald R. *The Church and the Age of Reason: 1648–1789*. London: Penguin Books, 1960.

Decree "Pastor Aeternus," of Vatican I, in J. Neuner and J. Dupuis, *The Christian Faith in the Doctrinal Documents of the Catholic Church*, rev. ed. New York: Alba House, 1982.

Vidler, Alec R. *The Church in an Age of Revolution: 1789 to the Present Day*. Baltimore: Penguin Books, 1961.

# Chapter 6

# Aggiornamento at Vatican II

For many of us the Second Vatican Council was an experience we lived through, but for others today, more than twenty-five years after the close of the council, it is history. It is part of our story that must be recalled. Our focus, of course, is the self-understanding of the Christian community, and Vatican II affected this immensely, not only by what it said but also by the event itself. Hence, in this chapter we will first describe the council as an *event*, then discuss the ecclesiologies (note the plural) in the documents themselves, and finally take up the reception and evaluation of the council at present.

## VATICAN II: AN ECCLESIAL EVENT

When, on January 25, 1959, Pope John XXIII announced to the cardinals in Rome his intention to call an ecumenical council, he was met with a stunned silence. Many saw no need for a council; many feared the consequences of a gathering of bishops in Rome; still others believed that the Roman curia were the ones best equipped to deal with the affairs of the universal church.

Although Pope John XXIII repeatedly referred to his "inspiration" to call a council, it was not a sudden revelation from on high. His personal secretary, Archbishop Loris F. Capovilla, recalls that the pope mentioned it to him only five days after becoming pope, and some cardinals claim that the idea was discussed even within the conclave.[1] He apparently

---

1. Loris F. Capovilla, "Reflections on the Twentieth Anniversary," in Alberic Stacpoole, ed., *Vatican II Revisited* (Minneapolis: Winston Press, 1986), 116; and Peter Hebblethwaite, *Pope John XXIII: Shepherd of the Modern World* (Garden City, N.Y.: Doubleday & Co., 1985), 306–8.

discussed it with several other advisers before making a firm decision. At any rate, the idea of summoning a council was there from the beginning and "was not accidental to the pontificate or a kind of afterthought; it was co-terminous with the pontificate as a whole, and acted as its goal, policy, programme and content."[2]

Considering his age (seventy-seven), Pope John did not want the council to be delayed very long and set the fall of 1963 as a target date for its convening, but, the story goes, each time a curial official offered reasons for delay, the pope set an earlier target date. For an undertaking of this size, much preparation was required. As the pope himself planned, the council took place in four phases: during the introductory, exploratory phase, called "ante-preparatory," 2,821 questionnaires were sent out to archbishops, bishops, abbots, heads of various clerical religious orders, and theological faculties around the world, soliciting their input; the second or preparatory phase properly speaking began in June 1960, with the appointment of preparatory commissions to draw up schemata to be presented to the council when it convened; the third phase was the general meeting of the council itself in all its solemnity, which took place in four sessions (in the fall seasons of 1962, 1963, 1964, and 1965); the final phase was the promulgation of the acts of the council.[3]

During the preparatory phase, more than eight hundred theologians, bishops, and other experts converged on Rome. Twelve preparatory commissions, and three secretariats were appointed, most of whose presidents and secretaries were from the Roman curia, although the pope made it plain that the council and the curia were distinct entities. While this work was going on in Rome, around the world expectations gradually rose, especially concerning the ecumenical thrust the pope had announced. The Secretariat for Christian Unity was organized under the direction of Cardinal Augustin Bea, a Jesuit Scripture scholar, in June 1960. This secretariat was a strange creature, for it was neither a preparatory commission for the council nor a curial congregation. Bea himself was a curial outsider, although he had been in Rome many years as rector of the Biblical Institute and had been personal confessor to Pius XII. Through voluminous correspondence and many meetings with Protestant and Orthodox representatives, Bea and those he gathered round him in the secretariat (Msgr. Jan Willebrands, for example) greatly influenced the preparatory work and helped guide the agenda

---

2. Ibid., 307.

3. Xavier Rynne, *Letters From Vatican City* (New York: Farrar, Straus & Company, 1963), 43, quoting from the pope's speech in St. Peter's, June 5, 1960, *Discorsi,* v. 2, 392. "Xavier Rynne" is a pseudonym for an unknown author (or authors) of several articles that appeared in the *New Yorker* during the first session of the council and were later complemented and published as this volume.

of the council in the direction of the quest for unity. As the pope probably intended, the secretariat also provided some balance to the Roman
curialists, who dominated the other preparatory commissions.[4]

Expectations were also raised by the media attention during this
phase. "Unlike the official preparations that were secret and therefore
invisible, the books, articles and television interviews about the Council carried the discussion to everyone in the church and beyond. This
media activity created expectations, gave rise to arguments about the
purpose of the Council, and reflected in however crude a manner the
*sensus fidelium,* that instinctive sense of what is right doctrine lodged
in the hearts of all the faithful."[5] In the United States, the council was
front-page news, and popular magazines such as *Time* were filled with
articles about it. Books such as Hans Küng's *The Council, Reform and
Reunion* (1960) urged greater use of Scripture in liturgy, the use of the
vernacular, abolition of the Index of Forbidden Books, and the reform
of the curia, thus specifying hopes and expectations even further.

With the possible exception of the British empire, no one is better at
putting on a spectacle than the Roman Catholic Church. The opening
of the council on October 11, 1962, was a spectacle made for the media.
A journalist's eyewitness account deserves to be quoted at length:

> At that moment (8 a.m.), two papal gendarmes, resplendent in
> parade uniform of white trousers and black topboots, coats, and
> busbies, slowly swung the great doors open, exposing to a por-
> tion of the crowd row upon row of bishops, clad in flowing white
> damask copes and miters, descending Bernini's majestic *scala re-
> gia* from the papal apartments. As brilliant television floodlights
> were switched on along the stairway, the intense light brought to
> mind Henry Vaughan's lines:
>
> > I saw Eternity the other night,
> > Like a great ring of pure and endless light.
>
> In rows of sixes, an apparently inexhaustible phalanx of prel-
> ates filed out of the Vatican Palace, swung to their right across
> St. Peter's Square, then wheeled right again, to mount the ramp-
> like steps leading into the basilica. Every now and then, this white
> mass was dotted with the black cassock, full beard, and round
> headdress of an oriental bishop, and here and there with the bul-
> bous gold crown and crossed pectoral reliquaries of a bishop of
> the Byzantine rite. Toward the end came the scarlet ranks of the
> Sacred College of Cardinals. Finally, the pope appeared, carried,

---

4. Hebblethwaite, *Pope John XXIII,* 375–85.
5. Ibid., 372.

in deference to the wishes of his entourage, on the *sedia gestatoria*, and looking rather timid, perhaps even frightened — as he always does when first mounting this oriental contraption — but gradually warming to the mild acclamation of the overawed crowd, and gently smiling and quietly weeping as he was carried undulantly forward, blessing the onlookers. At the entrance to the Council hall in the basilica, the procession halted while the pope dismounted and walked the length of the nave to the Confession of St. Peter.[6]

Pope John XXIII gave a now famous opening address in which he disagreed with "those prophets of gloom, who are always forecasting disaster," and saw in the modern world a new opportunity for the church. He made the helpful distinction between the "substance of the ancient doctrine of the deposit of faith...and the way in which it is presented" and stressed the pastoral character of the council.[7]

But if there was pageantry, there was also politics. Byzantine political scheming is a way of life at the Roman curia and had been going on throughout the preparatory phases, but the politics of the council began in earnest at the first general congregation, as the working sessions were called, on October 13, 1962. The first order of business was the election of the various conciliar commissions, successors to the preparatory commissions. A list of the names of those bishops who had served on the preparatory commissions was handed out with the expectation that they would be elected without further ado. But immediately, Cardinal Achille Liénart of Lille, primate of France, stood up without permission and moved that the voting be postponed until the various regional and national hierarchies could caucus and propose their own lists of nominees. Cardinal Josef Frings of Cologne seconded the motion to the vigorous applause of the bishops. After brief consultation, recognizing the will of the council fathers without need of a vote, Cardinal Eugéne Tisserant, who was presiding, adjourned the session, which had lasted only fifteen minutes. In those brief, dramatic moments what might have been a rubber stamp for the status quo became the free and open council that the pope had intended.

It was also a clear indication of the political divisions that would persist throughout the council, with the progressives led by Cardinals Liénart, Frings, Josef Léon Suenens of Malines, Bernard Alfrink of Utrecht, Julius Döpfner of Munich, Franz König of Vienna, Augustin Bea of the Secretariat for Christian Unity, Giovanni Montini of Milan, and Albert Meyer of Chicago, among others. The conservatives were led by

---

6. Rynne, *Letters from Vatican City,* 68–69.

7. "Pope John's Opening Speech to the Council," in Walter M. Abbott, S.J., ed., *The Documents of Vatican II* (New York: Crossroad, 1989, original, 1966), 715.

Cardinals Alfredo Ottaviani of the Holy Office, Giuseppe Siri of Genoa, Ernesto Ruffini of Sicily, Joseph Pizzardo of the Congregation of Seminaries and Universities, Paolo Marella of the Congregation for Bishops, and Archbishop Pericle Felici, general secretary of the council. It must be noted that terms like "progressive" and "conservative" are handy but generic designations and need to be nuanced in each usage.

Once the ten commissions of the council were elected, it was their task to go over the draft schemata, collect and collate suggested amendments, report back to the council, and include suggestions from the floor of the council. The commissions had theological experts (*periti*) who actually did much of the work. There was political jockeying to place progressive or conservative theologians on the various commissions. All of these maneuverings eventually leaked to the media, and people became acutely aware that the Roman Catholic Church was not a monolith, but was composed of fallible men (and very few women[8]). Despite it all, there was a palpable sense that this was indeed the work of the Spirit, a new Pentecost.

Pope John had said that just by coming together in council such a grand assemblage would itself be a statement about the church. He was right. The collegiality of the bishops, the cooperation of theologians and bishops, the active presence of the non-Catholic observers, and the pluralism even within the Roman Catholic communion, all were *experienced* before they were reflected in the official documents. Bishops who had been autonomous and isolated in their own dioceses discovered they had much in common and developed a sense of their own responsibility for the whole church. Theologians who had been under suspicion or at least on the periphery of official magisterial theology, such as Chenu, Congar, de Lubac, Rahner, Küng, and, posthumously, Teilhard de Chardin, were now influential participants in this central expression of the church. A massive but rapid theological education took place. Much of the scholarly work in Scripture, patristics, liturgy, and systematic theology that had been going on quietly since the post-Modernist witch hunt now bore fruit and was incorporated into the council documents. But already, before any documents were promulgated, the council as event had an immense impact on the

---

8. During the first session, Cardinal Suenens noted the absence of women from the conciliar deliberations, and, by the beginning of the second session some women "auditors" were appointed. By the end of the council there were twelve lay women and ten women religious, some of whom were appointed to commissions that drafted conciliar documents. Prominent among them was Sister Luke Tobin, superior of the Sisters of Loreto in the United States and then head of the Leadership Conference of Women Religious. See Rosemary Radford Ruether, "The Place of Women in the Church," in Adrian Hastings, ed., *Modern Catholicism: Vatican II and After* (New York: Oxford University Press, 1991), 260–66.

consciousness of the Christian community, Protestant, Orthodox, and Roman Catholic.

## ECCLESIOLOGIES IN THE DOCUMENTS

It is no exaggeration to say that the focus of Vatican II was ecclesiology. Neither was it an accident. The responses to the questionnaires sent out during the preparatory period resulted in 8,972 suggestions, wishes, or requests filling fifteen quarto volumes. The preparatory commissions distilled these into seventy-two schemata to be presented to the council fathers. Realizing that this was an overwhelming amount of material, "very uneven in value," that might prevent fruitful work at the council, Cardinal Suenens proposed to the pope that there be some overall plan for the council that would set it "on a truly pastoral course."[9] In a plan submitted to the pope and approved by him, Suenens recommended that the Second Vatican Council be linked to the First by beginning with a discussion of the schema *De Ecclesiae Christi mysterio*, dealing with the church both *ad intra* and *ad extra*, i.e., internally and in relation to the rest of the world. When Montini recommended such a plan for the council to the pope, he Montini said explicitly that the council should be centered around one theme: Holy Church.[10] Thus did it turn out. Vatican II has been called the Council on the Church. Issues affecting the doctrine on the church are reflected in all sixteen documents promulgated by the council, but the church is explicitly treated in the Dogmatic Constitution on the Church, *Lumen Gentium*, and the Pastoral Constitution on the Church in the Modern World, *Gaudium et Spes*. We shall concentrate our discussion on these two documents, with only passing references to others as seems appropriate.

### Lumen Gentium

The schema on the church prepared by a subcommittee of the theological commission, whose chair was Cardinal Ottaviani and whose secretary was Sebastian Tromp, S.J. (putative author of *Mystici Corporis*), not surprisingly followed the ecclesiology of that encyclical and that found in theological manuals in the first half of this century. This schema was debated on the floor of the council in early December and criticized as being too triumphalistic, juridical, and clerical by Bishop

---

9. Cardinal Léon-Josef Suenens, "A Plan for the Whole Council," in *Vatican II Revisited,* 88–105. Hebblethwaite attributes this plan to Cardinal Montini, *Pope John XXIII,* 442ff., but Suenens provides documentary evidence that he first proposed the plan in March 1962, and Montini and others later supported it.

10. Ibid., 103.

Emile Joseph de Smedt of Bruges. Others criticized the lack of a biblical and patristic emphasis (Cardinals Döpfner and Frings), and an abstract and legalistic terminology (Cardinal Bea and Bishop Blanchet). In sum, the council fathers urged a greater emphasis on the spirit of service and a more pastoral orientation.[11] The schema was sent back to the Theological Commission for revision between the first and second sessions.

A radically revised second draft was presented for discussion in the second session and occupied the council for the month of October 1963. The discussions focused on the notion of the collegiality of the bishops and concern that this might seem to weaken papal authority, and on the restoration of the permanent diaconate. There was also a fair amount of discussion of the general priesthood of the laity and its relationship to the hierarchy, as well as the relationship of religious priests to the local bishop, especially the notion of "exemption."[12] Finally, there was discussion of the chapter on Mary and whether it should be included in the schema on the church or be a separate document. All of the discussion on the floor had a profound impact on the revision of the draft between the 1963 and 1964 sessions, so that Gerard Philips remarks, "The Constitution on the Church is much more the work of the Council itself and of its most active members than is generally believed."[13] The final version was further refined in the fall of 1964; it was finally approved with a vote of 2,151 in favor and only 5 opposed and promulgated on November 21, 1964.

The Dogmatic Constitution on the Church begins by considering the church as a mystery (in Latin, *sacramentum*).[14] It is a sign of the unity of humanity with God and an instrument for achieving that union and unity.[15] The church is then presented in terms of various biblical images: Flock of Christ, Vineyard of God, Temple of the Holy Spirit, heavenly Jerusalem, spotless spouse of the spotless Lamb, pilgrim people, and, finally, Mystical Body of Christ (LG 6, 7). In explicating the latter image, the constitution marks a significant change from *Mystici Corporis*. After insisting that the hierarchical church and the Mystical Body of Christ, the visible assembly and the spiritual community, "form one interlocked

---

11. Gerard Philips, "Dogmatic Constitution on the Church: History of the Constitution," in Herbert Vorgrimler, ed., *Commentary on the Documents of Vatican II* (New York: Crossroad, 1989), 1:108–9.

12. "Exemption" refers to certain privileges granted to clerical religious orders that placed them outside the jurisdiction of the local ordinary.

13. Philips, "History of the Constitution," 126.

14. Only two of the council's decrees are called "Dogmatic Constitutions," this and the one on Revelation, *Dei Verbum*, to indicate the most solemn form of conciliar document, but it does not strictly define any new dogmas. It has the full weight of conciliar teaching, short of infallibility.

15. *Dogmatic Constitution on the Church, Lumen Gentium*, in Abbott, *Documents of Vatican II*, 1, 15. All further references will be in the text and will be abbreviated LG.

reality which is comprised of a divine and a human element," the constitution says that "this Church, constituted and organized in the world
as a society, *subsists in* the Catholic Church . . . although many elements
of sanctification and of truth can be found outside her visible structure"
(LG 8). Remember that *Mystici Corporis* had *identified* the true church
with the "holy, catholic, apostolic, Roman Church," and the 1963 draft
of the schema said that the true church "*is* [*est*]" the Catholic Church.
After discussion, the vague term "subsists in" was substituted to avoid
such identification and to leave open the question of the relationship
of one church to the many churches. This subtle shift in wording indicated a monumental change in the attitude of the Roman Catholic
Church toward other Christian confessions. For the first time since the
Reformation, the Catholic Church recognized other Christians not just
as individuals but as ecclesial bodies and applied the term "church" to
them. This would be spelled out further in the Decree on Ecumenism.[16]

The entire second chapter of the constitution is devoted to the image
that came to dominate the ecclesiology of the council, that of "People of
God." Referring to the total community of the church, bishops, clergy,
and laity, this image places greater emphasis on the human and communal aspects of the church than on the juridical and hierarchical aspects.
This chapter stresses the priesthood of all the baptized, as the Reformers
had, and the infallibility of the whole church (LG 10–12). It recognizes
that "within the Church particular Churches hold a rightful place," with
their own traditions and legitimate differences" (LG 13). It reaffirms that
the church in a wide sense is necessary for salvation, and recognizes that
the Catholic Church is "linked with those who, being baptized, are honored with the name of Christian," and calls them "Churches or ecclesial
communities" (LG 15; UR 3). Finally, this chapter asserts that "the plan
of salvation also includes those who acknowledge the Creator," Muslims and Jews, as well as those who sincerely seek God and "strive by
their deeds to do His will as it is known to them through the dictates
of conscience" (LG 16). The shift away from *Mystici Corporis* and the
ecumenical thrust of the document should be clear.

Following this communal and nonjuridical presentation of the
church as the People of God, chapter 3 situates the discussion of the
hierarchical structure and the episcopacy in this wider context. In accord with the plan for the council mentioned above, the constitution
stresses its continuity with Vatican I by reaffirming the dominical institution of the episcopacy and the Petrine primacy (LG 18). Being rather
cautious about historical claims, it asserts only that the episcopate runs
"back to the beginning," and that bishops are successors to the apostles

---

16. Aloys Grillmeier, "The Mystery of the Church," a commentary on chapter 1 of *Lumen
Gentium,* in Vorgrimler, *Commentary,* 1:149–50.

by divine institution (LG 20). The constitution settled a dispute in the
history of doctrine by affirming that "by episcopal consecration is conferred the fullness of the sacrament of orders," laying to rest the opinion
that a bishop is just a priest with greater powers of jurisdiction (LG 21).

Perhaps the most important contribution toward redressing the imbalance in the ecclesiology of Vatican I is the strong assertion of the
collegial nature of the episcopacy. Just as St. Peter and the other apostles
were "constituted one apostolic college, so in a similar way the Roman
Pontiff as the successor of Peter, and the bishops as the successors of
the apostles are joined together." This collegial nature and meaning
of the episcopal order found expression in ecumenical councils and
in the ancient practice of conciliar assemblies as well as in the custom
of new bishops being consecrated by neighboring bishops. "Together
with its head, the Roman Pontiff, and never without this head, the episcopal order is the subject of supreme and full power over the universal
Church." This supreme authority is exercised in a solemn way in an ecumenical council but also "by the bishops living in all parts of the world,
provided that the head of the college calls them to collegiate action, or
at least so approves or freely accepts the united action of the dispersed
bishops, that it is made a true collegiate act" (LG 22).

Individually a bishop is the "visible principle and foundation of unity
in his particular church," citing Cyprian, and "from such individual
churches there comes into being the one and only Catholic Church."
Thus further recognition is given to the place of the local churches and
the fact that they "enjoy their own discipline, their own liturgical usage,
and their own theological and spiritual heritage," especially the ancient
patriarchal churches (LG 23). Episcopal bodies today are encouraged
to put this collegiate sense into practical application, thus giving official
recognition to territorial episcopal conferences.[17]

Bishops have the duty to preach and teach, and this obligation is
called "a true service," *diakonia,* or ministry. They teach with the "authority of Christ," and this teaching is to be received by the faithful
with "a religious assent of soul." The constitution then discusses the
infallibility of the bishops:

> Although the individual bishops do not enjoy the prerogative of
> infallibility, they can nevertheless proclaim Christ's doctrine infal-
> libly. This is so, even when they are dispersed around the world,
> provided that while maintaining the bond of unity among them-
> selves and with Peter's successor, and while teaching authentically
> on a matter of faith or morals, they concur in a single viewpoint

---

17. LG 23, n. 115. Explicit affirmation and further specification of national and regional episcopal conferences is found in the Decree on the Bishops' Pastoral Office in
the Church, *Christus Dominus,* nos. 37–38.

as the one which must be held conclusively. This authority is even more clearly verified when, gathered together in an ecumenical council, they are teachers and judges of faith and morals for the universal church. Their definitions must then be adhered to with the submission of faith. (LG 25)

The document then repeats verbatim the definition of papal infallibility in *Pastor Aeternus* of Vatican I and immediately says that "the infallibility promised to the Church resides also in the body of bishops when that body exercises supreme teaching authority with the successor of Peter." When "either the Roman Pontiff or the body of bishops together with him defines a judgment, they pronounce it in accord with revelation itself," and they must painstakingly inquire into that revelation and strive to give apt expression to its contents, but do not allow for any new public revelation (LG 25). The council did not envision the possibility that we have seen in the history of the church of a conflict between the Roman Pontiff and a council in the exercise of infallible teaching authority and made no attempt to give priority to one over the other. Conciliarism and Gallicanism were not the concerns of this council. Restoration of the rightful place of the bishops in the governance of the church was their intention.

With this in mind, the constitution again stresses that the "Church of Christ is truly present in all legitimate local congregations of the faithful which, united with their pastors, are themselves called churches in the New Testament." "Bishops govern the particular churches entrusted to them as the vicars and ambassadors of Christ" and are not to be "regarded as vicars of the Roman Pontiff, for they exercise an authority which is proper to them, and are quite correctly called 'prelates,' heads of the people whom they govern" (LG 26–27). Thus did the council respond to the impression in the minds of some after Vatican I that bishops had been reduced to mere emissaries of the pope, though this was never the actual teaching of Vatican I.[18] Further, the recovery of the emphasis on the local church balances the concern for unity, sometimes misunderstood as uniformity, that underlay the definition of papal infallibility of Vatican I, as we saw in the previous chapter.

The third chapter of *Lumen Gentium* then treats the other ranks of the hierarchy, simple priests and deacons. Of priests it says, "Although priests do not possess the highest degree of the priesthood,

---

18. The German Chancellor Otto von Bismarck had asserted such a position in 1872 and the German hierarchy responded in a collective declaration in 1875 to the contrary. Pope Pius IX confirmed this position in an apostolic brief of 1875 saying that "the bishops are not mere tools of the Pope, nor papal officials without responsibility of their own," and that the episcopate is of divine institution and has rights and duties that the pope cannot change. See J. Neuner and J. Dupuis, eds., *The Christian Faith in the Doctrinal Documents of the Catholic Church*, rev. ed. (New York: Alba House, 1982), nn. 840–41.

and although they are dependent on the bishops in the exercise of their power, they are nevertheless united with the bishops in sacerdotal dignity." This association with and dependency on the bishops is true of both diocesan and religious priests (LG 28). Deacons are also ordained "unto a ministry of service" and are necessary for the life of the church. The constitution then says that "the diaconate can in the future be restored as a proper and permanent rank of the hierarchy," as seems appropriate to "competent territorial bodies of bishops," with the approval of the Supreme Pontiff. This applies also to married men of mature age.[19]

If chapter 3 recovers the rightful place of bishops in the life of the church, chapter 4 does the same for the laity. It stresses that "everything which has been said so far concerning the People of God applies equally to the laity, religious, and clergy. But there are certain things which pertain in a particular way to the laity, both men and women, by reason of their situation and mission" (LG 30). The laity are established among the People of God by reason of their baptism and share "in the priestly, prophetic, and kingly functions of Christ." But there is a "secular quality proper and special to laymen." By their vocation they seek the kingdom of God by engaging in temporal affairs and "work for the sanctification of the world from within, in the manner of leaven." They have the same grace and vocation to perfection as all the other members of the People of God and "share a true equality with regard to the dignity and to the activity common to all the faithful for the building up of the Body of Christ" (LG 32). The "lay apostolate" is now described as "a participation in the saving mission of the Church itself," in contrast to the language used prior to the council in which the lay apostolate was described as participation in the work of the hierarchy. This apostolic work is commissioned through the sacraments of baptism and confirmation (LG 33). In addition to this general apostolic calling, "laymen have the capacity to be deputed by the hierarchy to exercise certain church functions for a spiritual purpose." Thus the council opened the door to the expansion of lay ministries that has occurred since the council, as we will see in the next chapter. But the document recognizes that the special sphere for lay activity is in temporal affairs, which though governed by their own principles, cannot be "withdrawn from God's dominion" (LG 36). All of these themes were later expanded and deepened in the Decree on the Apostolate of the Laity, *Apostolicam Actuositatem*.

Chapter 5, entitled "The Call of the Whole Church to Holiness," does just what it says, asserting that "all the faithful of Christ of whatever

---

19. LG 29. For restoration of the diaconate in the Eastern churches see the Decree on Eastern Catholic Churches 17. The topic is also dealt with in the Decree on the Church's Missionary Activity 16.

rank or status are called to the fullness of the Christian life and to the perfection of charity" (LG 40). The special place of religious in the life of the church is affirmed in the following chapter. The religious life is "not an intermediate one between the clerical and lay states." It is primarily "a sign which can and ought to attract all the members of the Church to an effective and prompt fulfillment of the duties of their Christian vocation" (LG 43–44).

From the time of Robert Bellarmine through the neo-scholastic manuals of the early twentieth century, the church had been described as a "perfect society."[20] But chapter 7 of *Lumen Gentium* described the church as a "pilgrim church," which will "attain her full perfection only in the glory of heaven." Until that time, "the pilgrim Church in her sacraments and institutions, which pertain to this present time, takes on the appearance of this passing world. She herself dwells among creatures who groan and travail in pain until now and await the revelation of the sons of God" (LG 48). It affirms the unity of the wayfarer church with the church triumphant in heaven and urges all to work to correct "any abuses, excesses, or defects which may have crept in here and there." This is a definite attempt to overcome the "triumphalism" that had been denounced on the council floor.

Finally, after the council decided not to issue a separate document on Mary, the last chapter discusses the role of the Blessed Virgin Mary in the mystery of Christ and the church. Mary is "hailed as a pre-eminent and altogether singular member of the Church, and as the Church's model and excellent exemplar in faith and charity" (LG 53). The document reaffirms the doctrines of the Immaculate Conception and the Assumption and mentions the various titles accorded to Mary but stresses that there is only one Mediator between God and humans. Citing St. Ambrose, it calls Mary "a model of the Church in the matter of faith, charity, and perfect union with Christ" (LG 63).

I think it is clear that the Dogmatic Constitution on the Church marks some major and dramatic shifts in the self-understanding of the Roman Catholic Church. Though stressing continuity with Vatican I, it restored the episcopal college to its rightful place in the governance of the church, including sharing in the infallibility "with which Christ wished his church to be endowed," though always joined to the successor of Peter; it recognized the place and function of the local churches as well as their diverse traditions; it affirmed the ecclesial nature of other Christian bodies and that they possess some means of grace and salvation; it no longer identified the mystical Body of Christ with the

---

20. Although a technical term in scholasticism meaning that the society contained within itself all the means necessary to achieve its end, the term "perfect society" connoted the lack of imperfections and led to the triumphalistic attitude the council wished to correct.

Roman Catholic Church alone; it relocated the hierarchical structure of the church within the whole People of God; it stressed the equality and apostolic vocation of the laity and that all ministry in the church is service, *diakonia;* it recognized the human imperfections in the church and its need for reform until it completes its pilgrimage on earth; and it balanced the tendency to divinize Mary by locating her too within the People of God.

As the council progressed, these themes were further developed in other documents on more specific topics such as ecumenism and the laity, but *Lumen Gentium* remains the core programmatic statement of Vatican II on the church.

## *Gaudium et Spes*

Cardinal Suenens, as mentioned above, had proposed to Pope John an overall plan for the council focusing on the church both *ad intra* and *ad extra. Lumen Gentium* dealt with the church *ad intra.* Suenens's speech proposing his plan to the council fathers on December 4, 1962, was the stimulus for the document on the church *ad extra,* the Pastoral Constitution on the Church, *Gaudium et Spes.* Dom Helder Camara, auxiliary bishop of Rio de Janeiro, had also urged that the council express its concern about the great problems of people around the world.

There had been no preparatory document specifically on this topic, though there were draft schemata on the social order and on the laity that dealt with some of the same issues. Using some of the material from these schemata, a mixed commission appointed during the council did prepare what came to be called Schema XIII, which went through several drafts. Cardinal Suenens continued to be its main shepherd. The final version was approved by the council on December 4, 1965, by an overwhelming majority.[21]

The Pastoral Constitution on the Church in the Modern World is lengthy, sometimes repetitive, and divided into two parts. Part 1 deals with more doctrinal issues and will concern us here, while part 2 is a series of pastoral applications to contemporary issues that do not themselves contribute to the ongoing self-understanding of the church. It is consciously in continuity with *Lumen Gentium,* which it frequently cites, and does not offer a new or different ecclesiology.

What is striking and startlingly new is the council's attitude toward the modern world. In stark contrast to the posture of Vatican I, which saw the "gates of hell . . . rising up everywhere against the Church's di-

---

21. For a detailed history of the text see Charles Moeller, "History of the Constitution," in Vorgrimler, *Commentary,* 5:1–76.

vinely established foundation with the intention of overthrowing the
Church,"[22] this constitution positively affirms and is open to "the dimensions of human culture opened up by advances in the historical, social,
and psychological sciences."[23] The siege mentality of the nineteenth and
early twentieth centuries noted in the last chapter is abandoned. The
council "now addresses itself without hesitation, not only to the sons of
the Church and to all who invoke the name of Christ, but *to the whole
of humanity*" (*Gaudium et Spes* GS 2; hereafter GS). It affirms its "solidarity with the entire human family" and conceives of its mission as
continuing the work of Christ who "entered this world to give witness
to the truth, to rescue and not to sit in judgment, to serve and not to
be served" (GS 3).

In describing "The Situation of Men in the Modern World," it recognizes the church's "duty of scrutinizing the signs of the times," a phrase
frequently used by John XXIII. It acknowledges a "true social and cultural transformation" that has profound repercussions on the religious
sphere of human life. Science and technology have transformed the face
of the earth and extended human dominion over space and time. The
"human community has become all of a piece" and "has passed from
a rather static concept of reality to a more dynamic, evolutionary one"
(GS 5). This dynamic and evolutionary worldview reflects the profound
influence of the thought of Teilhard de Chardin on the document and
pervades it in many ways (GS 6, n. 11). The document goes on to describe changes in the social order, as well as psychological, moral, and
religious changes, and affirms "that humanity can and should increasingly consolidate its control over creation." "Man is slowly becoming
aware," it states, "that it is his responsibility to guide aright the forces
which he has unleashed and which can enslave him or minister to him,"
again reflecting a Teilhardian perspective (GS 9). Hence, "the Council
wishes to speak to all men in order to illuminate the mystery of man
and to cooperate in finding the solution to the outstanding problems
of our time" (GS 10).

In contrast with the preconciliar ecclesiology that conceived of the
church as the *societas perfecta* standing apart from and over against the
"City of Man," the constitution now understands the church as the People of God deciphering "authentic signs of God's presence and purpose
in the happenings, needs, and desires in which this People has a part
along with other men of our age . . . in whose midst it lives [to] render
service to each other" (GS 11).

Chapter 1 affirms the dignity of the human person based on the

---

22. *Pastor Aeternus*, in Neuner and Dupuis, *Doctrinal Documents*, n. 818.
23. Donald R. Campion, S.J., "The Church Today," an introduction to the constitution
in Abbott, *Documents of Vatican II*, 185.

scriptural teaching that humans were created in the image of God, not "as a solitary" but as a social being in interpersonal communion with others. Though recognizing that "man is split within himself" and, as a result, human life is a struggle between good and evil, it affirms the "progress in the practical sciences, technology, and the liberal arts" that humans have accomplished, "especially in his probing of the material world and in subjecting it to himself" (GS 15). In contrast to the 1864 *Syllabus of Errors*, the council viewed "authentic freedom [as] an exceptional sign of the divine image within man," a theme developed further in the Decree on Religious Liberty. In discussing the church's response to atheism it recommends that a believer bear witness by making faith penetrate his or her entire life, including the worldly dimensions "by activating him toward justice and love, especially regarding the needy." Finally, this chapter asserts the possibility of the ultimate salvation for all humans (GS 22).

Chapter 2 calls to mind Christian doctrine about human society found in recent papal encyclicals, especially *Mater et Magistra, Pacem in Terris,* and *Ecclesiam Suam.* It reaffirms human interdependence and the consequent responsibility of each social group for the welfare of other groups and of the "entire human family" (GS 25–26). It affirms the basic equality of all and the basic human rights to education, to found a family, to employment, to a good reputation and respect, to follow one's conscience, to privacy, and to religious freedom. But more than a "merely individualistic morality" is required. Because of the solidarity of the human race, one must "count social necessities among the primary duties of modern man" and seek to become "artisans of a new humanity" (GS 30).

Chapter 3 recognizes the "autonomy of earthly affairs ... which enjoy their own laws and values," and therefore genuine scientific investigation "never truly conflicts with faith" (GS 36). Again this contrasts sharply with the suspicion and hostility with which historical and scientific methods were viewed in the nineteenth and early twentieth centuries, especially in the Modernist crisis. Although the document carefully distinguishes earthly progress from the growth of Christ's kingdom, "Nevertheless, to the extent that the former can contribute to the better ordering of human society, it is of vital concern to the kingdom of God" (GS 39). We will see that this distinction without separation will be developed after the council by Latin American liberation theology.

The last chapter in part 1 explicitly deals with "The Role of the Church in the Modern World," again referring to Cardinal Suenens's speech on the council floor. The church "serves as a leaven and as a kind of soul for human society as it is to be renewed in Christ and transformed into God's family" (GS 40). The earthly and the heavenly city penetrate each other. The "Church believes she can contribute greatly toward making the family of man and its history more human. At the same time, she is firmly convinced that she can be abundantly and variously helped by the world in the matter of preparing the ground for the gospel." The council wishes to foster "this mutual exchange and assistance in concerns which are in some way common to the church and the world."

The constitution recognizes that "Christ . . . gave His Church no proper mission in the political, economic, or social order." The church's purpose is a religious one, but in certain circumstances, the church "can and indeed should initiate activities on behalf of all men," particularly for the needy. At the same time it makes clear that "in virtue of her mission and nature, she is bound to no particular form of human culture, not to any political, economic, or social system" (GS 42). Neither does the church have the solution to all particular problems in the social order. The council thus walks a fine line between describing the mission of the church as a religious one and encouraging the pursuit of a just social order as a consequence of the Gospel spirit. "They are mistaken who, knowing that we have here no abiding city but seek one which is to come, think that they may therefore shirk their earthly responsibilities. For they are forgetting that by the faith itself they are more than ever obliged to measure up to these duties, each according to his proper vocation" (GS 43). Religion does not consist in acts of worship alone nor only certain moral obligations. The council says that the "split between the faith which many profess and their daily lives deserves to be counted among the more serious errors of our age." Secular activities, however, "belong properly although not exclusively to laymen." The council admits that this witness to the Gospel in the world, this mission to be the "sign of salvation on earth," is hampered by the unfaithfulness of her members, both clerical and lay and that a "great distance lies between the message she offers and the human failings of those to whom the gospel is entrusted."

Finally, the document affirms "The Help Which the Church Receives from the Modern World," especially in learning to express the message of Christ and accommodating it to diverse cultures as well as in interpreting "the many voices of our age . . . to judge them in the light of the divine Word." Also, since the church has a visible and social structure, "she can and ought to be enriched by the development of human social life" (GS 44). Referring to *Lumen Gentium,* part 1 closes by asserting once again that the church is "the universal sacrament of salvation," manifesting and exercising God's love for humankind.

The second part of the document is predominantly pastoral and deals with specific topics of concern today: marriage and family life, human culture, life in its economic, social, and political dimensions, war and peace, and the formation of a family of nations. In these areas the council summarizes recent papal social teaching but does not deal with ecclesiology as such.

*Gaudium et Spes* marks a major shift in the self-understanding of the Roman Catholic community in its relationship to the modern world. It takes a positive view of advances in the human sciences, locates itself within the whole human community, and specifically puts itself in service to that community. It ends the ghetto mentality and urges dialogue with the world, with all its diverse voices. It no longer conceives of itself as a "perfect society" but recognizes its failures and limitations as well as its need to learn from developments in the human sciences. It recognizes that it does not have all the answers but must search for solutions to contemporary problems along with the rest of humanity. It recognizes and accepts change and a dynamic and evolutionary view of the world and the social order. Its mission is to witness to the Gospel and to serve the common good of all humankind, the second following from the first and not in conflict with it. Thus the church's self-understanding *ad extra* is a dramatic reversal of the siege mentality that dominated the preceding century and a half.

Other dramatic reversals of course were manifested in the council's Decree on Ecumenism, *Unitatis Redintegratio,* and in the Decree on Religious Freedom, *Dignitatis Humanae,* both of which we will comment on briefly.

## Other Documents

We have already mentioned the shift in *Lumen Gentium* from the simple identification of the Mystical Body of Christ with the Roman Catholic Church found in *Mystici Corporis* to the more nuanced phraseology of *subsistit in* of the Dogmatic Constitution and the willingness to attribute ecclesial characteristics to other Christian bodies. We have noted also the overall influence on the council of the Secretariat for Christian Unity and the importance of the active participation of the official Protestant and Orthodox observers. But the council fathers clearly wished to pursue further the quest for unity among Christians that John XXIII had announced as a goal of the council.

Reversing almost four hundred years of polemics, the Decree on Ecumenism, *Unitatis Redintegratio,* admits that "men of both sides were to blame" for the separations that had rent the seamless garment of Christ, and now accepts "with respect and affection as brothers" those whom it had previously regarded as heretics or schismatics and as adversaries to be refuted in theological manuals. Now the council affirms that actions carried out in these separated churches and communities "can truly engender a life of grace, and can be rightly described as capable of providing access to the community of salvation." Nevertheless, it main-

tains that the "fullness of the means of salvation" can be found in the
Catholic Church alone (UR 3). In contrast to the Catholic Church's earlier refusal to participate in the World Council of Churches (1948), the
decree now urges "all the Catholic faithful to recognize the signs of the
times and to participate fully in the work of ecumenism." They are urged
to dialogue with, cooperate with, and pray with different churches and
communities.

The decree envisions a great deal of freedom within the unity it
seeks:

> While preserving unity in essentials, let all members of the Church,
> according to the office entrusted to each, preserve a proper free-
> dom in the various forms of spiritual life and discipline, in the
> variety of liturgical rites, and even in the theological elaborations
> of revealed truth (UR 4).

The decree recognizes that renewal and reform within the Catholic Church itself is a necessary prerequisite for this movement toward
unity to take place. It admits that there have been "deficiencies in conduct, in church discipline, or even in the formulation of doctrine" which
should be rectified, and in humble prayer begs "pardon of God and of
our separated brethren" for past failures (UR 6–7). After urging that the
theological education of future bishops and priests be presented from
an ecumenical viewpoint, it reminds Catholic theologians engaged in
ecumenical dialogue that "they should remember that in Catholic teaching there exists an order or 'hierarchy' of truths, since they vary in their
relationship to the foundation of the Christian faith" (UR 11). This is
perhaps one of the most significant advances for theology put forth
by the council. Finally, the decree approves of the diversity of customs
and observances of the Eastern churches and extends this approbation
to "differences in theological expressions of doctrine," saying that they
should be "considered as complementary rather than conflicting" (UR
17). All in all, the Decree on Ecumenism is a remarkable reversal of
the previously prevailing positions and attitudes toward other Christian
churches.

The Decree on Religious Freedom, *Dignitatis Humanae*, originally
a chapter in the Decree on Ecumenism, offers another example of a
significant change in the position of the church vis-à-vis the temporal
society. Pius IX in the *Syllabus of Errors* in 1864 had condemned the
propositions that "every one is free to embrace and profess the religion
which by the light of reason he judges to be true" and that "in our age
it is no longer advisable that the Catholic religion be the only State religion, excluding all other cults."[24] And in 1885, Leo XIII had said in the

---

24. *Syllabus of Errors*, in Neuner and Dupuis, *Doctrinal Documents*, 283–84.

encyclical *Immortale Dei* that "the Church does not consider it licit that various forms of worship of God should have the same rights as the true religion." He recognized, however, that some states "tolerate in practice and by custom" all religions and they all have equal rights. Thus the Catholic Church seemed to operate on a double standard: "freedom for the Church when Catholics are a minority, privilege for the Church and intolerance for others when Catholics are a majority."[25] Unless this ambiguity were cleared up, the council felt, further ecumenical movement would be difficult.

The Decree on Religious Freedom declares "that the human person has a right to religious freedom. This freedom means that all men are to be immune from coercion on the part of individual or of social groups and of any human power, in such wise that in matters religious no one is to be forced to act in a manner contrary to his own beliefs. Nor is anyone to be restrained from acting in accordance with his own beliefs, whether privately or publicly, whether alone or in association with others, within due limits" (DH 2). Thus the Catholic Church claims for all churches the freedoms she had previously claimed for herself, arguing that this right is founded "in the very dignity of the human person."

Such a clear departure from the teaching of previous popes made the document, as John Courtney Murray said, "the most controversial document of the whole Council, largely because it raised with sharp emphasis the issue that lay continually below the surface of all the conciliar debates — the issue of the development of doctrine."[26] It was this notion of development, not the notion of religious freedom, that caused controversy and opposition to the document, but the final version states clearly that "this sacred Synod intends to develop the doctrine of recent Popes on the inviolable rights of the human person and on the constitutional order of society" (DH 1). This formal sanctioning of the validity of development was, Murray notes, "a doctrinal event of high importance for theological thought in many other areas." In addition, I would suggest that the Decree on Religious Freedom marks the end of the last vestiges of the integral relationship of church and state that we call Christendom.

We have dealt individually with only four of the sixteen documents promulgated by Vatican II, but these indicate the major consequences for the self-understanding of the Roman Catholic community to be found in the documents as a whole. By way of summary, let me indicate what I consider to be the major shifts in this ecclesial self-understanding:

---

25. John Courtney Murray, S.J., "Religious Freedom," an introduction to the Decree on Religious Freedom in Abbott, *Documents of Vatican II*, 673.

26. Ibid., 673.

1. The church is no longer seen as a "perfect society" but rather as a "pilgrim church," making its way with human sinfulness, imperfections, and weaknesses, partly responsible for its internal disunity as well as for atheism and unbelief in the contemporary world.

2. While the church is still the guardian of the "deposit of faith," it recognizes that there is a distinction between the substance of the deposit and the way in which it is presented, that no one formulation captures all truth, that diverse formulations may complement one another, and that there is a "hierarchy of truths."

3. The Roman Catholic Church no longer sees itself as the sole channel of grace, but some means of salvation are to be found in other churches and ecclesial bodies; there is, in effect, salvation outside the Roman Catholic Church.

4. In contrast to the immutability defended by Billot, the church recognizes a more dynamic and evolutionary worldview. Development of doctrine is affirmed by both word and the actions of the council, and the ancient principle of *ecclesia semper reformanda* was embraced.

5. Although the teaching of Vatican I is reaffirmed, the documents recognize the rights and duties of local churches and local bishops as well as the participation of all bishops as a college in the governance of the church.

6. The concern for the unity of the church evidenced in Vatican I is not abandoned, but freedom, diversity, and pluralism in observances, customs, and even in doctrinal expressions is recognized as contributing to the richness of the church.

7. The mission of the church is not to preserve the faithful from the world, but to serve all of humanity. It is to proclaim and witness to the Gospel, but this entails active participation in the search for justice in the secular sphere. Openness to and dialogue with the world, other Christian communions, non-Christians, and atheists contrasts with the previous defensive posture of the church.

These were major shifts from the preconciliar self-understanding of the Roman Catholic community. But these shifts did not repudiate earlier ecclesiological understandings. Although the dominant image for the church was the communal one of "People of God," the hierarchical structure of the church was reaffirmed. Vatican I's doctrine of papal primacy and infallibility was placed side by side with the affirmation of episcopal collegiality and episcopal infallibility. The necessity of the church for salvation was affirmed simultaneously with the recognition of some means of salvation outside the church. The religious nature of the church's mission was asserted along with its mission of service to all humanity. The documents were written by committees and reflect it. There was a large progressive majority but the concerns of conservatives were also considered. These unresolved ambiguities and diverse emphases lead us to conclude that there is not one coherent ecclesiology in the documents, but a plurality of ecclesiologies. We will suggest a way of understanding this situation below. In chapter 1 we briefly sketched the effects the council had on the daily lives of Roman Catholics in forms of piety, attitudes, and ecclesial structures. In the following chapters we will discuss some of the challenges and possibilities that have developed since the council, but let us first say a few words about how the council was received and evaluated.

## RECEPTION AND EVALUATION OF VATICAN II

The most fundamental "reception" of Vatican II was that of the participants themselves, who overwhelmingly experienced it as the work of the Holy Spirit.[27] They clearly felt that the council was a gift and a grace that could be explained in no other way than as the movement of the Spirit. They knew they were participating in an extraordinary event and making history. This perception gradually came to be shared by nonparticipants as well. Protestant observers such as Albert C. Outler and George A. Lindbeck regarded the council as an "epochal event" offering a "genuinely new vision of the world" for Roman Catholics, leading to "notable transformations."[28]

The solemn closing of the council on December 8, 1965, marked a beginning, not an end. The work of implementing the initiatives of the council remained to be carried out by the various national hierarchies. Their meetings as national hierarchies throughout the council had given them a new sense of unity and of their responsibility as conferences for the church of their nation or region. Practical changes such as the vernacular in the liturgy required collective action in approving translations, revisions in the sacramentary, and so on. Episcopal collegiality moved from the documents to lived experience.

Much of the burden for the reception and implementation of the council fell on the shoulders of the local parish clergy, whose theological education had not prepared them for the changes, nor indeed, for change at all. Many frequently followed instructions from national or

---

27. *Vatican II Revisited, passim.*

28. Albert C. Outler, "Strangers within the Gates: An Observer's Memories," in *Vatican II Revisited*, 170–83, and George A. Lindbeck, *The Future of Roman Catholic Theology* (Philadelphia: Fortress Press, 1966), 1.

diocesan offices without a deeper understanding of what was being implemented and, consequently, were unable to prepare the people for
the changes. They dutifully turned the altar around, removed the altar rail, and told the faithful to shake hands at the kiss of peace, but
in the same authoritarian manner that had characterized much clerical
behavior before the council.

Although Vatican II had spoken of collegiality only with reference to
the episcopate, local priests soon concluded that something analogous
should happen on the diocesan level, and local laity expected the same
on the parish level. Participation and consultation became the order of
the day. In general, both clergy and laity approved of the changes initiated by the council even if they did not fully understand the theological
underpinnings. A 1977 survey found that U.S. Catholics "approved of
the Council's reforms by 67–23 percent."[29] Among younger Catholics
the approval rate was even higher, and now we have a whole generation
who have known only the postconciliar church.

As the council recedes into history, there have been many ventures
to evaluate and assess its significance.[30] Our interest here is not to assess the council as a whole but only its impact on the self-understanding
of the Christian community. Perhaps one of the most insightful and influential assessments was that of Karl Rahner in 1979. "Vatican II," he
wrote, was "the first major official event in which the Church actualized
itself precisely as a *world Church*." By this he understood that at Vatican II the church took its first official, though initial and diffident, steps
away from a Eurocentric church, which for centuries had acted as "an
export firm which exported a European religion as a commodity it did
not really want to change but sent throughout the world together with
the rest of the culture and civilization it considered superior." With Vatican II, it "begins to act through the reciprocal influence excercised by all
its components."[31] He argues that it was an epochal change, comparable
to the church's move from Jewish Christianity into Hellenistic and European culture and civilization, initiating an essentially different situation
for Christianity. Since Rahner's assessment, it has become commonplace
to speak of the "emergent global church." We will discuss this further
in chapter 9.

---

29. George Gallup, Jr., and Jim Castelli, *The American Catholic People: Their Beliefs,
Practices, and Values* (New York: Doubleday & Co., 1987), 49ff.

30. Among others see *Vatican II Revisited by Those Who Were There*, previously cited;
Giuseppe Alberigo, Jean-Pierre Jossua, and Joseph A. Komonchak, eds., *The Reception of
Vatican II*, trans. Matthew J. O'Connell (Washington, D.C.: Catholic University of America
Press, 1987); René Latourelle, ed., *Vatican II: Assessment and Perspectives*, 3 vols. (New
York: Paulist Press, 1988); and John W. O'Malley, S.J., *Tradition and Transition: Historical
Perspectives on Vatican II* (Wilmington, Del.: Michael Glazier, 1989).

31. Karl Rahner, S.J., "Towards a Fundamental Theological Interpretation of Vatican II,"
*Theological Studies* 40, no. 4 (December 1979): 716–27.

From a historical perspective, John W. O'Malley compared Vatican II with two other great reformations, the Gregorian and the Lutheran, under four aspects: content, rhetoric, quality of leadership, and institutional grounding.[32] With regard to content, he suggests that Vatican II constitutes a "new ecclesiological or theological paradigm" constituted not by a single issue, but by the underlying shift from an ahistorical to a historical mode of treating all issues.[33] Unlike the two earlier reformations, the rhetoric of Vatican II is not confrontational but conciliatory and reassuring. It is a "rhetoric of congratulation" rather than a "rhetoric of reproach" and for that reason lacks "dramatic force."[34] The two earlier reformations were led by charismatic individuals, while the leadership of Vatican II, though it has been called Pope John's Council, was in fact a committee "whose members went home to resume life pretty much as usual once the work was done. Gregory and Luther never 'went home.' "[35]

On the issue of institutional grounding, both the earlier reformations had created a new social class that had high stakes in the success of the reformation — "for the Gregorians, the creation of the college of cardinals, and for the Lutherans, the married clergy."[36] Vatican II, however, seems to have created no such class with a vested interest in its success, although various candidates such as the Synod of Bishops or national episcopal conferences have been suggested. The laity and/or lay ministry could possibly emerge as such a class, but as yet cannot be said to have the "institutional grounding" necessary for it to continue reforms over time.[37] O'Malley concludes that "despite the complexity of its rhetoric, despite the weakness of its leadership and institutional grounding," he is inclined to call Vatican II another "great reformation" though significantly different from his two historical models.

I find O'Malley's analysis very helpful and I am inclined to agree with much of what he says. I have argued, however, in my earlier work that Vatican II was not itself a paradigm shift, but was an excellent example of an institution in the *process of a paradigm shift*.[38] The council unseated the dominant hierarchical and juridical approach to the church but did not replace it completely. Instead, it placed a more communal, sacramental understanding epitomized by the "People of God" side by side with the older view without resolving apparent contradictions. We

---

32. John W. O'Malley, *Tradition and Transition*, and in *Theological Studies* 44, no. 3 (September 1983): 373–406, to which page references are made here.
33. Ibid., 392–94.
34. Ibid., 396.
35. Ibid., 399.
36. Ibid., 390.
37. Ibid., 400–402.
38. See my *Authority in the Church: A Study in Changing Paradigms*, previously cited.

have seen that there are several ecclesiologies in the documents. The ahistorical or classicist approach to theology was no longer regnant at the council, but it has not yet completely disappeared. We are still, after twenty-five years, witnessing the struggle of these two mindsets. I share, however, O'Malley's view that the new historical consciousness will eventually prevail within the church because it is already, and has been for a century, pervasive in the reality "out there" of the rest of our culture. Vatican II only belatedly recognized it.

Writing twenty years after the council, Hermann J. Pottmeyer suggested that the postconciliar reception can be described in two phases. The first, the "phase of excitement," which we have alluded to above, and the second, the "phase of disillusionment," during which the enthusiasts discovered "the inertia characteristic of so great an institution and its historical forms" and the "weight of tradition . . . present in the conciliar texts and their footnotes."[39] The task that remains for us, he argues, is "to incorporate what is still binding in preconciliar theology into the newly acquired foundation, that is, into a *communio* ecclesiology and a Christian anthropology that calls for commitment to human dignity." Such a task requires time and "giving the Spirit of God enough freedom to lead the church along new paths," including the freedom to make mistakes.[40]

Pottmeyer also makes the point, with which I concur, that the juxtaposition of the two ecclesiologies is itself progress because it at least relativized the Tridentine and Vatican I ecclesiology "in the sense that it no longer regarded their formulations as the absolutely final stage of development in the understanding of the faith, but instead located them within the whole tradition of faith."[41] An authentic interpretation of the conciliar documents must keep in mind that the views of the minority, although incorporated into the documents, "do not represent the will of the Council in the same degree as the theses that passed by an overwhelming majority." This point is ignored by some "Restoration" interpreters.

Just as there was a conservative minority during the council, approximately 220 of the 2,200 in average attendance, so there has been a minority opposed to the initiatives of the council ever since.[42] Many of these were and continue to be members of the Roman curia and, therefore, exert influence beyond their numbers. International organizations such as Credo, Communion and Liberation, Catholics United for the

---

39. Hermann J. Pottmeyer, "A New Phase in the Reception of Vatican II: Twenty Years of Interpretation of the Council," in Alberigo, et al., *The Reception of Vatican II*, 34.
40. Ibid.
41. Ibid., 40.
42. Michael J. Walsh, "The Conservative Reaction," in Hastings, *Modern Catholicism*, 283–88.

Faith, and Tradition, Family, Property, have been formed to try to direct the church back to a preconciliar mode. They have publications like the *Wanderer* and *Le pensée catholique* that promote their views. Perhaps the most extreme and notorious of the reactionary groups was that led by Archbishop Marcel Lefebvre and his Fraternité Sacerdotale S. Pie X, which has claimed that Vatican II was a schismatic council and the work of Satan.[43] Lefebvre was suspended *a divinis* (forbidden to say Mass or administer the sacraments) and his fraternity suppressed in 1976. He defiantly consecrated four traditionalist bishops in 1988, which entailed automatic excommunication. He died in 1991, unreconciled to the church.

Criticism of the council also came from the left with organizations like "Christians for Socialism," claiming that Vatican II "had represented the high point in the Church's effort to adapt itself to the bourgeois form of society."[44] This movement was not very widespread nor long-lived, however.

Since the election of John Paul II as pope on October 16, 1978, many observers believe there has been a concerted effort at what is being called the "Restoration." The leader of this Restoration is perceived to be Cardinal Joseph Ratzinger, the prefect of the Congregation for the Doctrine of the Faith. Although a "progressive" theologian at Vatican II when he was theological advisor to Cardinal Frings of Cologne, Ratzinger has manifested an increasingly gloomy view of the world and the openness to it affirmed by Vatican II. In his now famous *Report on the Faith,* he said, "After the phase of indiscriminate 'openness' it is time that the Christian reacquire the consciousness of belonging to a minority and of often being in opposition to what is obvious, plausible and natural for that mentality . . . [called] the 'spirit of the world.' "[45]

Under Ratzinger's leadership the congregation has taken repressive measures against such progressive theologians as Jacques Pohier, Hans Küng, Edward Schillebeeckx, Leonardo Boff, and Charles Curran, has attacked liberation theology, and has called into question the teaching authority of national episcopal conferences. The appointment of conservatives as bishops around the world is strong evidence of something like a Restoration.[46] When asked directly about the Restoration, Ratz-

---

43. For a concise summary of this and other opposition movements see Daniele Menozzi, "Opposition to the Council (1966–84)," in Alberigo, et al., *The Reception of Vatican II,* 325–48.

44. Ibid., 341.

45. Cardinal Joseph Ratzinger with Vittorio Messori, *The Ratzinger Report,* trans. Salvator Attanasio and Graham Harrison (San Francisco: Ignatius Press, 1985), 36.

46. For a journalistic but well-documented account of the Restoration see Penny Lernoux, *People of God: The Struggle for World Catholicism* (New York: Viking Press, 1989), and Hans Küng and Leonard Swidler, eds., *The Church in Anguish: Has the Vatican Betrayed Vatican II?* (San Francisco: Harper & Row, 1987).

inger replied, "If by 'restoration' is meant a turning back, no restoration of such kind is possible.... But if by *restoration* we understand the search for a new balance after all the exaggerations of an indiscriminate opening to the world, after the overly positive interpretations of an agnostic and atheistic world, well, then a *restoration* . . . is altogether desirable and, for that matter, is already in operation in the Church. In this sense it can be said that the first phase after Vatican II has come to a close."[47]

If such a Restoration is already operative in the church, it was not evidently shared by all the fathers of the Extraordinary Synod of 1985, summoned by Pope John Paul II to assess the council. In his insightful analysis of that synod, Dulles discerned basically three groups of opinions or perspectives represented there. The first, led by Ratzinger and Cardinal Joseph Höffner, he calls "neo-Augustinian." This group saw the "church as an island of grace in a world given over to sin." For them the "world is falling into misery, division, and violence," and the openness of the postconciliar period allowed the church to be contaminated.[48] The second viewpoint, called "communitarian" and led by Cardinal Basil Hume of England and the presidents of the episcopal conferences of the United States and Canada, Bishops James Malone and Bernard Hubert respectively, were convinced that "great progress had been made as a result of the council, but they attributed the main difficulties to the failure of conservative prelates to carry through the reforms of Vatican II." A third group, "coming from Third World countries, shared neither the sacralism of the Augustinians nor the secular optimism of the communitarians. They wanted a politically involved church that was confrontational and militant."[49] All three groups, however, used the language of "communion" in their speeches, indicating that this *communio* ecclesiology has become common since the council.

The final report of the synod blended aspects from all three viewpoints, the emphasis on mystery and sacred authority of the neo-Augustinians, the concern for pluriformity, communion, and participation of the communitarians, and the option for the poor and oppressed of the Third World theologians. It did not repudiate Vatican II as some had feared, nor did it call for a Restoration.

The assessment and reception of the council will continue. But there is no doubt that it was a major event, if not *the* major religious event of the twentieth century. I think it is important to maintain a historical perspective on it also. Congar, citing Cardinal John Henry Newman,

---

47. *The Ratzinger Report*, 37–38.
48. Avery Dulles, "The Extraordinary Synod of 1985," in his *The Reshaping of Catholicism: Current Challenges in the Theology of the Church* (San Francisco: Harper & Row, 1988), 191.
49. Ibid., 192–93.

remarks that " 'it is rare for a council not to be followed by great confusion' " and notes that the First Council of Nicaea (325) "was followed by fifty-six years of contentions punctuated by synods, excommunications, exiles, ... interventions and imperial acts of violence."[50] The impact of the Second Vatican Council will be felt for many more years, and we will be dealing with issues it raised for the foreseeable future.

My own assessment is that the council, although it did not completely shift paradigms, initiated a massive "reversal of course," the course the church had been following since Trent and the Counter-Reformation, and that it signalled the end of the siege or ghetto mentality of the previous century and a half in the wake of the French Revolution. Its juxtaposition of diverse ecclesiologies, its internal incoherence and ambiguity, resulted in a lack of clarity of vision, a lack of certainty, and a massive identity crisis. It blurred the boundaries between the church and the world, between the sacred and the secular, between clergy and laity, between pastoral activity and political action. But this is not all bad. The council moved from a preoccupation with certainty and the church's authority to a concern for truth, understanding, and service. The documents legitimated change and freedom of inquiry, and while this may frighten some, I doubt that it can be reversed. It does, however, leave us at present with many challenges and opportunities, which we will discuss in the following chapters.

## RECOMMENDED READINGS

Abbott, Walter M., S.J., general editor. *The Documents of Vatican II*. New York: Crossroad, 1989, original, 1966, especially the Dogmatic Constitution on the Church, the Pastoral Constitution on the Church in the Modern World, the Decree on Ecumenism, and the Declaration on Religious Freedom.

Alberigo, Giuseppe, Jean-Pierre Jossua, and Joseph A. Komonchak, eds. *The Reception of Vatican II*. Trans. Matthew J. O'Connell. Washington, D.C.: Catholic University of America Press, 1987.

O'Malley, John W., S.J. *Tradition and Transition: Historical Perspectives on Vatican II*. Wilmington, Del.: Michael Glazier, 1989.

---

50. Yves Congar, O.P., "A Last Look at the Council," in *Vatican II Revisited*, 349.

# PART III

# Challenges and Possibilities

# Chapter 7

# Changing Forms of Ministry

Vatican II unsettled the previously established certainties in many areas of church life but did not provide answers to all the questions raised. Although it legitimated change and development, the council gave only very general lines for the development to follow. We should not expect solutions to problems to come only at the level of theory or theology, however. As we saw in chapter 2, theology and the lived experience of the Christian community are dialectically related. Some issues can be clarified only by the further experience of the community. The openness of Vatican II encouraged experimentation in various areas, resulting in many new experiences, which, in turn, require further reflection. This is an ongoing dialectical process. Thus, in this and the following chapters of the section we will describe some new experiences and review some current reflections on them, indicating both the challenges and the possibilities for the future. This chapter will deal specifically with the changes occurring in the leadership roles within the Roman Catholic Christian community.

## CRISIS IN ORDAINED MINISTRY

From a purely sociological point of view, it is not surprising that the changes initiated by Vatican II should have been felt most acutely among the clergy and religious, those in the professional roles of leadership in the community. The affirmation by the council of the priesthood of all believers, its emphasis on church leadership as service, *diakonia*, its call for collegiality and participation in decision making and for the church to exercise its mission in the world for the sake of all humanity, all produced a profound "sociological ambivalence" and a massive identity crisis among the clergy, both individually and collectively.

"Sociological ambivalence" is not just a matter of social psychology or of personal conflicts. It is a result of the role structure and the expectations surrounding it.[1] Vatican II had shifted the attitudes and expectations surrounding the role of priest without providing a theology of priesthood to support it. Changes in style and structure need to be accompanied by a rationale, without which only ambiguity and confusion result.

Prior to the council, an authoritarian style had characterized the behavior of the bishop toward his priests, and the behavior of the priests toward the people, even when tempered by the personal kindness and gentleness of many bishops and priests. We have mentioned that post–Vatican II reforms were frequently imposed in an authoritarian manner. But the council had called on bishops to regard their priests as brothers and friends, and on priests to be "as a brother among brothers" vis-à-vis the laity.[2] Clergy trained to think of obedience as the primary virtue were now expected to adopt a collegial and participatory style.[3] Those who had been separated and isolated from "the world" of everyday affairs were now expected to live among their fellow humans and to be in touch with the modern world. The virtues to be cultivated are "goodness of heart, sincerity, strength and constancy of character, zealous pursuit of justice, civility" (PO 3).[4]

Since the late Middle Ages, great emphasis had been placed on the cultic aspects of priesthood, the correct, valid, and licit administration of sacraments, especially the offering of the sacrifice of the Mass, and the hearing of confessions. But the council said that the primary duty of priests was the "proclamation of the gospel of God to all" (PO 4). In most seminaries, dogmatic theology and canon law had been emphasized more than Scripture, so many priests were ill-prepared for the proclamation of the word. Homilies were rare and Sunday sermons were frequently replaced by appeals for building funds and letters from the local chancery. Suddenly, priests were expected to be well informed

---

1. The term "role structure" includes those factors that determine a social role: the social circle or set of persons who interact with the person; the social self or characteristics attributed to the person because of the role; the social functions or the person's contribution to the social circle; and the social status or the privileges and immunities attributed to the social role. For further discussion, see Robert K. Merton and Elinor Barber, "Sociological Ambivalence," in *Sociological Ambivalence and Other Essays* (New York: Free Press, 1976), 1–48.

2. Decree on the Ministry and Life of Priests, *Presbyterorum Ordinis*, in the *Documents of Vatican II*, 3, n. 29. Further references will be abbreviated PO.

3. For a discussion of the emphasis on obedience in Christian thinking see Dorothee Sölle, *Beyond Mere Obedience: Reflections on a Christian Ethic for the Future*, trans. Lawrence W. Denef (Minneapolis: Augsburg, 1970).

4. There is, however, a brief paragraph on obedience, n. 15.

on the latest in biblical studies and to deliver well-crafted and rele-
vant homilies. Such expectations came from the people, but were also
internalized. Priests felt increasingly inadequate.

The council's renewed emphasis on the participation of the laity in
the mission of the church and the idea that the call to holiness was for
all, not just for the religious or clerical caste, further called into question the notion of the special or higher "vocation" of the priesthood. The
gap between clergy and laity, that had developed ever since the Middle
Ages, was overcome, at least in theory, at Vatican II. The whole spirituality of the priesthood which had prevailed since Trent, greatly influenced
by Père de Berulle, Jean-Jacques Olier, the Oratory, and Saint-Sulpice,
namely, that "the priest is the one who is set apart from the people, and
priestly celibacy is the only adequate expression of this essential separation," was called into question.[5] This left many priests wondering just
why they had sacrificed family life and personal fulfillment if holiness
and union with God could be attained just as well by the laity.

The most visible result of this sociological ambivalence was a massive
exodus from the active ministry, both secular and religious. Although exact figures are difficult to find, in the United States it is estimated that
"since 1968 approximately ten thousand priests have resigned (as well
as fifty thousand sisters and four thousand brothers)." Furthermore, sociologists estimate that there will be a 40 percent decline in the number
of active priests from 1980 to 2000, and that by the year 2000 only thirty
thousand priests will be available for sixty-five million Catholics.[6] Concomitantly, the number of seminarians preparing for ordination at the
theologate level dropped from 7,855 in 1968–69 to 3,934 in 1987–88.[7]
As of 1990, 10 percent of all parishes in the United States were without
a full-time resident priest (the percentage is much higher worldwide).
The clergy crisis is frequently presented in terms of such statistics, but
I believe these figures are just the evidence of a problem that lies much
deeper.

---

5. Edward Schillebeeckx, *Ministry: Leadership in the Community of Jesus Christ* (New
York: Crossroad, 1981), 58–59.

6. Jay P. Dolan, R. Scott Appleby, Patricia Byrne, and Debra Campbell, *Transforming
Parish Ministry: The Changing Roles of Catholic Clergy, Laity, and Women Religious* (New
York: Crossroad, 1990), 90. Exact numbers are unavailable, but a sociologist who has
studied the issue says, "The best estimate of total resignations is that about 15 percent
to 17 percent of all religious priests active in 1970 resigned in the following decade,
and about 12.5 percent to 13.5 percent of all diocesan priests in 1970 resigned in the
following decade" (Dean R. Hoge, *The Future of Catholic Leadership: Responses to the
Priest Shortage* [Kansas City, Mo.: Sheed & Ward, 1987], 10). According to the official
*Statistical Yearbook of the Church*, approximately fifty thousand priests left the active
ministry between 1964 and 1986; and other groups estimate the total to be closer to one
hundred thousand. See Michael Gaine, "The State of the Priesthood," in Adrian Hastings,
ed., *Modern Catholicism: Vatican II and After* (New York: Oxford University Press, 1991),
246–55.

7. Figures are from the *CARA Seminary Forum*, 15, 3–4, 1987.

A recent study by the Committee on Priestly Life and Ministry of the National Conference of Catholic Bishops analyzed some of the major reasons for the contemporary problem. The study pointed to such factors as "unhealthy role expectations, declining numbers, differing views and diverse ecclesiologies, loneliness and the need for affirmation," as sources of poor morale among priests. It said, "Many feel they have worked hard and long to implement, or at least adjust to, the practical consequences of Vatican II. They sense that much of that effort is now being blunted or even betrayed and they elect to drop out quietly."[8] Priests are overworked, lonely, and discouraged. One source of the discouragement, the study concluded, was that "some solutions to the clergy shortage are precluded from discussion and that not all pastoral solutions and options can be explored."[9]

In addition, there have been changed expectations concerning lifestyle and priestly spirituality. The view of the priest as one set apart and protected from worldly matters, perhaps served by an elderly housekeeper or devoted nuns who catered to "Father's" every wish, became unacceptable and implausible. The "sacred hands of the priest" were now expected to wash the car, buy the groceries, and fix his own meals. He was expected to share the joys and sorrows of his people and participate in their lives. Many priests found this a relief, but the previous training they had internalized did not prepare them for these changes in lifestyle.

Something similar happened in the case of priestly spirituality. Although Vatican II recognized that celibacy is not "demanded by the very nature of the priesthood," it did not alter the discipline of celibacy (PO 16), which had been the major expression of separation from the world. The council did urge a more positive attitude, "free of any taint of Manicheism," toward human values and created goods (PO 17). There was a need for a spirituality that integrated these positive human values with the ascetical tradition. The Curé d'Ars was no longer an adequate model for the holy priest.

It is not only the negative experiences of dwindling numbers and low morale among the ordained that raise the question of other "pastoral solutions and options." There have been many positive experiences of leadership in Christian communities around the world by married men and women (we will discuss base ecclesial communities in the next

---

8. NCCB's Committee on Priestly Life and Ministry, "Reflections on the Morale of Priests," *Origins* 18, no. 31 (January 12, 1989): 498–505.

9. Another survey of those ordained from 1980 to 1984 provided a somewhat more positive attitude toward the priesthood: "Most priests are very happy to pretty happy about the 'way things are these days' in their lives, and over 80 percent would definitely or probably enter the priesthood again if they had their choice" (Eugene F. Hemrick and Dean R. Hoge, *A Survey of Priests Ordained Five to Nine Years* [Washington: National Catholic Education Association, 1991], vii).

chapter) that suggest the present discipline of confining ordination to celibate males is questionable. The experience of catechists and pastoral agents exercising all the forms of leadership in their communities except those of presiding at the Eucharist and hearing confessions forces the question: Why not ordain them? Many bishops at the Synod of Bishops in 1971 argued that the ordination of married men was a pastoral necessity in their dioceses and that compulsory celibacy was a countersign in their cultures, but the synod was afraid of the "principle of escalation." Any relaxation in the law of celibacy would lead to an abandonment of this longstanding Western discipline, they feared.[10] This position was reaffirmed in the synod of 1990.

From both a historical and a theological perspective, the Dutch theologian Edward Schillebeeckx has argued that the law of celibacy for priests in the Western church, as a disciplinary law of purely human origin, should give way to the prior right of the Christian community to the Eucharist. If a community is deprived of this central expression of the presence of Christ in the community because of a lack of celibate clergy, then the church should change its discipline. "As a result of the present coupling of celibacy and ministry," he says, "at least in the Western church, in many places the apostolic vitality of the community and the celebration of the eucharist are endangered. In such a situation, church legislation, which can in any case be changed, must give way to the more urgent right to the apostolic and eucharistic building up the community."[11]

I suspect that the anomaly to which Schillebeeckx points has not become critical enough worldwide for the church to change its legislation yet. Rather than discuss such a change, the U.S. bishops conference recently approved a Rite for Sunday Liturgy without a Priest. One retired bishop opposed it on the grounds that it only obscured the real issue they should be discussing. Pope John Paul II has said that discussion of the issue of celibacy is "untimely," but prohibiting discussion will not make the question go away. The motivation offered by Vatican II for celibacy — that "they can more easily devote their entire selves to God alone with undivided heart" (LG 42) — is called into question by the counterexperience of married clergy in the Uniate churches and other Christian communions such as the Orthodox and Episcopal. Vatican II has admitted celibacy "is not, indeed, demanded by the very nature of

---

10. For a brief discussion of the history of the law of celibacy see Edward Schillebeeckx, *The Church with a Human Face* (New York: Crossroad, 1985), 240–44. He states, "The law of celibacy, at first implicit in the Latin church at the First Lateran Council (1123) and then promulgated explicitly in canons 6 and 7 of the Second Lateran Council in 1139, was the conclusion of a long history in which there was simply a law of abstinence, applying to married priests."

11. Ibid., 48, and *Ministry*, 37.

the priesthood" (PO 16). As long as we have a discipline of compulsory celibacy, it will continue to be a problem for the ordained clergy and for future recruitment. But the law of celibacy is not the only factor in the clergy crisis.

The ambiguity about the functions of the ordained priest and the relationship of ordained to nonordained ministry are other major factors in the sociological ambivalence at present. If the exclusive identification of the priesthood with its cultic functions was overcome in Vatican II, the way in which these could be integrated with other social functions in the pursuit of justice has not been resolved. Working with the poor through community organizing, providing sanctuary for refugees, sheltering the homeless, ministering to street gangs, are all now understood to be legitimate areas of priestly ministry. But how these are related to sacramental and cultic functions is not clear. Perhaps the difficulty lies in expecting all these various forms of ministry to be exercised by the ordained priest. We will discuss the possibility of a greater diversification of ministries below.

Another experience of ordained ministry that has occurred in the last twenty-five years is that of the restored permanent diaconate. It was authorized by Vatican II and officially reinstated by Pope Paul VI on August 15, 1972. In the United States by 1990, there were 9,497 permanent deacons,[12] sometimes referred to as "married deacons," although the diaconate is open to both married and single men. The typical deacon in this country "is white, middle aged, married with children still residing at home and has a socio-economic status which is middle class as measured by education, occupation, and neighborhood of residence."[13] Some work in their own parishes and others in parishes where they do not reside. In general, this has been a positive experience in the United States. Many are good preachers and serve as a bridge between the clerical and lay worlds, between the spiritual and the secular realms. Although they are most active in sacramental ministry and proclaiming the word, they also engage in charitable activities and social action.[14] There is some concern that the ministry of service, distinctive of the diaconate, should be receiving greater emphasis than it has.[15]

On the negative side, some seem to have been absorbed into the clerical caste and become part of the hierarchical establishment (al-

---

12. Worldwide there were 14,737, with the next largest concentration in Europe with 3,447, which together with the United States is 88 percent of the total.

13. *A National Study of the Permanent Diaconate in the United States* (Washington, D.C.: USCC Office of Publishing and Promotion Services, 1981), 49–50.

14. Ibid., 20.

15. See, for example, Timothy J. Shugrue, *Service Ministry of the Deacon* (Washington, D.C.: USCC, 1988), and for a personal reflection by one deacon, LaRue H. Velott, "The Permanent Diaconate Today: Theology and Actuality," *Deacon Digest* 6, no. 3 (August 1989): 11ff.

most one-third wear the Roman collar always or sometimes). In some cases, they are not accepted by priests and laity for a variety of reasons.[16] Underlying this ambivalence is the lack of a clear role description for the permanent deacon. In any case, the permanent diaconate is one more step in bridging the gap between clergy and laity and one more factor contributing to the ambivalence surrounding the ordained priesthood. It is instructive to note that the experience of the permanent diaconate has been confined almost exclusively to the church in the First World.

Another experience, much rarer in the United States than the permanent diaconate, has been the acceptance of married Episcopal priests into the active priesthood in the Roman Catholic Church. Permitted by Pope John Paul II in 1982, these married priests, though somewhat of a novelty, seem to be accepted by Roman Catholics when they work in regular parish ministry.

All of the above experiences have made the post-Tridentine image of the priest as a person set apart from the world and from the community, with the sacral power to consecrate the Eucharist and hear confessions, implausible in today's church. The ambiguity about the nature and function of ordained ministry has occasioned much theological research and reflection.[17] One thing has become clear, however: ordained priesthood is now discussed in the wider context of *ministry* in the church. Hence, before suggesting some elements of a theology of ministry, we must consider the experiences of nonordained, or lay, ministry in the Christian community.

## LAY MINISTRIES

When Vatican II said that "the laity, too, share in the priestly, prophetic, and royal office of Christ and therefore have their own role to play in the mission of the whole People of God in the Church and in the world," it gave great impetus to the active participation of the laity in all aspects of the community's life.[18] Although the council had stressed the "secular

---

16. *A National Study*, 48.

17. In addition to the two Schillebeeckx books already noted, see Bernard Cooke, *Ministry to Word and Sacraments* (Philadelphia: Fortress Press, 1977), Raymond E. Brown, *Priest and Bishop: Biblical Reflections* (New York: Paulist Press, 1970), Urban T. Holmes, *The Priest in Community* (New York: Seabury Press, 1978), William R. Burrows *New Ministries: The Global Context* (Maryknoll, N.Y.: Orbis Books, 1980), Thomas F. O'Meara, *Theology of Ministry* (New York: Paulist Press, 1983), and Kenan B. Osborne, *Priesthood: A History of Ordained Ministry in the Roman Catholic Church* (New York: Paulist Press, 1988).

18. Decree on the Apostolate of the Laity, *Apostolicam Actuositatem*, in *Documents of Vatican II*, no. 2. It is important to remember that discussion of the "lay apostolate" antedated the council and prepared for it. See Jay P. Dolan et al., *Transforming Parish Ministry*, 254.

quality [that] is proper and special to laymen," it recognized that "lay-men have the capacity to be deputed by the hierarchy to exercise certain church functions for a spiritual purpose" (LG 33). In the last twenty-five years, we have seen a virtual explosion in lay ministry in the church.[19]

The emergence of lay ministry has been part of the overall restruc-turing of ministry in the church. In 1972, Pope Paul VI suppressed what had been called the "minor orders" of exorcist and porter and estab-lished the other two liturgical functions of lector and acolyte as lay ministries common to the whole Western church. The same year, the German bishops allowed lay preaching under well-defined conditions, and the following year local ordinaries were allowed to designate lay men and women as "extraordinary" ministers of the Eucharist. All of these ministries entailed some official recognition in a rite of installation or commissioning and pertain to liturgical services.

But we have also seen the burgeoning of other forms of lay min-istry not directly connected with the liturgy. Youth ministry, ministry to the elderly and to the widowed and divorced, catechists, pastoral agents, leaders of *comunidades eclesiales de base*, social justice min-istry, ministries of healing and counseling, ministry to the homeless and to battered women and administrative and financial ministries, most of which express the church's responsibility and concern in the temporal sphere, have all developed in recent years. Sometimes these ministries are recognized by the community with a blessing or some other cere-mony, and sometimes not. These ministries have emerged as the needs of the local community have warranted them. They may differ from re-gion to region; in Asia, for example, the bishops have listed a ministry of interreligious dialogue because of the need for Christians in a minority position to engage their neighbors of other religious traditions.

The very fact that we use the word "ministry" to apply to all these forms of service is indicative of a change in our way of thinking.[20] The documents of Vatican II had confined the use of *ministerium* to or-dained ministry, but their stress on the fact that these ministries, bishop, priest, deacon, were to be understood in terms of service, *diakonia*, rather than power, *potestas*, led naturally to the recognition that there were other forms of service in the Christian community as well as the ordained ones. Despite the fact that *Lumen Gentium* had maintained that "the common priesthood of the faithful and the ministerial or hier-archical priesthood . . . differ from one another in essence and not only in degree" (LG 10), common usage suggested that they were closely re-

---

19. For a fuller discussion of this from 1970 to the present see Dolan and colleagues, *Transforming Parish Ministry*, chap. 14.
20. John A. Coleman, "The Future of Ministry," *America* (March 28, 1981): 243–49.

lated. All Christians were called to holiness, all Christians were called to ministry by the very fact of their baptism and confirmation.

Further evidence of the laity's desire to serve in some capacity may be found in the rapid growth of voluntary service organizations such as the Jesuit Volunteer Corps, Maryknoll Lay Missioners, and Glenmary Associates. These are organizations that provide an opportunity for limited periods of service, usually from one to five years, for laypersons both within the United States and abroad. More than six thousand young people have participated in the Jesuit Volunteer Corps alone in the past fifteen years.

## THE FEMINIST MOVEMENT

Recent developments in ministry have been shaped not only by the impetus given by the Second Vatican Council and by the generosity of so many laypersons, but also by developments in society outside the church. Perhaps the most obvious example of this is the feminist movement in the United States and elsewhere. The increased consciousness of discrimination against women in all areas of social, economic, and political life has had its impact on the position of women in the Christian community. The exclusion of women from positions of power and decision making in the church is perceived as a clear injustice. For so many years of recent church history, women, especially religious women, have been the backbone and mainstay of religious education, health care, and service to the poor and marginalized that their service came to be taken for granted. They were undervalued and underpaid. Only when women's religious orders and congregations dramatically declined in numbers and they were no longer able or willing to carry the burden of staffing thousands of schools and hospitals with nuns and these institutions had to hire laypersons to take their place did the full realization of their immense contribution dawn on the church.

Further, women's religious orders have been in the forefront of adapting themselves to the post–Vatican II church, especially in terms of a more participatory and collegial style of governance. Women are no longer willing to be excluded from decision making in other areas of church life. This exclusion has caused much pain. Archbishop Rembert Weakland has put it well:

> There are no words to explain so much pain on the part of so many competent women today who feel that they are second-class citizens in a Church they love. That pain turns easily to anger and is often shared and transmitted to the younger generation of men and women. Women do not want to be treated as stereotypes of

sexual inferiority, but want to be seen as necessary to the full life of a Church that teaches and shows by example the co-discipleship of the sexes as instruments of God's kingdom. They seek a Church where the gifts of women are equally accepted and appreciated.[21]

Though much of the discussion has focused on the issue of the ordination of women, other positions of power and decision making, such as diocesan chancellors, superintendents of education, judges on diocesan courts, members of diocesan synods, and professors in seminaries, are gradually being filled by women.

Although the feminist movement is not as strong or as organized in many Third World countries as in the United States, women's position in those societies is also changing dramatically. Many of the leaders of *comunidades eclesiales de base* are women, many pastoral agents and catechists are women, and many of those martyred for their commitment to the poor are women. This experience of women's leadership within the Christian community poses the question of the ordination of women all the more sharply. We will discuss the issues surrounding this below.

All these experiences — decline in numbers and real ambivalence among ordained clergy, positive experiences of lay leadership, a proliferation of ministries, the voluntary participation of the laity, the raised consciousness of the position of women in society — provide the basis for some ongoing theological reflection and pose challenges and opportunities for the future.

## CHALLENGES AND POSSIBILITIES

The questions raised by these recent experiences of ministry have forced theologians to retrieve anew the historical development of ministry in the Christian community in order to situate the present in a larger context. I have mentioned a number of studies already, and I will not attempt to review all the recent research, but permit me to summarize some conclusions that may help us deal with our contemporary issues.

Just as there was a plurality of ecclesiologies in the early church, as we saw in chapter 3, so there was diversity and plurality in ministries in the various churches. The Pauline lists of different gifts, different forms of service, include apostles, prophets, teachers, gifts of healing, assistance, administration, tongues, and mighty deeds (1 Cor. 12:27–31, Rom. 12:6–8, Eph. 4:11–15), but all are for the "building up of the body of Christ." All are gifts of the same Spirit; all are the work of God. Hence,

---

21. Archbishop Rembert Weakland, interview in *Origins* (October 1, 1987): 262.

our first conclusion is that there was diversity and plurality of ministries from the beginning, but they were all for one purpose, the building up of the community, and they all had one source, the Spirit.

Secondly, these various forms of service emerged only gradually into structured offices with a variety of terminological designations. This development was not uniform nor did it follow a standard pattern among the various churches. For example, the function of "overseership," or supervision, *episkopē*, seems to have been present in most communities, but those who exercised it were sometimes individuals, variously designated *diakonoi, episkopoi,* or *presbyteroi,* and in other places supervision was exercised by a group, again under various designations.[22] Pastoral supervision seems to have been exercised by a college of *presbyteroi/episkopoi* at Rome until well into the second century. There is no mention of a single bishop of Rome as late as 150.[23] Hence, a second conclusion we may draw from the experience of the early Christian communities is that ministry developed from necessary *functions* and charisms into *offices,* and later those occupying these offices assumed a separate *status,* that of the clergy. Other charisms remained operative in the community but did not become officially designated offices.

In the second and third centuries, as the ecumenical Lima document states, "a threefold pattern of bishop, presbyter and deacon became established as the pattern of ordained ministry throughout the Church. In succeeding centuries, the ministry by bishop, presbyter and deacon underwent considerable changes in its practical exercise." The document goes on to say that "nevertheless the threefold ministry of bishop, presbyter and deacon may serve today as an expression of the unity we seek and also as a means for achieving it."[24]

A third principle culled from the historical retrieval is that ordained ministry (but I would also add nonordained ministries) involves two elements: a grace (charism) from God and appointment to and a call from a community. Ministry is always related to a community. Schillebeeckx points out that the Council of Chalcedon (451) declares that "no one may be 'ordained' priest or deacon in an absolute manner...unless a local community is clearly assigned to him, whether in the city or in the country, whether in a martyrdom [burial place where a martyr was venerated] or in a monastery."[25] This relationship to a community has, over the years, been lost in practice if not in theory. When priesthood

---

22. Raymond E. Brown, S.S., "Episkopē and Episkopos," *Theological Studies* 41, no. 2 (June 1980): 322–38.

23. Jay, *The Church,* 37–42.

24. *Baptism, Eucharist and Ministry,* Faith and Order Paper no. 111 (Geneva: World Council of Churches, 1982), 19, 22.

25. Edward Schillebeeckx, *Ministry,* 38.

was understood primarily as the power of sacramental consecration as something conferred on the priest *soli*, then it seemed to be a power that could be exercised independently of the community. The relationship to a community has been preserved in the Lutheran practice of permitting ordination only after a candidate has been called by a community. In the Roman Catholic tradition, this relationship is reflected in the rite of ordination but not in the prevailing practice of assigning priests to communities which have no say in the matter and to which the priest may have no previous relationship. The practice of "private" masses obscured this relationship to a community, although the presence of a "server" was supposed to represent the community.

This ecclesial element in ministry, the relationship of the minister to the community, makes a number of other current practices anomalous. In many places leaders emerging from within small or local communities cannot be ordained because of the current church discipline. An ordained priest may visit the community intermittently, but has no other relationship to the community than to celebrate the Eucharist and hear confessions. Again Schillebeeckx says, "This means that the modern situation in which a community might not be able to celebrate the eucharist because no priest is present is theologically inconceivable in the early church; the community chooses a president for itself and has hands laid on him so that they can also be a community which celebrates the eucharist, i.e., a 'community of God.' "[26] The practice of appointing a bishop to a local church without the consent and, at times, over the objections of the local church is another practice that is anomalous in the light of this ancient principle.[27] Some form of calling by the community should be an essential part of any official ministry in the church. In the case of nonordained ministries, at least some recognition by the community should be present.

The historical development of ministry in the church also reveals that there has been a great deal of fluidity and flexibility in the actual practice of the various ministries. At one time, only the bishop could preside at the Eucharist and preach. Then, as Christianity spread outside of urban centers, presbyters took over these functions for the local communities. At another time, the diaconate fell into disuse and became just a step on the way to priesthood, only to be restored after Vatican II. Even today, as noted above, the permanent diaconate does not seem to respond to the churches' needs in the Third World. There has been a long history of dispute over who could preach; sometimes lay preaching has been allowed and other times this ministry has been confined to

---

26. Ibid., 41.
27. This was a major issue raised by European theologians in the "Cologne Declaration," *Origins* 18, no. 8 (March 2, 1989): 633–34.

the ordained. The minor orders evolved over time, but were suppressed after Vatican II. Religious orders have been founded for particular ministries, for example, the Trinitarians for the Redemption of Captives, the Hospitallers of St. Joseph for nursing, the Order of Preachers.

This historical fluidity and flexibility demonstrates that ministries arose in response to needs in the community at a particular time and, when the situation changed, some fell into desuetude. Such flexibility should continue to characterize the restructuring of ministries in our time.

A historical overview also suggests that the diverse ministries of the early church suffered a gradual narrowing to the notion that ministry was almost exclusively cultic and liturgical. O'Meara points out that "not only did the ministry become the activity of a small group of Christians but ministry itself tended to appear as liturgy and ministers sought out their places therein. It is hardly surprising that the diaconate should have suffered as a result of the process of sacralization. The field of social welfare that had been the diaconate's chief *raison d'être* now began to be entrusted to priests or lay people. In 595, the Synod of Rome complained that the deacons were no longer looking after the poor but were chanting psalms instead: the liturgy had become their main sphere of activity."[28]

Today we are experiencing a reversal of that tendency with the expansion and diversification of ministry back into the public and temporal arena. Care for the poor, the oppressed, the marginalized is once again at the heart of the church's ministry. The needs of particular churches, for example in Latin America, are calling both ordained and nonordained to new forms of ministry beyond the sacristy and the sanctuary. The split between faith and daily life that *Gaudium et Spes* (43) deplored is being overcome.

The history of the development of ministry in the Christian community has shown us that there has been a plurality and diversity of ministries from the earliest time, that ministries began with the needs of the community and the gifts of the Spirit but gradually turned into fixed offices with a separate status, that there has nonetheless been fluidity and flexibility in these functions and offices, and that there was a gradual narrowing of ministry to cultic and liturgical activity exercised by a very select group in the Christian community. Since Vatican II, we have been engaged in a restructuring of ministry, especially but not exclusively in the Roman Catholic Church. We have experienced a "blurring of the boundaries" between the sacred and the secular, between the ordained and the nonordained, and an expansion and diversifica-

---

28. O'Meara, *Theology of Ministry*, 199–200.

tion of ministries. We are still faced with some challenges and some possibilities.

If the ordained priesthood is now seen as part of the larger ministry of all baptized Christians, what is or ought to be the functions specific to it? What is the relation between the ordained and the nonordained ministries? What are, or might be, the criteria for distinguishing the two? What of the current discipline of confining ordination to celibate males? How does the culture in which we live affect our practice and understanding of ministry? Without attempting a complete answer to these questions, let me propose some elements that should guide us in the continuing restructuring of ministry.

First, and most obviously, all ministry is service, service to the community, and, on behalf of the community, service to the world. It is for the building up of the community and for furthering the community's mission to the world. It should not be thought of in terms of power, dignity, status, or the distribution of rights and obligations, but in terms of the gifts of the Spirit and the needs of the community.

Second, ministry should always further the mission of the church, proclaiming and bringing about the kingdom of God. It should not be turned inward, concerned only with intraecclesial affairs.

Third, ministry involves discipleship, the following and imitation of Christ, as well as apostleship, being sent out by Christ as a witness to the Gospel in both word and deed.

Fourth, ministry is always based in the gifts of the Spirit and the needs of the community. These gifts and these needs will vary from place to place and from time to time. We must be careful to allow the Spirit the freedom to "breathe where it wills," and to discern the needs of the times for our own particular community.

Fifth, ministry should be publicly recognized by the community, indicating its need for and approval of a particular ministry. This may be the most solemn and longstanding rite of ordination, or some other form of commissioning or installation. Ministry is not a private affair, nor something one arrogates to oneself.[29]

With these five principles in mind, what can be said about the contemporary challenges facing the church today? First, what is distinctive about ordained ministry? I would propose that we reverse the form of the question and ask: What functions and needs are so vital to the Christian community that they should be recognized by the rite of ordination? From a historical, sociological, and theological perspective, we can answer clearly: "supervision," or "overseership," and presiding over the community and its eucharistic celebration. Bishop and priest are the ti-

---

29. These principles are similar to the six characteristics of ministry proposed by O'Meara, *Theology of Ministry*, 136.

tles we have traditionally given to those who fulfill these vital functions in the Christian community.

There has not been much questioning of the bishop's function as supervisor of a particular, local, or regional church. Some would argue that the geographical size of most dioceses is too large and that we should have much smaller dioceses and many more bishops. Certainly in the early church the size of a diocese was closer to what we now call a parish, and there were many more bishops who had a much closer relationship with their clergy and people. Further, today there are incredible demands and expectations placed on the bishops — to preside and preach at many liturgical functions, represent the church in many public forums, participate in unlimited committee meetings, sit on boards of institutions, etc. Though there have been a number of structures instituted to assist the bishop, such as clergy personnel boards and diocesan liturgical commissions, still the demands on a bishop in an average diocese are excessive. Again, this would suggest that we should have many more bishops or that many of his current obligations should be delegated to other clergy, as has happened with the administration of the sacrament of confirmation. This is a possibility and a challenge.

The real crisis in ordained ministry since Vatican II has been in the priesthood. It seems that presiding over a local community and at the Eucharist is a necessary and vital function that merits ordination. Presiding means leadership, ability to inspire and motivate, to reconcile differences, to foster collaboration, to promote dialogue, and to discern needs. It involves special responsibility for teaching and preaching the word of God. These functions correspond to the functions of the ancient Israelite priesthood: to discern God's will by consulting the *Urim* and *Thummim* (the sacred lots), to teach the law or provide moral exhortation (thus the *rabbi*), and to offer sacrifice or the cultic function.[30] Brown comments that the first two functions "were shifted over to the prophet and the scribe respectively," and only the sacrificial function remained at the end of the Old Testament period. There seems to be a parallel with the narrowing of the function of priest to a cultic one in late medieval Catholicism. A recovery of the other functions may now be in order. Certainly, today people expect the priest to be knowledgeable about the Scriptures and to be able to preach and teach effectively. They also expect spiritual direction and counseling or help in discerning the will of God. There is still great need for liturgical and sacramental practice that is theologically well grounded and meaningful to people's daily lives. All of these functions seem appropriate to the priesthood today.

---

30. Raymond E. Brown, *Priest and Bishop,* 10–13.

What then of the diaconate? This seems to be a title in search of a function. We have seen above that the function of the deacon in the early church seems to have been the area of social welfare, but this faded into the background and the deacon became primarily a liturgical functionary. Recent experience has displayed a similar tendency in the permanent diaconate. Vatican II restored it without clearly indicating what needs of the community it was designed to meet. Unless some clarification of the role and functions of the deacon can be achieved, it is not clear that we should ordain people to this office. An office in search of a function is an anomaly.

What then is the relationship between these ordained ministries in the church and the other, nonordained ministries? Vatican II had said that "though they differ from one another in essence and not only in degree, the common priesthood of the faithful and the ministerial or hierarchical priesthood are nonetheless interrelated" (LG 10). That language can be, and probably was, understood in terms of the scholastic categories of substance and accident: that an ontological change takes place through ordination and not just an accidental one, or one of degree. But it could also be understood in terms of an organic analogy, as suggested in *Christifideles Laici:* "Ecclesial communion is more precisely likened to an 'organic' communion, analogous to that of a living and functioning body. In fact, at one and the same time it is characterized by a diversity and complementarity of vocations and states in life, of ministries, of charisms and responsibility. Because of this diversity and complementarity, every member of the lay faithful is seen in relation to the whole body and offers a totally unique contribution on behalf of the whole body."[31] Using this organic analogy, I have suggested that some functions are so essential to the life of the community that they can be called *vital,* i.e., necessary and fundamental, for its continued life. These vital functions are the ones the community solemnly recognizes and authorizes by ordination. The other functions are diverse and complementary, as the pope says, but not vital. Historically, in fact, we have seen them emerge and decline without the death of the body of Christ. Ministries arise in response to the gifts of the Spirit and the needs of a particular church at a particular time and place. Such ministries are unique contributions and necessary, but not vitally so. I think this organic functional analogy based on the needs of the community is more helpful and intelligible than ontological essences or a permanent *character.* Just as we speak of "vital functions" or "vital signs" without which an organism cannot live, so we can understand the functions of supervision and presiding as vital

---

31. Pope John Paul II, *Christifideles Laici,* in *Origins* 18, no. 35 (February 9, 1989): 570, n. 20.

for the life of a Christian community. We cannot have a true Christian community without them.[32] I think it could also be argued that ministry to the poor is vital to any Christian community, and perhaps that should be specified as the function of the diaconate. How vital a particular ministry is to the life of a Christian community, then, is the criterion I am suggesting for distinguishing ordained from nonordained ministries.

What of the current discipline in the Roman Catholic Church of confining ordination to celibate males? These issues have been discussed for some time (at the official level, in the Synods of 1971 and 1990) and will continue to be discussed, over Vatican objections, because of the experiences referred to above. Schillebeeckx's position that the right of the community to eucharistic celebration takes precedence over church law is a very persuasive one. The claims that the exclusion of married persons and women from the presbyterate is of dominical origin do not stand up to the findings of biblical and historical scholarship.[33] The weight of tradition is the main argument for maintaining the discipline. The tradition of compulsory celibacy is a highly variegated one, as Schillebeeckx and others have pointed out.

The tradition of not ordaining women to the presbyterate is much stronger. Although the Pontifical Biblical Commission said that "it does not seem that the New Testament by itself alone will permit us to settle in a clear way and once and for all the problem of the possible accession of women to the presbyterate,"[34] the Congregation for the Doctrine of the Faith in its declaration of October 15, 1976, argued from the constant tradition of the church, the attitude of Christ himself, and the practice of the Apostles to conclude:

> This practice of the Church therefore has a normative character: in the fact of conferring priestly ordination only on men, it is a question of an unbroken tradition throughout the history of the Church, universal in the East and in the West, and alert to repress abuses immediately. This norm, based on Christ's example, has

---

32. I am not suggesting that these vital functions must be carried out or structured in the same way in all Christian communities. In fact, they have been expressed in a variety of forms throughout the history of the church. Of those communions that have not maintained the threefold pattern of episcopacy, presbyterate, and diaconate, the Lima document says, "They will further need to ask themselves whether the threefold pattern as developed does not have a powerful claim to be accepted by them" (*Baptism, Eucharist and Ministry*, 25). It also recognized that "the threefold pattern stands evidently in need of reform."

33. See the Report of the Pontifical Biblical Commission on the question of the ordination of women, *Origins* 6, no. 6, 92–96.

34. Ibid., 96.

been and is still observed because it is considered to conform to God's plan for his Church.[35]

Biblical scholars have pointed out that, on historical grounds, "the example of the Lord" is very difficult to come by. The evidence indicates that women exercised many of the functions that later came to be identified with the ordained priesthood. It is not clear that Jesus intentionally excluded anyone from these functions.[36]

The other argument of the declaration is based on the sacramental nature of the priesthood, which requires a "natural resemblance" between Christ and his minister that would be lacking "if the role of Christ were not taken by a man."[37] Many Catholic theologians have not found these arguments persuasive.[38] In particular, they have pointed out that "the sacramental sign necessary to act *in persona Christi* is to be located within the human person rather than within masculine or feminine sexuality."[39] This issue will continue to challenge the church for the foreseeable future because injustice toward and oppression of women is a problem for contemporary cultures around the globe. It is not just an ecclesial issue.

How does our cultural context in the United States affect how we think and act with regard to ministry in the church? Recalling some of the characteristics of our social and cultural context from chapter 1, let me briefly suggest some implications for our thinking and our practice of ministry.

First, our pluralistic and relativistic culture makes it difficult for us to believe that there is only one way in which ministry can be structured or organized. Our historical consciousness reinforces this because we know that in fact ministry in the Christian community has taken many different forms over time. The structure of ministry appropriate to the late Middle Ages or to post-Tridentine Catholicism is not seen as universally and absolutely normative for all times and places. Ministry, like the church it serves, is culturally conditioned and always has been. Such a perspective suggests that in the future there could be a married clergy in some cultures, Africa and Latin America perhaps, and not in others. Could not women be ordained to the presbyterate where that would enhance the church's mission, but not in cultures where it would not? Can

---

35. Sacred Congregation for the Doctrine of the Faith, *Declaratio circa quaestionem admissionis mulierum ad sacerdotium ministeriale*, 14.

36. Sandra M. Schneiders, "Did Jesus Exclude Women from Priesthood?" in Leonard Swidler and Arlene Swidler, eds. *Women Priests: A Catholic Commentary on the Vatican Declaration* (New York: Paulist Press, 1977), 230.

37. Ibid., 15–16.

38. See Schillebeeckx, *Ministry*, 96–98, and "An Open Letter to the Apostolic Delegate," by the Pontifical Faculty of the Jesuit School of Theology at Berkeley, *Commonweal* (April 1, 1977): 204–6.

39. Ibid., 205.

even longstanding tradition be understood as immutable? The problems posed for the unity of the church by such cultural differentiation will be discussed in chapter 9.

The individualism so characteristic of society in the United States poses other difficulties if the purpose of ministry is understood as the building up of the community. That function of leadership will be more difficult when a sense of community is lacking. Liturgy by itself will not turn a parish into a community. Individualism is not easily overcome by communal rituals. The rights of individuals can seem to take precedence over the rights of the community. The liturgy, instead of being the fundamental celebration of Christian unity, can become a very divisive experience if a group feels its rights have been denied.

A third characteristic, which Bellah and his fellow authors termed the "therapeutic model," has a definite impact on ministry, as we suggested in chapter 1. The priest can be seen primarily as a counselor whose purpose is to foster personal integration in his clients, rather than as a representative of the community, acting both *in persona Christi* and *in persona ecclesiae*. This can lead to confused expectations of the sacrament of reconciliation, for example, on the part of both the priest and the penitent. It can also constrain any prophetic function that might be needed in the community. Is the function of the priest to comfort or to challenge?[40] Thus, the therapeutic model emphasizes ministries to individuals, and activities on behalf of social justice that may challenge the system, such as community organizing, are not viewed as "ministry."

Finally, our cultural traditions of freedom and participation make suspect a process of choosing leaders in the Christian community at any level, bishop or priest, that does not include the participation of the people. This also applies to the style of leadership. The participatory and consultative process that was employed by the U.S. bishops in drafting their pastoral letters on nuclear weapons and the economy only enhanced their authority in the United States, whereas other cultures perceived it as diminishing that authority.

The church in the United States with its form of leadership or ministry does not live in isolation, however. We are increasingly influenced by developments in other parts of the globe. One of the most important of these is the liberation theology emanating from Latin America to which we turn in the next chapter.

---

40. For a discussion of this issue among Protestant churches see Jeffrey K. Hadden, *The Gathering Storm in the Churches* (Garden City, N.Y.: Doubleday & Co., 1969).

# RECOMMENDED READINGS

Dolan, Jay P., R. Scott Appleby, Patricia Byrne, and Debra Campbell. *Transforming Parish Ministry: The Changing Roles of Catholic Clergy, Laity, and Women Religious*. New York: Crossroad, 1990.

O'Meara, Thomas F. *Theology of Ministry*. New York: Paulist Press, 1983.

Osborne, Kenan B. *Priesthood: A History of Ordained Ministry in the Roman Catholic Church*. New York: Paulist Press, 1988.

Schillebeeckx, Edward. *The Church with a Human Face*. New York: Crossroad, 1985.

# Chapter 8

# Liberating Ecclesiology

Without doubt the most interesting, stimulating, and challenging theology of the church in the last twenty years has emerged in Latin America among the liberation theologians. The dialectical relationship between experience and theology, to which we have previously referred, is well exemplified there. The experience of the *comunidades eclesiales de base*, the Christian base communities, has provided the experiential basis for further reflection on the church, and this reflection has, in turn, offered guidance and understanding to these communities. Although base communities, at least in Brazil, began before the theology of liberation was articulated, they are correlative and have developed concomitantly. In this chapter, then, we will briefly introduce liberation theology, describe the experience of the *comunidades eclesiales de base* (CEBs), then offer a summary of the ecclesiology of liberation theology, focusing on Juan Luis Segundo, Gustavo Gutiérrez, Leonardo Boff, and the two meetings of the Council of Latin American Episcopacies (CELAM) at Medellín, Colombia, in 1968 and Puebla, Mexico, in 1979. Finally we will discuss the challenges and possibilities of this ecclesiology for the churches in the First World, especially in the United States.

## BACKGROUND OF LIBERATION THEOLOGY

During Vatican II the Latin American bishops were known as the "Church of Silence" because of their general lack of active participation in the deliberations of the council,[1] but even while the council was in session they made plans to adapt the teachings of the council to the

---

1. There were some individual bishops such as Dom Helder Camara of Brazil, Bishop Manuel Larraín of Chile, and Archbishop Juan Landázuri of Peru, who made significant contributions.

situation in Latin America. By the time the second CELAM conference convened in Medellín in 1968, they had begun to read the "signs of the times" for the Latin American continent. They realized that the dialogue partner for the theology of Vatican II had been the nonbeliever of the Western European world. It became very clear that the situation in Latin America was quite different. There they were concerned not with the *nonbeliever*, but with the *nonperson*.[2]

The "modern world" with which Vatican II opened a dialogue was the world of secularized Western Europe and North America. It was the world dominated by science and technology that we described in chapter 1. But the "modern world" in Latin America, and most of the rest of the southern hemisphere, is dominated by massive poverty and oppression. It seemed to the liberation theologians that the mission of the church in their world was necessarily different from that in the First World countries. Most of the liberation theologians had been educated in Europe and knew the best of recent Roman Catholic theology. They knew Rahner, Congar, Chenu, de Lubac, and Metz. They knew Moltmann and Pannenberg, but they were not satisfied that these theologians were addressing the Latin American situation.

The actual term "theology of liberation" was first used by Gustavo Gutiérrez in a lecture in Chimbote, Peru, in July 1968, shortly before the beginning of the Medellín conference. He had a major hand in drafting the documents of Medellín, and so the theology of liberation very quickly appeared in the documents of the Latin American episcopacy. But the antecedents of liberation theology were much older and broader than Gutiérrez's famous talk. Edward L. Cleary lists six factors that contributed to the development of an indigenous theology in Latin America and the modernization of the church there: lay movements, the influx of foreign religious personnel, the formation of transnational and national structures, papal nuncios, new ecclesial leadership groups, and John XXIII and Vatican II.[3]

Cardinal Giacomo Lercaro, at the end of the first session of the council, gave a stirring speech urging that the church should become the "church of the poor." Although the council did not develop this theme, it certainly resonated with the bishops and theologians from Latin America. They recognized that the church on that continent had been identified for centuries with the upper classes and had neglected the poor who were the vast majority. Hence the call for the church to focus its mission and ministry on the poor. Further, even before Vatican II, many recognized that the evangelization of the people had been

---

2. Gustavo Gutiérrez, *The Power of the Poor in History* (Maryknoll, N.Y.: Orbis, 1983), 57.

3. Edward L. Cleary, *Crisis and Change in the Church in Latin America Today* (Maryknoll, N.Y.: Orbis, 1985), 3.

very truncated. In contrast to North America, neither the indigenous peoples nor the *mestizos* and later European immigrants had been educated in the faith. There was nothing like the parochial school system developed for immigrants in the United States; popular religiosity was the usual mode of education in the faith. The territorial parishes were vast geographically, and the infrastructure of transportation and communication was poor. Many nominally Catholic people had no idea of what Catholicism was all about. There was an overwhelming need for evangelization.

It was also clear that the church in Latin America had been overly concerned with life after death and tended to regard the time here on earth as merely a period of testing. The neglect of the actual historical situation of the majority of believers was appalling. With the arrival of the foreign religious personnel that had been called for by Pope John XXIII in 1961, the awareness of this situation became all the more acute.

The formation of lay movements to which Cleary refers was also important. In the 1940s and 1950s, the models of Catholic Action, such as the Young Christian Workers, developed in Belgium and France were imported and had a great impact on middle-class Catholics in Latin America. Their procedure — to see, to judge, and to act — can still be found in the methods of the CEBs. A little later, the Cursillo movement was also influential in getting laypersons involved in the life of the church.

Cleary comments, "North Americans do not realize how organizationally weak the Latin American church has been."[4] The formation of the Council of Latin American Episcopacies in 1955 was a major factor in developing a sense of transnational consciousness in the church in Latin America. Bishops who had previously been isolated by lack of contact and communication soon found that they shared many concerns and problems. The first meeting in 1955 was, as Cleary remarks, "forgettable," but the second meeting at Medellín, Colombia, in 1968, was a landmark in the life of the Latin American church.

The most significant aspect of Medellín was not that the church discovered the world of the poor; rather "its importance was to institutionalize in its decrees the experience and practice of a significant number of Catholics in every stratum of the church from peasants to archbishops."[5] The bishops at Medellín perceived themselves to be "on the threshold of a new epoch in the history of our continent. It appears to be a time full of zeal for full emancipation, of liberation from every

---

4. Ibid., 11.
5. Alfred T. Hennelly, ed., *Liberation Theology: A Documentary History* (Maryknoll, N.Y.: Orbis, 1990), 89.

form of servitude, of personal maturity and of collective integration. In
these signs we perceive the first indications of the painful birth of a new
civilization."[6] There was a sense of urgency, of hope, and of new beginnings. It was clearly a *kairos,* a decisive moment, in the life of the church
in Latin America, and the formation of this transnational structure was
a significant factor for its future development.[7]

Another factor in the development of liberation theology during the
1960s was the actual political, social, and economic situation of Latin
America. The United Nations had declared the 1960s the "decade of
development," and in 1961 President John F. Kennedy had announced
the "Alliance for Progress," a program designed to foster development
in Latin America. Although some Latin Americans were skeptical, in
general expectations were raised that at last development would occur on that continent. By the end of the 1960s these expectations
were frustrated. Not only was there no "trickle-down effect" as had
been predicted, but the gap between the rich and the poor only increased. Democratic reformist governments in a number of countries
were replaced by military regimes. In Chile, for example, the show-
case of the Alliance for Progress, reform efforts produced few results,
and the young and the intellectuals began looking to more radical solutions. The Allende government was the first popularly elected Marxist
government in the Western hemisphere and had a lot of Christian support. By that time it had become clear that development really meant
dependency. The North American banks that had invested heavily in
Latin America made huge profits. "Development" was good for business. It was another name for liberal capitalism. Hence, it was not
surprising that "dependency theory" was accepted by the liberation theologians as an explanation of their situation and was incorporated into
the documents of Medellín, although they have since recognized its
limitations.[8]

Liberation theology, then, was the result of a convergence of ecclesial, theological, social, political, and economic factors. The affirmation
of Vatican II that the church should share the joys and hopes of humankind, that it should be involved in the affairs of the world, in the
situation of massive poverty and oppression in Latin America, in the
overall dehumanizing social and political situation that caused many to
"die before their time," in the poignant phrase that Gutiérrez borrowed

---

6. Ibid., "Introduction to the Final Documents," 95.

7. For a discussion of the role of papal nuncios, another factor Cleary mentions, see
Penny Lernoux, *People of God: The Struggle for World Catholicism* (New York: Viking,
1989), *passim,* and Emilio F. Mignone, *Witness to the Truth: The Complicity of Church and
Dictatorship in Argentina, 1976–1983,* trans. Phillip Berryman (Maryknoll, N.Y.: Orbis,
1988).

8. For example see Gustavo Gutiérrez in the introduction to the revised edition of *A
Theology of Liberation* (Maryknoll, N.Y.: Orbis, 1988), xxiv.

from sixteenth-century Spanish missionary Bartolomé de Las Casas, led theologians to read the signs of the times and to reread Scripture and the Christian tradition from the perspective of the poor.

## MAJOR THEMES OF LIBERATION THEOLOGY

Our focus is on the self-understanding of the Christian community, its ecclesiology, but in order to understand this, it is necessary to summarize briefly the major concerns of liberation theology.

First, the liberation theologians have reacted against the seeming dichotomy in Latin American Catholicism between this world and the next, between the natural and the supernatural, between secular history and salvation history. Instead, they insist on the *unity of history*. There are not two separate spheres of activity. What we do here on earth, in human history, has salvific value and significance. We are citizens of two worlds, as Vatican II reminded us, but they cannot be separated in fact or in human consciousness. Christianity is not primarily a test, a preparation for life after death. It is rather the necessary but insufficient condition for the coming of the kingdom of God.

Second, if our activity in this world does have salvific value, then Christians must concern themselves with the actual historical situation here and now. This entails a description and analysis of the political, economic, social, and cultural situation in which we are to carry on the work of evangelization. The use of the social sciences is a major methodological starting point for liberation theology. They found that dependency theory and the Marxist categories of class conflict and class struggle seemed particularly apt descriptions of the Latin American situation.

Third, if our activity here on earth and in human history is necessary but insufficient for bringing about the kingdom of God, then it inevitably overflows into political activity. It cannot remain in the private or purely spiritual domain. The blurring of the boundaries we mentioned as an after-effect of Vatican II found its expression here also. What some considered political activity, others considered pastoral practice. The experience of the base communities, as we will see, bears this out.

Fourth, concomitant with their emphasis on social-cultural analysis and political activity as part of pastoral practice was the awareness that the social and political situation in Latin America was one of conflict and institutionalized violence. The liberation theologians were not advocating violence, but merely recognizing that it is a fact of life in Latin America. The fact that "class conflict" and "class struggle" were Marxist terms contributed to much misunderstanding, but such terms did seem to capture the actual situation on that continent.

Fifth, if there is a class struggle, the theologians of liberation could

not help but ask on which side God is to be found. Their rereading of
Scripture made it clear that God was on the side of the poor; the preference of God, and therefore of the church, should be with the poor.
The basis for this was not political expediency nor historical reality, but
the Gospel. Thus, by the time of CELAM III in 1979, the Latin American
bishops could speak of a "preferential option for the poor." This meant
that the church should preach the Gospel to the poor, should live in
solidarity with the poor, and should assume the viewpoint of the poor,
seeing history from the "underside." Further, the church should be prepared to be evangelized by the poor. Because of God's option for the
poor, the church must follow.

Finally, there was the explicit theme of liberation. What could salvation in Jesus Christ mean in a situation of massive poverty and oppression? How to speak of God to the poor, to those "who die before their
time"? Does the Christian message have anything to say to Latin America? Gutiérrez's answer was to translate "salvation" into "liberation" —
not a doctrinal innovation but a semantic one of major importance. The
correlative to oppression and subjection is liberation. "Salvation" had
taken on such otherworldly connotations that the Good News seemed
to have no relevance for the daily life of Latin America. As we will see,
Gutiérrez did not reduce the theological concept of salvation/liberation
to the purely this-worldly realms of politics and economics, but rather
included these levels of human activity in the Christian project of complete, integral liberation. Liberation from sin was still the most radical
and fundamental form of salvation, but it was no longer disconnected
from the social and political aspects of human life.[9]

The liberation theologians believed that their reflections on and
reinterpretation of Scripture coincided with a popular movement for
revolutionary change in Latin America and that they were on the cutting
edge of change in a continent that was both believing and oppressed.
Hence, their writings exude a sense of urgency and of hope. They were
more concerned with praxis than with theory, more with change than
with the status quo, more with evangelization of the poor than the comfort of the middle and upper classes, and more concerned with the local
church than the worldwide church.

They intended to deal with all the major themes of Christian theology from a liberation perspective and realized that this was a long-term
project. Thus, they have written on Christology, ecclesiology, grace and
the human condition, the Trinity, the sacraments, and social ethics.[10]

9. Gustavo Gutiérrez, *A Theology of Liberation* (Maryknoll, N.Y.: Orbis, 1973), 36–37,
176–77, and *passim*.

10. For example, see the early five-volume series by Juan Luis Segundo subtitled *A Theology for Artisans of a New Humanity:* vol. 1, *The Community Called Church;* vol. 2,
*Grace and the Human Condition;* vol. 3, *Our Idea of God;* vol. 4, *The Sacraments Today;*

Before outlining the ecclesiology of liberation theology, let us say something about the lived experience of the new forms of church in Latin
America: the *comunidades eclesiales de base*.

## COMUNIDADES ECLESIALES DE BASE

Not only was the lived experience of the base communities in dialectical
relationship with liberation theology, they arose almost simultaneously.
In 1964 in Brazil, for which we have the best available documentation,[11]
while the Brazilian bishops were drafting their first Joint Pastoral Plan
for 1965–1970, there was a meeting of theologians to discuss what eventually became liberation theology. This plan attempted to address the
problems of the Brazilian church regarding evangelization in a country
whose dioceses were vast and which had a severe shortage of priests.
The hierarchy was looking for a strategy to make use of laypersons in the
evangelization of Brazil. The result was what we now call basic Christian communities. They were inspired by and usually initiated by clergy
and religious. They did not spring spontaneously from the grassroots,
as is sometimes portrayed. Marcello Azevedo defines a basic ecclesial
community as

> a group of persons, or a combination of groups, in which there is
> a primary, fraternal, and personal relationship and which lives the
> totality of the life of the church expressed in service, celebration,
> and evangelization.[12]

Typically, according to Boff's somewhat romanticized description, "the
group may meet under a huge tree and every week they are found there,
reading the sacred texts, sharing their commentaries, praying, talking
of life, and making decisions about common projects. It is an event,
and the Church of Jesus and the Holy Spirit takes shape under that
tree."[13] Historically, these communities have been successful mainly in
rural areas and the slum areas surrounding large cities.

Such a community is called *of the base*, "insofar as it is made up of
poor, simple people, marginalized by the organization of society and
yet part of that society as production force and labor force, but without

---

vol. 5, *Evolution and Guilt* (Maryknoll, N.Y.: Orbis, 1973–74). See also the current series
*Theology and Liberation*, which includes such titles as Leonardo Boff, *Trinity and Society*
(Maryknoll, N.Y.: Orbis, 1988), and Enrique Dussel, *Ethics and Community* (Maryknoll,
N.Y.: Orbis, 1988).

11. Marcello de Carvalho Azevedo, S.J., *Basic Ecclesial Communities in Brazil*, trans.
John Drury (Washington, D.C.: Georgetown University Press, 1987).

12. Ibid., 74.

13. Leonardo Boff, *Church: Charism and Power*, trans. John W. Diercksmeier (New
York: Crossroad, 1985), 128.

voice or viable options."[14] It is *ecclesial* because there is communion in the faith and communion with the pastors of the church.[15] Communion with the pastors is characteristic of the base communities in Brazil, but not necessarily in all other countries of Latin America. In Nicaragua, for example, because the hierarchy was deeply divided, some bishops supported the base communities and others did not. The episcopacies of Latin America in general, however, as expressed in the documents of Medellín and Puebla, have been very supportive.[16] Although Pope Paul VI had praised base communities in his apostolic exhortation *Evangelii Nuntiandi*, some Vatican critics have contended recently that these communities are not really "church."[17]

Arthur McGovern observes that such communities most resemble what in North America we call "community organizations," but with the significant difference that the CEBs are communities of believers who focus on scriptural reflection as an illumination of their own situation.[18] Azevedo and Boff have argued that such communities are a concrete experience of the local church and an exemplification of the universal church on the local level. They are the church of the poor, of the people. In Latin America, they are not a rejection of the institutional or universal church, although the danger of sectarianism remains a possibility.

Again, Azevedo and Boff believe that the CEBs are a new way of being church. "The fact is that the [CEBs] are a new way of *living* as Church, of *being* Church and *acting* as Church, in Brazil. This way of being Church is *not* new insofar as [CEBs] are reviving and reliving many elements of the most authentic tradition of the Church from its very beginnings. . . . But this way of being Church *is* new when compared with the earlier model that has actually been operative during the almost five centuries of the Church's presence in Brazil."[19]

In Brazil alone, it is estimated that there are between seventy thousand and eighty thousand such communities. But, Azevedo points out, the CEBs

> have not found a place in a markedly urban milieu. They are still confined to an age group averaging well above the markedly young population of Brazil. They are also limited to the traditional frame of the rural, agricultural world, whether the members live in the

---

14. Azevedo, *Basic Ecclesial Communities*, 78.

15. Ibid., 72.

16. See in Hennelly, *Documentary History*, from Medellín, the "Document on Justice," 20, the "Document on Peace," 27, and from Puebla, the "Final Document," 96–98, 261–63, 629, 641–43.

17. T. Howland Sanks, "Forms of Ecclesiality: The Analogical Church," *Theological Studies* 49 (1988): 695–708.

18. Arthur F. McGovern, *Liberation Theology and Its Critics: Toward an Assessment* (Maryknoll, N.Y.: Orbis, 1989), 211.

19. Azevedo, *Basic Ecclesial Communities*, 5.

nonurban interior or carry that frame to urban peripheries and live it for a time.[20]

Azevedo suggests that this may be due to the secularizing and modernizing influences among large portions of the population in Latin America.

It is also true that CEBs are not as numerous in other countries of Latin America as they are in Brazil, but the phenomenon is widespread enough to make it a significant experiential source for further theological reflection. Let us now turn to the explicit ecclesiology of liberation theology.

## LIBERATION ECCLESIOLOGY

Even though there is some diversity among the liberation theologians, there is great convergence in their views of the church. Here we will briefly outline the ecclesiologies of Segundo, Gutiérrez, and Boff, and see how they are reflected in the documents of Medellín and Puebla.

In line with Vatican II, the liberation theologians regard the church primarily as a *sign, a sacrament of salvation* for the world. Segundo begins his reflection in *The Community Called Church* (1968) with the seemingly contradictory facts that the church is and always will be *particular,* a historically limited community, but one that makes claims to *universality*.[21] If the function of the church is not to funnel as many persons as possible into itself, and if there are ecclesial elements in other Christian bodies, and if salvation is possible outside the church, what is the *function,* what is the *mission* of the church? He suggests that there are two lines of thought on this matter in the New Testament. The first, epitomized by Mark 16:15–16 (Go into the whole world and proclaim the Gospel to every creature), suggests that salvation is attained by entering the church through faith and baptism and remaining faithful to the end. In this view, the mission of the church is to "preach the gospel to the whole world," and to incorporate as many as possible into the visible church. Universality meant wide geographical distribution and the greatest number of members possible.

In Matthew 25:31–46 we find another description of salvation. Here, salvation depends on human behavior toward others: feeding the hungry, clothing the naked, visiting the sick and lonely, caring for the least

---

20. Ibid., 168–69.
21. Juan Luis Segundo, S.J., *The Community Called Church*, trans. John Drury (Maryknoll, N.Y.: Orbis, 1973). See also T. Howland Sanks and Brian H. Smith, "Liberation Ecclesiology: Praxis, Theory, Praxis," *Theological Studies* 38 (1977): 3–38, and McGovern, *Liberation Theology*, 213–14.

of the brothers and sisters. Such deeds can be performed by all humans without a conscious awareness of their significance for "eternal life." Indeed, Segundo points out the element of surprise in the Gospel narrative: "Lord, when did we feed you?" This line of thought would seem to diminish the particularity of the church, since all persons are to be judged by the same criteria and all are capable of the deeds and attitudes necessary for salvation whether or not they are members of a visible community.

Segundo brings these two lines of thought together by saying that the Christian is distinguished by the fact that he or she will *not be surprised* by the criteria of judgment.

> For if he is a believer, he is so precisely because he has accepted the revelation of this universal plan which culminated in the last judgment. The Christian is he *who already knows*. This, undoubtedly, is what distinguishes and defines him.[22]

Thus, the church is the community of those who know the universal plan of salvation, possess the "secret of what is happening in human history." Or again, the church is the consciousness of humanity — that part of humanity fully aware of what is taking place in it.[23]

For Segundo, the meaning of the universality of the church is not that it should be the sole channel of grace (through faith and the sacraments) for all. It does not have a monopoly on the means of grace and salvation for which all are destined. Rather, it is to do the works of love in the world, to be in the service of all humanity, but to do so consciously, with full awareness of the significance of these actions in the universal plan of salvation. The Christian community is to make manifest to the rest of humanity with whom it makes its way in the world the mystery of God's plan of salvation for all. The church is essentially a *sign*, "placed here precisely and exclusively to pass on to men a certain signification, i.e., a message, something that is to be grasped, comprehended, and incorporated to a greater or lesser degree into the fashioning of history and the world."[24]

Membership in the church is not necessary for salvation. Indeed, those who become members assume the obligations and the risks that the sign-function of the church entails. It could even make their salvation more difficult: "membership in the ecclesial community saves people when it is shouldered as a new and more profound responsibility."[25] This means, further, that the "primary preoccupation of the

---

22. Segundo, *The Community Called Church*, 11.
23. Ibid., 29–30.
24. Ibid., 81.
25. Ibid., 82.

Church is not directed toward her own inner life but toward people outside." Gutiérrez will refer to this as an "uncentering" of the church.

This sign-bearing function of the church is not only the unilateral proclamation of the Gospel, but also Christians must engage in dialogue with the rest of the world and learn to "read the signs of the times." Segundo says,

A church which dialogues and works with the rest of mankind is a church that knows she is part of humanity; a church that knows she is the conscious portion of the deeper mystery that is being worked out in every human life, and in all of humanity taken together in its process of historical becoming. A church that dialogues is a church that knows she is, by definition, in the service of humanity.[26]

Finally, in Segundo's ecclesiology the church is primarily a congregation of many base communities (i.e., grassroots communities) small enough to permit face-to-face personal relations with real giving and real sharing.[27] He is more concerned with the local church than with the large institutional church, which, he believes, has been preoccupied with maintaining its position of dominance in Latin American society. For him, the church should be a means of salvation, not an end in itself.

Published three years after Segundo's work on the church, Gutiérrez's *A Theology of Liberation* (1971) remains the *magna carta* of liberation theology.[28] Although his later works have developed and explicitated his thought, the basic lines of his ecclesiology were already clear. His major concern is the "classic question of the relation between faith and human existence, between faith and social reality, between faith and political action, or in other words, between the Kingdom of God and the building up of the world" (45). He believes that, in the history of Christianity, there have been three basic answers to this question. First, "the Christendom mentality," in which temporal realities lack autonomy and the "plan for the Kingdom of God has no room for a profane, historical plan." In this view, the church is the exclusive means of salvation, and its work is directed primarily to the benefit of its own members.

The second answer, which he calls the "New Christendom," is epitomized by Jacques Maritain; in it the church is still the "center of the work of salvation," but the task of creating a just society, a society inspired by Christian principles, is recognized as a proper function of Christians, especially the laity.

---

26. Ibid., 131.
27. Juan Luis Segundo, *The Sacraments Today* (Maryknoll, N.Y.: Orbis, 1974), 32.
28. Gustavo Gutiérrez, *A Theology of Liberation,* references in the text are to the 1973 English translation.

Evolving from this view was the third response, the one dominating the documents of Vatican II, which he calls the "distinction of planes" model. Here, a clear distinction is drawn between the church and the world, and the autonomy of the temporal sphere is recognized. The church should not interfere in temporal matters except through moral teaching, and it "has two missions: evangelization and the inspiration of the temporal sphere." The church is an order apart, the order of salvation and holiness in the world (53–58).

In contrast to these three responses, Gutiérrez argues that there is only one history and that the sacred and the profane, the natural and the supernatural, the temporal and the spiritual, cannot be separated. There has been a "rediscovery of the single convocation to salvation," which reaffirms the possibility of the presence of grace in all and the *integral* vocation to salvation, giving "religious value in a completely new way to the action of man in history, Christian and non-Christian alike." As a consequence, "the frontiers between the life of faith and temporal works, between Church and world, become more fluid. . . . The building of a just society has worth in terms of the Kingdom, or in more current phraseology, to participate in the process of liberation is already, in a certain sense, a salvific work" (72). For Gutiérrez, salvation is "not something other-worldly, in regard to which the present life is merely a test. Salvation — the communion of men with God and the communion of men among themselves — is something which embraces all human reality, transforms it, and leads it to its fullness in Christ" (151). Hence, the mission of the church is determined more by the political context of the society in which it exists concretely than by "intra-ecclesial problems." The "liberating action of Christ is at the heart of the historical current of humanity; the struggle for a just society is in its own right very much a part of salvation history" (168).

The mission of the church — conscientizing evangelization (liberation) — is *ad extra* and this determines the shape of its inner life. "The notion of evangelization, indeed, provides the key to Gutiérrez's ecclesiology."[29] For Gutiérrez, evangelization and conscientization are correlative terms. This does not mean, however, that salvation/liberation is a purely intrahistorical, a purely political, social, or economic affair. There is an intimate relationship between the liberation of humans on the social and political level and their liberation from sin. "One is not present without the others, but they are distinct: they are all part of a single, all-encompassing salvific process, but they are to be found at different levels" (176). Gutiérrez does not collapse political liberation

---

29. James B. Nickoloff, "The Church and Human Liberation: The Ecclesiology of Gustavo Gutiérrez," Ph.D. dissertation at the Graduate Theological Union, October 1988, 288. This is an excellent, thorough presentation and evaluation of Gutiérrez's ecclesiology.

or the work of humanizing the social situation into the coming of the kingdom of God, as some critics have charged. To cite his earliest work:

> Temporal progress — or, to avoid this aseptic term, the liberation of man — and the growth of the Kingdom both are directed toward complete communion of men with God and of men among themselves. They have the same goal, but they do not follow the same parallel roads, not even convergent ones. The growth of the Kingdom is a process which occurs historically *in* liberation, insofar as liberation means greater fulfillment of man. Liberation is a precondition for the new society, but this is not all it is. While liberation is implemented in liberating historical events, it also denounces their limitations and ambiguities, proclaims their fulfillment, and impels them effectively towards total communion. This is not identification. Without liberating historical events, there would be no growth of the Kingdom. But the process of liberation will not have conquered the very roots of oppression and exploitation of man by man without the coming of the Kingdom, which is above all a gift. (177)

This integral relationship between liberation from sin and political, social, and economic liberation has obvious consequences for the self-understanding of the community called church and for its mission.

As in Segundo's ecclesiology, there is an "uncentering" of the church in Gutiérrez's view. The church must cease considering itself as the exclusive place of salvation and orient itself toward a new and radical service of humanity (256–58). The church does not exist for itself but for others. Its function is to be a sign, "a sacrament of history," for *all* humanity, not only for those within its institutional structure.

> Through the people who explicitly accept his Word, the Lord reveals the world to itself. He rescues it from anonymity and enables it to know the ultimate meaning of its historical future and the value of every human act. (260)

Like Segundo, Gutiérrez quotes Teilhard's phrase that the church is the "reflectively Christified portion of the world." It is not "nonworld" but the conscious part of the world that "knows" the plan of salvation for all humanity. It is the church's function to manifest this possibility of communion among humans and of humans with God in its life and actions. The church itself "in its concrete existence ought to be a place of liberation . . . it has all the more obligation to manifest in its visible structures the message that it bears" (261). It also must manifest this possibility in its concrete historical context. In Latin America, this means denouncing the unjust social system and announcing the Good New of other possibilities (265–72).

In later writings, Gutiérrez has stressed that the church must be, or become, the church of the poor. In *The Power of the Poor in History* (1979) he argued that "history has been written from the viewpoint of the dominating sectors.... We must recover the memory of the 'scourged Christs of America,' as Bartolomé de Las Casas called the Indians of our continent."[30] But a rereading of history means a remaking of history. The Gospel read from the viewpoint of the poor "calls for a church to be gathered from among the poor, the marginalized." Such a church will spring from the people who will "snatch the gospel out of the hands of their dominators." They will become the evangelizers. Such a popular church, or church of the people, is being born from the *comunidades eclesiales de base*.[31]

But the identification or solidarity of the church with the poor will bring accusations that it is forsaking its "spiritual mission" and will entail a "reexamination of the church's own structures and of the life of its members."[32] Such a perspective, seeing reality from the side of the poor, is one of the two fundamental insights of liberation theology. The other is that, involvement in the liberation process is the starting point, or the first moment in theological reflection. Theology is always the "second act."[33] The evangelizing mission of the church will be carried out by the poor on behalf of the poor. The poor, in the CEBs, participate in this evangelizing mission and in the transformation of the world that it entails. There are not two separate functions of the church; the poor are the bearers of this one fundamental mission. Thus, the church must be not the church *for* the poor, nor a church *with* the poor, but the church *of* the poor.

A similar emphasis on the church of the poor is found in Leonardo Boff's two works on the church, *Ecclesiogenesis* and *Church: Charism and Power*. Boff argues that there is a new form of church being born from the base communities. What is taking place in Latin America is "a true ecclesiogenesis, the genesis of a new Church, but one that is not apart from the Church of the apostles and tradition, taking place in the base of the Church and in the grassroots of society, that is, among the lower classes who are religiously as well as socially deprived of power."[34] He contrasts this new church with the institutional church, which was epitomized by Bellarmine in the sixteenth century and which has been operative in Latin America through most of its history.

---

30. Gustavo Gutiérrez, *The Power of the Poor in History*, 20–21; see also *The Truth Shall Make You Free* (Maryknoll, N.Y.: Orbis, 1990), 141–52.
31. Gutiérrez, *The Power of the Poor,* 98.
32. Ibid., 156–57.
33. Ibid., 200.
34. Leonardo Boff, *Church: Charism and Power: Liberation Theology and the Institutional Church,* trans. John W. Diercksmeier (New York: Crossroad, 1985), 116.

In this work, Boff is more concerned with the internal structures of the church than are Segundo and Gutiérrez. He points out that the church cannot fulfill its sign-bearing function as long as there are injustice and inequality *within* the church itself. He compares the institutional church to the society inherited from the Industrial Revolution. "In terms of the Church, those who hold the means of religious production, the realm of the symbolic, also hold power and so create and control official discussion." This leads to an undeniable inequality in the church: "one group produces the symbolic goods and another consumes them. There are the ordained who can produce, celebrate, and decide and the nonordained who associate with and assist the ordained."[35] The group in control develops a "corresponding theology that justifies, reinforces, and socializes its power by attributing divine origin to its historical exercise of that power."

In contrast to this institutionalized inequality in the church, the church being born of the base communities is the "true creation of an ecclesial reality, of communal witness, of organization and missionary responsibility. The lay people take the word in their own hands, create symbols and rites, and rebuild the Church with grassroot materials."[36] This inevitably creates a tension with the hierarchical church, but does not entail a break with the institutional church. "The Church at large, structured as a network of institutional services, converges with the Church as a network of base communities. The latter receives the symbolic 'capital' of faith from the former, its link with tradition and its dimension of universality."[37] These base communities need not be restricted to the poor as a social class: "everyone, no matter what class, who opts for justice and identifies with the struggles of the community will find a place there."[38]

Boff's critique of the institutional church is based in his conviction that the Christian community must be a witness, a sign, of love in the world. Hence, the base communities cannot be "an underground organization or a sect." They must manifest a new way of being a community that will be a model and an influence on the society outside the church.

Boff's strident critique understandably evoked a strong response from the hierarchical church in Rome. In a document released in March 1985, the Congregation for the Doctrine of the Faith rejected his comparison of the church with industrial production and consumption. It said,

---

35. Ibid., 43.
36. Ibid., 118–19.
37. Ibid., 121.
38. Ibid., 122.

One ought not impoverish the reality of the sacraments and the word of God by reducing them to the "production and consumption" pattern, thus reducing the communion of faith to a mere sociological phenomenon. The sacraments are not "symbolic material," their administration is not production, their reception is not consumption. The sacraments are gifts of God, no one "produces" them, all receive the grace of God in them, which are the signs of eternal love.[39]

The document reasserted the hierarchy's right to judge the various charisms in the church, especially that of prophecy, saying that "the supreme criterion for judging not only its ordinary exercise but also its genuineness pertains to the hierarchy." Boff accepted the criticisms and was later silenced for a year.

Since the liberation theologians, especially Gutiérrez, were instrumental in drafting the documents of Medellín, it is not surprising that their ecclesiology should be reflected in the documents. At that time the bishops committed themselves "to live a true scriptural poverty expressed in authentic manifestations that may be clear signs for our peoples," and "to promote a new evangelization and intensive catechesis that reach the elite and the masses," thus echoing the concern for the church to identify with the poor and its mission of evangelization.[40] They call for the development of base communities: "It is necessary that small basic communities be developed in order to establish a balance with minority groups, which are the groups in power. This is possible only through vitalization of these very communities by means of the natural innate elements in their environment."[41] And again, in the "Document on Peace," they say that one of their pastoral goals is "to encourage and favor the efforts of the people to create and develop their own grassroots organizations for the redress and consolidation of their rights and the search for true justice."[42]

In the years between the second General Conference at Medellín in 1968 and the third at Puebla in 1979, there were reactions among some groups of bishops to the directions laid out at Medellín. The conservative Archbishop (now Cardinal) Alfonso López Trujillo had been elected secretary general of CELAM in 1972 and, together with a number of European and Latin American theologians and bishops, orchestrated an attack on liberation theology. Hence, there was some

---

39. Congregation for the Doctrine of the Faith, "Notification Sent to Fr. Leonardo Boff regarding Errors in His Book, *Church: Charism and Power*" (March 11, 1985), as cited in Hennelly, *Documentary History*, 429.

40. "Message to the Peoples of Latin America," as cited in Hennelly, *Documentary History*, 93.

41. "Document on Justice," 20, as cited in Hennelly, *Documentary History*, 104.

42. "Document on Peace," 27, as cited in Hennelly, *Documentary History*, 112.

expectation that Puebla would retract the church's commitment to the poor and condemn basic ecclesial communities. In fact, it did just the opposite.

It was Puebla that first used the now famous phrase "preferential option for the poor" and renewed the church's solidarity with the poor and marginalized of Latin America. Of base communities the bishops said,

> In 1968 base-level ecclesial communities [CEBs: *comunidades eclesiales de base*] were just coming into being. Over the past ten years they have multiplied and matured, particularly in some countries, so that now they are one of the causes for joy and hope in the Church. In communion with their bishops, and in line with Medellín's request, they have become centers of evangelization and moving forces for liberation and development.
>
> The vitality of the CEBs is now beginning to bear fruit. They have been one of the sources for the increase in lay ministers, who are now acting as leaders and organizers of their communities, as catechists, and as missionaries.
>
> In some places insufficient attention has been paid to the work required to develop CEBs. It is regrettable that, in some areas, clearly political interests try to manipulate them and to sever them from authentic communion with their bishops.[43]

In addition to the danger of manipulation of the CEBs for political purposes, the conference also warned against the risk of sectarianism. They recall Vatican II's notion of the church as the pilgrim People of God and say, "Insofar as the Church is a historical, institutional People, it represents the broader, more universal, and better defined structure in which the life of the CEBs must be inscribed if they are not to fall prey to the danger of organizational anarchy or narrow-minded, sectarian elitism."[44] Finally, Puebla refuted the charge of some critics that a base community was not really a *church* or an ecclesial community, saying that, "as an ecclesial reality, it is a community of faith, hope, and charity. It celebrates the Word of God and takes its nourishment from the Eucharist... and through the service of approved coordinators, it makes present and operative the mission of the Church and its visible communion with the legitimate pastors."[45]

In summary, the three liberation theologians we have discussed, together with the statements of the second and third general meetings

---

43. "Final Document," in John Eagleson and Philip Scharper, eds. *Puebla and Beyond: Documentation and Commentary*, trans. John Drury (Maryknoll, N.Y.: Orbis, 1979), no. 6, 135–36.

44. Ibid., no. 261, 157.

45. Ibid., no. 641, 212.

of the Council of Latin American Episcopacies, present an ecclesiology with four distinguishing characteristics: (1) the church is a sign, the sacrament of God's saving love for the world; (2) its mission is evangelization for integral liberation; (3) the church must be "de-centered," because it is not the exclusive means of salvation and not an end in itself; and (4) it must be a church *of* the poor, committed to and in solidarity with the oppressed of Latin America.

Critics of this ecclesiology point out several dangers. We have already mentioned the Vatican's letter to Leonardo Boff, which vigorously opposed his critique of the unequal distribution of power within the church, and Puebla's warning about the danger of sectarianism. In its 1984 "Instruction on Certain Aspects of the 'Theology of Liberation,'" the Vatican warned against a "disastrous confusion between the *poor* of the Scripture and the *proletariat* of Marx." It said that for some liberation theologians, although no specific theologians were named, "the *Church of the poor* signifies the Church of the class which has become aware of the requirements of the revolutionary struggle as a step toward liberation and which celebrates this liberation in its liturgy."[46] They feared that the language of "class struggle" and "class conflict" would be divisive for the church.

This instruction also criticized the liberation theologians for "a critique of the very structures of the Church," saying that this "has to do with a challenge to the *sacramental and hierarchical structure* of the Church, which was willed by the Lord Himself."[47]

In 1986, the Vatican issued another instruction, entitled "Instruction on Christian Freedom and Liberation," which was much more positive in its evaluation of liberation theology as a whole and of its understanding of the church in particular. In contrast to the 1984 document, it said, "The special option for the poor, far from being a sign of particularism, or sectarianism, manifests the universality of the church's being and mission. This option excludes no one."[48] This is the reason the church rejects "reductive sociological and ideological categories" that would suggest exclusivity. It further praised the "new basic communities" as witnesses to evangelical love and "a source of great hope for the church."

---

46. Sacred Congregation for the Doctrine of the Faith, "Instruction on Certain Aspects of the 'Theology of Liberation,'" (Vatican City, 1984), no. 10, 25.

47. Ibid., no. 13, 25.

48. The Congregation for the Doctrine of the Faith, "Instruction on Christian Freedom and Liberation" (Vatican City, 1986), as cited in *Origins* no. 68 (April 17, 1986): 723.

## CHALLENGES AND POSSIBILITIES

Christians in the First World and in the United States in particular cannot help but ask how this self-understanding of the church could be applied or adapted to their own situation. The liberation theologians have consistently warned against the simple transposition of their theology to another context. Their theology is deeply rooted in the Latin American situation. Indeed, that is why it is so powerful and attractive. The liberation theologians have enabled the traditional Christian symbols to speak to and energize the daily lives of their people. Liberation theology seems to have overcome that gap between faith and daily life that Vatican II lamented.

What can we in North America learn from them?

First, we can agree rather readily that the church should be a sign, a sacrament of integral salvation in and for the world. What that would mean concretely in our historical context cannot be easily summarized. We need to do the kind of social and cultural analysis of our context that the liberation theologians have done in their situation. We can, I believe, adopt their method of doing theology. This method sees theological reflection as the "second act," the first being commitment to and solidarity with the poor and oppressed. As Gutiérrez says at the end of *A Theology of Liberation,* "all the political theologies, the theologies of hope, of revolution, and of liberation, are not worth one act of genuine solidarity with the exploited social classes" (308). Such a "preferential option for the poor" may be particularly difficult in a society that is basically middle class. Even recognizing that we are a "bourgeois" church, as Metz puts it, is the beginning of a new awareness, however.

Second, the Christian community in the First World can accept, and to some extent already has accepted, the mission of the church as evangelization for integral liberation. Again, the question becomes what does "integral liberation" mean in the concrete in our context? What are the sources of oppression in our context from which we need liberation? Robert McAfee Brown suggests that "our oppressor is not a group within our social-economic system so much as it is the very socio-economic system itself." This system includes such things as,

> the necessity of upward mobility, both personally and professionally; the willingness to compete, by fair means or foul, against those who threaten our success or our job or our nation; a commitment to "looking out for Number One," for no one else will; a conviction that the payoff for hard work is material comfort of an increasingly lavish sort; a willingness to put our jobs ahead of our families; a belief that it is both appropriate and necessary to check

our moral values at the entrance to the work place, for the bottom
line is always profit, and nothing must interfere with that.[49]

This may be a bit harsh, but some critical reflection on and counter-
witness to such values would seem to be necessary for the sign/
sacramental function of the church in our context.

Third, the liberation theologians challenge us to recognize the role
that the United States and other First World countries play in their position of dependency. They call upon the church in the First World to
denounce the policies of their governments and their transnational corporations that support and are in complicity with oppressive regimes
and structures in Central and South America. This has begun to happen,
for example, when church leaders in the United States, in conjunction
with the bishops of Central America, strongly condemned United States
foreign policy and aid to such countries as El Salvador. A much broader
critique of corporate policies that make dependency so profitable for
U.S. transnationals is needed.

Fourth, could the model of the CEBs be adopted and adapted in
the United States? The National Conference of Catholic Bishops in the
United States explicitly encouraged the formation of CEBs as a strategy
for the pastoral care of Hispanics in their 1983 pastoral letter on the
subject.[50] But the attempts to form CEBs have met with only limited success. Allan Deck suggests two factors that may inhibit their success in the
United States: "the highly urban and mobile character of U.S. Hispanics"
and the fact that "the institutional strength of the parish in most pastoral contexts in the U.S. makes it extremely difficult to introduce and
sustain models of Church that do not clearly reaffirm the parish structure."[51] Nevertheless, there does seem to be some quest for smaller,
more communitarian groupings among Hispanics, as evidenced by the
"leakage" to fundamentalist and pentecostal churches. How healthy the
parish structure is in the United States and whether or not something
like the CEBs is needed, we will discuss further in chapter 10.

Fifth, the need for the internal structure of the church to manifest
justice and equality, as Boff argues, poses a challenge to the church in
the United States. As Roger Haight remarks, "The Church risks hypocrisy,
vacuous moralism and the appearance of sheer ridiculousness if it does

---

49. Robert McAfee Brown, "Reflections of a North American: The Future of Liberation
Theology," in Marc H. Ellis and Otto Maduro, eds., *The Future of Liberation Theology:
Essays in Honor of Gustavo Gutiérrez* (Maryknoll, N.Y.: Orbis, 1989), 496–97.
50. *The Hispanic Presence: Challenge and Commitment* (Washington, D.C.: United
States Catholic Conference, 1983), 27.
51. Allan Figueroa Deck, S.J., *The Second Wave: Hispanic Ministry and the Evangelization of Cultures* (New York: Paulist Press, 1989), 73.

not respond to the social injustices within its own institution."[52] This is most clearly evident in the position of blacks and women in the church.

Finally, I agree with Robert McAfee Brown when he concludes, "The task is not to decide that Latin American liberation theology is the way of the future, and seek to import it. The task is rather to discover where our own areas of need for liberation are located, and begin to create a liberation theology for North America."[53]

## RECOMMENDED READINGS

Boff, Leonardo. *Church: Charism and Power*. New York: Crossroad, 1985.

Cleary, Edward L. *Crisis and Change in the Church in Latin America Today*. Maryknoll, N.Y.: Orbis, 1985.

Gutiérrez, Gustavo. *A Theology of Liberation*, rev. ed. Maryknoll, N.Y.: Orbis, 1988.

Segundo, Juan Luis. *The Community Called Church*. Maryknoll, N.Y.: Orbis, 1973.

---

52. Roger Haight, *An Alternative Vision: An Interpretation of Liberation Theology* (New York: Paulist Press, 1985), 184.
53. Brown, "Reflections of a North American," 494.

# Chapter 9

# Global Church
# and Inculturation

The theology of liberation that has emerged in Latin America was a reflection of the increasing self-awareness and self-confidence of the Christian community in that region. This phenomenon, paralleled in Africa and Asia, was stimulated in part by the renewed emphasis on the local church and on the diversity of cultures in the documents of Vatican II. But it was also occasioned by the demise of colonial empires in the 1950s and 1960s, as well as the tremendous demographic increase of Christianity in these regions. Walbert Bühlmann has pointed out that in 1900 85 percent of all Christians lived in Europe and North America, but by 1980 49 percent lived in the Third World, and this figure is expected to rise to 60 percent by the year 2000.[1] At present, there are more Christians in Africa than in North America and more Roman Catholics in Latin America than in Europe and North America combined.[2] Such factors have led Bühlmann and others to talk about an emerging world church or global church. Paradoxically, increasing *regional* awareness has been accompanied by increasing *global* awareness. In this chapter, then, we will discuss the meaning and experience of the global church, the meaning and process of inculturation, the implications for the self-understanding of the Christian community of these recent phenomena, and the challenges and possibilities they present for the future of the church.

---

1. Walbert Bühlmann, *With Eyes to See: Church and World in the Third Millennium*, trans. Robert R. Barr (Maryknoll, N.Y.: Orbis, 1990), 6–7.

2. According to the *1989 Encyclopaedia Britannica Book of the Year*, there are 282,526,720 Christians in Africa, 232,557,080 Christians in North America, 377,753,520 Roman Catholics in Latin America, and 354,732,840 Roman Catholics in Europe and North America (United States and Canada).

# THE GLOBAL CHURCH

What does it mean to speak of a global or worldwide church? We have referred in chapter 1 to Karl Rahner's theological interpretation of Vatican II as "the Church's first official self-actualization *as* a world Church."[3] He meant that the church was beginning to be "de-Europeanized," to move out from European culture as the only embodiment of the faith. Even though Christianity had taken root in Latin America, Africa, Asia, and Oceania centuries before, it was an exported European religion that was "sent throughout the world together with the rest of the culture and civilization it considered superior." Now, "a world Church as such begins to act through the reciprocal influence exercised by all its components."[4] As evidence for this mutual influence at Vatican II, Rahner cites the presence of indigenous bishops, the use of the vernacular in the liturgy, the encouraging of regional episcopal conferences, and the "truly positive evaluation of the great world religions." He rightly insists that at Vatican II this was only an incipient and diffident movement, but it initiated an agenda for the church in the future, that is, the inculturation of the faith in all the cultures of the world. When that happens, we will have what Rahner meant by a world church.

A global church implies that the various regional churches would be not independent but *interdependent*. They would mutually influence one another and recognize regional and cultural differences in liturgical practice, doctrinal expression, law, and church governance. True recognition of cultural diversity implies the principle of *subsidiarity*, i.e., that no decisions should be made at a higher level that can be made at a lower one. A global church would be somewhat decentralized, or, as some say, polycentric.

The term "global church" also implies a shift in attitude or perspective. It would entail asking new questions or reframing older ones, not insisting on policies or formulations based on a European framework, allowing the agenda to be set by the local or regional churches.[5] If other cultures are taken seriously, for example, questions about marriage would be posed differently in Africa than in North America, questions about social equality would be formulated differently in India with its caste tradition than in Britain or France.[6] A global church, in other words, implies the end of European ethnocentrism in the church.

---

3. Karl Rahner, S.J., "Towards a Fundamental Theological Interpretation of Vatican II," *Theological Studies* 40, no. 4 (December 1979): 716–27; see our discussion of this article in chapter 4 of this volume.

4. Ibid., 717.

5. See Robert J. Schreiter, C.PP.S., *Constructing Local Theologies* (Maryknoll, N.Y.: Orbis, 1985), 1–5.

6. See for example, Lisa Sowle Cahill, "Moral Theology and the World Church," *Proceedings of the Catholic Theological Society of America* 39 (1984): 35–51.

Those who speak of a global or world church, however, do not intend it in a triumphalistic sense, as if the church will take over the world. Rahner and Bühlmann are acutely aware that Christians are only 32 percent of the world's population and the proportion is decreasing with rising birth rates in countries that are primarily Hindu, Buddhist, and Muslim. Bühlmann says, "In many countries of the third world, Christianity seems little more than an insignificant sect, and even in the West the age of the 'Christian nations' is a thing of the past."[7]

When we speak of a global or world church, in summary, we mean a church that is de-Europeanized, multicultural, polycentric, interdependent, and influenced by all the world's cultures in its liturgy, law, doctrine, structure, and practice. Is such a church just wishful thinking, or is there some experiential basis for talking about a global church?

## EXPERIENCE OF THE GLOBAL CHURCH

Within the Roman Catholic community, the institution of the international Synod of Bishops by Pope Paul VI in 1965 provided a forum for the voices of the various regional churches to be heard at the highest level. Called by the pope, the synod has met at regular intervals of two or three years from 1967 through 1990 and dealt with such topics as Justice (1971), Evangelization (1974), the Laity (1987), and Priestly Formation (1990). Its purposes are to "encourage close union and valued assistance between the Sovereign Pontiff and the bishops of the entire world," "to insure that direct and real information is provided" on issues internal to the church and its activity in the world, and "to facilitate agreement on essential points of doctrine and on methods of procedure in the life of the Church."[8] It is an advisory and consultative body, although many expected that it would eventually become a legislative branch of the church's government. This has not happened, but the synod has provided input from the bishops around the world on major issues facing the church. Some meetings of the Synod have been more influential than others. Thus, the 1971 Synod on Justice in the World, with leadership from the bishops of the Third World, said that "action on behalf of justice and participation in the transformation of the world fully appear to us as a constitutive dimension of the preaching of the Gospel."[9]

---

7. Bühlmann, *With Eyes to See*, 8.

8. Pope Paul VI, "Apostolica Sollicitudo," September 15, 1965, as cited in Abbott, *Documents of Vatican II*, 721.

9. Synod of Bishops, *Convenientes ex universo*, November 30, 1971, in Austin Flannery, O.P., ed., *Vatican Council II: More Post Conciliar Documents* (Northport, N.Y.: Costello Publishing Co., 1982), 696.

The 1974 Synod on Evangelization and the Apostolic Exhortation of Pope Paul VI the following year, *Evangelii Nuntiandi*, made a major contribution and gave great impetus to inculturation and the move toward a global church. At that synod, the bishops of Africa and Madagascar made a strong collective statement "concerning what they termed 'the task of religious acculturation.' "[10] They considered a "theology of adaptation" to be out of date, and urged what they called a "theology of incarnation." They said that "the young churches of Africa and Madagascar must take over more and more the responsibility for their own evangelization and total development."[11] We will discuss the papal exhortation that flowed from the synod below, but this synod was clearly an experience of the global church.

The Extraordinary Synod of 1985, called by Pope John Paul II to assess the Second Vatican Council, provided another example of input from churches around the world. In analyzing that synod, Avery Dulles said that there were three major schools of thought, but that "there were many different perspectives, reflecting concerns from a variety of nations and continents."[12] Thus, the Synod of Bishops has provided some experience of churches from different continents and cultures influencing one another and, thus, forming a global church.

That same synod debated another experience of the global church in the form of national and regional episcopal conferences. As we have seen in chapter 6, these were encouraged by Vatican II (LG 23 and CD 38) and were given clear juridical status in the 1983 revised Code of Canon Law (447–459 and 753). Perhaps most significant has been the experience of CELAM in Latin America, as we indicated in the previous chapter.

Episcopal conferences in Southeast Asia, Africa, and North America have also provided experiences of how the national and regional churches are becoming more self-aware and self-confident. This has not always pleased the Vatican, and a working paper (*instrumentum laboris*) from the Congregation for Bishops tried to denigrate their significance and teaching authority. This document received almost universally negative responses from both theologians and bishops.[13] This

---

10. Aylward Shorter, *Toward a Theology of Inculturation* (Maryknoll, N.Y.: Orbis, 1988), 212.

11. Ibid., 213.

12. Avery Dulles, "The Extraordinary Synod of 1985," in *The Reshaping of Catholicism* (San Francisco: Harper & Row, 1988), 191.

13. Congregation for Bishops, "Theological and Juridical Status of Episcopal Conferences," January 12, 1988. For responses, see the articles in *America* (March 19, 1988): 292–304, and the response of the National Conference of Catholic Bishops, "Response of the Episcopal Conference of the United States to the *Instrumentum Laboris* on Episcopal Conferences, November 16, 1988, and Avery Dulles, "Episcopal Conferences: Their Teaching Authority," *America* (January 13, 1990): 7–9.

ongoing discussion is one very clear example of the tension between unity and pluralism in this emerging global church, which we will discuss further below.

Other experiences of the mutual influence of churches from different continents and cultures have occurred in various international meetings of theologians, such as the Ecumenical Association of Third World Theologians (EATWOT), which began at Dar-es-Salaam in 1976 and held regular meetings through 1983,[14] the five interecclesial conventions of CEBs, and the Theology of the Americas conference in Detroit in 1975 and its follow-up. The many trips to various local and regional churches of Pope John Paul II have certainly given visible expression to the global church and have provided opportunities for an exchange of views between the pope and the local churches. Some have felt that the pope spoke too much and listened too little; nevertheless, he gained firsthand knowledge of the difficulties and needs of the church around the world.

Since the incipient and hesitant actualization of the global church at Vatican II as Rahner suggested, we have had these and other experiences which give some further evidence that, in fact, a global church is in the making. The above examples are all from the Roman Catholic experience, but Protestant Christians have also been concerned with the interaction of the Gospel and the local cultures, as we will see below. But because the Protestant traditions give much greater emphasis to the local church, they have not been as willing to speak of a global or worldwide church as have Roman Catholics.

As should be clear, a global church entails that local or particular churches be truly embedded in their own cultures, although not isolated in them. To this process of inculturation and the problems it raises, let us now turn.

## INCULTURATION

From a theological point of view, some form of inculturation is implied by the mystery of the incarnation. Christians understand that God's self-communication takes place in and through matter, in and through human words, symbols, and actions. We saw above that the African bishops at the 1974 synod used the language of a "theology of incarnation" to refer to this process of inculturation.

As a matter of practice, from the time of Paul's speech on the Areopagus to the Athenians (Acts 17:22–34), the church has attempted to

---

14. For a discussion of the origin and growth of EATWOT, see Rosino Gibellini, *The Liberation Theology Debate* (Maryknoll, N.Y.: Orbis, 1988), chap. 4, 61–78.

present the Gospel to persons of diverse cultures in a manner they could understand and accept. Once they decided that converts to Christianity did not have to adopt all the forms of Jewish culture, the church was engaged in inculturation. But it is only recently that the church has appropriated a more sophisticated understanding of culture as developed by the social sciences.

Although there are a variety of approaches to culture,[15] we understand it as defined by anthropologist Clifford Geertz: "an historically transmitted pattern of meanings embodied in symbols, a system of inherited conceptions expressed in symbolic forms by means of which men communicate, perpetuate, and develop their knowledge about and attitudes toward life."[16] As the church has gradually appropriated such an understanding of culture, it has become clear that there is more than one culture, that no one culture is normative for the others or superior to them. Such a "classicist" mindset had prevailed among European missionaries through the nineteenth and early twentieth centuries. By the time of Vatican II, Pope John XXIII in his opening address made a distinction between "the substance of the ancient doctrine of the deposit of the faith" and "the way in which it is presented."[17] This recognition of a distinction between the faith and its cultural forms underlies the discussion of culture in *Gaudium et Spes* (53–63) and *Ad Gentes* (19–22), where the diversity of cultures was explicitly recognized and greater emphasis was given to the local churches.[18] Hence, the dialogue between faith and a multiplicity of cultures has become a major concern in recent years.

Although a variety of terms has been used to describe this dialogue between faith and cultures — adaptation, accommodation, incarnation, contextualization, and indigenization — among Roman Catholic theologians, the word "inculturation" has become increasingly more common.[19] Protestants are more inclined to use "contextualization."[20] The term "inculturation" needs to be distinguished from "enculturation" (the process by which an individual is inserted into his or her own culture, similar to "socialization") and "acculturation" (the encounter

---

15. For a discussion of these approaches, see Schreiter, *Constructing Local Theologies*, 45–49.

16. Clifford Geertz, *The Interpretation of Cultures* (New York: Basic Books, 1973), 89.

17. Pope John's Opening Speech to the Council, October 11, 1962, in Abbott, *Documents of Vatican II*, 715.

18. For a fuller discussion of the teaching of Vatican II and Popes Paul VI and John Paul II, see Aylward Shorter, *Toward a Theology of Inculturation* (Maryknoll, N.Y.: Orbis, 1988), chaps. 14, 15, and 16.

19. Shorter, *Toward a Theology of Inculturation*, 3–16, and Robert J. Schreiter, "Faith and Cultures: Challenges to a World Church," *Theological Studies* 50 (1989): 745–48.

20. See, for example, David J. Hesslegrave and Edward Rommen, *Contextualization: Meanings, Methods, and Models* (Grand Rapids: Baker Book House, 1989).

between two or more cultures).[21] Aylward Shorter suggests that the term "inculturation" was introduced and popularized largely by the Society of Jesus, and hence he cites the former superior general of the Jesuits for a definition:

> the incarnation of Christian life and of the Christian message in a particular cultural context, in such a way that this experience not only finds expression through elements proper to the culture in question (this alone would be no more than a superficial adaptation) but becomes a principle that animates, directs and unifies the culture, transforming it and remaking it so as to bring about a "new creation."[22]

Such an inculturation is not a once-and-for-all event that takes place the first time Christianity encounters a particular culture, but is an ongoing process. It must continue to occur in the older, more established churches as well as in the younger or newer churches. Second, and following from this ongoing process, inculturation is not the work of the missionary but of the local church, the local Christian community. Further, if it is truly a dialogue, the Christian message will not only animate and transform the local culture, but will itself be penetrated by the local culture. If it is a true dialogue, both partners will be changed.

Avery Dulles has suggested that Christianity itself has some of the characteristics of a culture: "Like a culture, it is a system of meanings, historically transmitted, embodied in symbols, and instilled into new members of the group so that they are inclined to think, judge, and act in characteristic ways."[23] Hence, when Christianity encounters a particular culture initially a process of "acculturation" takes place insofar as it is an encounter of two cultures. In a pluralistic society, Christianity may be considered a "subculture."

Yet Christianity transcends, in one sense, all particular cultures. In the words of *Gaudium et Spes,* "the Church, sent to all peoples of every time and place, is not bound exclusively and indissolubly to any race or nation, nor to any particular way of life or any customary pattern of living, ancient or recent. Faithful to her own tradition and at the same time conscious of her universal mission, she can enter into communion with various cultural modes, to her own enrichment and theirs too."[24]

---

21. Shorter, *Toward a Theology of Inculturation,* 5–7.

22. Ibid., 11, citing Pedro Arrupe, S.J., "Letter to the Whole Society on Inculturation," 1978, in J. Aixala, ed., *Other Apostolates Today: Selected Letters and Addresses of Pedro Arrupe, S.J.* (St. Louis, 1981), 172.

23. Avery Dulles, "The Emerging World Church: A Theological Reflection," *Proceedings of the Catholic Theological Society of America* 39 (1984): 5–6. For a fuller discussion of this notion, see Clifford Geertz, "Religion as a Cultural System," in *The Interpretation of Cultures,* 87–125.

24. *Gaudium et Spes,* 58, in Abbott, *Documents of Vatican II,* 264.

In another sense, however, Christianity is never independent of culture. It is always expressed in some cultural forms. There is no such thing as a disembodied faith. Historically, the process of inculturation has taken place when the faith, expressed in one cultural form, its Jewish form for example, moves to embed itself in another culture, the Graeco-Roman for example.

According to Ary Roest Crollius, inculturation takes place in three stages. The first stage he calls *translation,* when the church comes into contact with a new culture while still presenting the Christian message in the forms of another culture. At this stage, "Though minor adaptations are made and translations prepared, the Church has a foreign outlook, and so becoming a Christian often implies leaving behind one's own culture."[25] In the second stage, *assimilation,* with larger numbers and an indigenous clergy, inculturation proper begins, though it may be somewhat passive. In the third stage, *transformation,* the church will take a more active role in transforming the local culture. He concludes that "the entire process of inculturation is one of *integration,* both in the sense of integration of the Christian faith and life in a given culture and of integration of a new expression of the Christian experience in the life of the universal Church."[26] These three stages may occur concomitantly, and the whole is an ongoing and dynamic process.

The process of inculturation is dynamic and continuous precisely because cultures themselves are not static. Cultures are living and dynamic. They are always in the process of change. This is especially true today when rapid communication and transportation enable, indeed force, many cultures to impact on one another. Acculturation, the encounter of two or more cultures, has been dramatically speeded up. Many cultures in Asia, Oceania, and Africa are in the process of modernization (read Westernization) at a time when they are rediscovering their own cultural heritages long suppressed by colonialism. They are in turmoil and very fragile. In this situation, it is doubly difficult for Christianity to engage in a process of inculturation.

## EXPERIENCE OF INCULTURATION

As indicated above, Christianity experienced inculturation as soon as it accepted Gentiles as Christians and began the move out of the Judaean culture, which itself was not homogeneous. The Apologists of the second century, such as Clement of Alexandria and Justin Martyr,

---

25. Ary Roest Crollius, S.J., "Inculturation: Newness and Ongoing Process," in J. M. Waliggo, A. Roest Crollius, S.J., T. Nkeramihigo, S.J., J. Mutiso-Mbinda, *Inculturation: Its Meaning and Urgency* (St. Paul Publications, 1986), 42.

26. Ibid.

made use of Vergil's *Aeneid* and his *Fourth Eclogue* to show that there
were prophecies anticipating Christ's birth and his second coming in
Gentile literature and philosophy.[27] With the conversion of the emperor
Constantine and the establishment of Christianity as the religion of the
empire, Christianity became so immersed in Byzantine culture as to be
almost indistinguishable from it. In the Western empire Greek culture
gradually gave way to Latin culture, and the church became the bearer
of this culture throughout the period we call Christendom, as we saw
in chapter 4. In the East, the missionaries to the Slavs, Saints Cyril and
Methodius, helped create a Slavonic culture by developing an alpha-
bet, now called the Cyrillic, and a written form of Slavonic into which
they translated the Greek and Roman liturgies, civil and canon law, and
eventually the entire Bible.

The symbiosis of Western Latin culture and Christianity began to
break up at the time of the Reformation, the beginning of the sixteenth
century. Shorter points out that "national vernaculars had developed
to the point of becoming written languages with a growing corpus of
literature behind them. . . . Moreover, Europe had resolved itself into a
collection of nation-states, with a growing sense of national identity
and self-sufficiency."[28] This coincided with the circumnavigation of the
globe, the discovery of the New World, and its subsequent colonization
and evangelization.

The Roman Catholic Church's reaction to the Reformation was to
insist on the unity of the church and to do everything to enforce this by
strict uniformity in liturgy, law, and theology. Further, one of the major
reforms initiated by Trent, as we have seen, was its institution of seminaries for the training of clergy. Again Shorter says, "Seminary training
was to be uniform throughout the world, making no cultural distinc-
tions whatever. Not only did the uniform training of priests in the world
widen the gap between clergy and laity; it also prevented the training
of priests in many of the mission countries where it was well-nigh impossible to create the necessary educational facilities on the Western
model."[29]

To deal with problems created by Catholic missionary activity as
well as to centralize control of it, Pope Urban VIII created the Sacred
Congregation *de Propaganda Fide* in 1622. According to Shorter, "The
congregation tried valiantly to oppose wholesale cultural domination,
but it distinguished between the religious and secular aspects of culture.
Secular culture was not to be touched, but whatever did not conform

---

27. In this brief historical sketch I am following the fuller treatment in Shorter, *Toward
a Theology of Inculturation*, chaps. 10, 11, and 12.
28. Ibid., 152.
29. Ibid., 154.

to Catholic faith and morals must be uprooted."[30] Such a distinction, however, was very difficult to apply in practice, especially in cultural systems in which religion permeates the system as a whole. The most famous attempt to apply such a distinction was the case of Matteo Ricci and the Chinese rites.

Although Ricci himself died twelve years before the founding of the *Propaganda Fide,* the controversy he initiated continued into the twentieth century. Ricci and his fellow Jesuits arrived in China in 1581 and embarked "on a profound dialogue with the religious culture of the Chinese" and aimed at "nothing more nor less than inculturation in the true sense of the word. The goal was to achieve a Christian reinterpretation of Chinese culture which would, in turn, provoke a Chinese interpretation of Christianity presented in this sympathetic Chinese form."[31] Ricci insinuated himself into the highest levels of Chinese culture by his knowledge of Western science, mathematics, and astronomy. He was the author of more than twenty scholarly works in Chinese. In his attempt to distinguish and appropriate those aspects and practices of Chinese culture that were not incompatible with Christianity, he approved "of the application of the traditional Chinese title 'Lord of Heaven' to the God of Christianity" and authorized the traditional ceremonies honoring Confucius and the cult of the familial ancestors. After Ricci's death in 1610, missionaries from other religious congregations attacked these and other practices as incompatible with Christianity. In the following century, a commission of cardinals was appointed to examine the dispute. As a result Pope Clement IX condemned the Chinese rites in 1704, and this was later finalized by Pope Benedict XIV in 1742. Only in 1935 was Ricci's position vindicated when Pope Pius XI approved the cult of Confucius, and four years later his successor, Pius XII, approved traditional funeral rites and the cult of the ancestors. Similar attempts at inculturation occurred in India with Roberto de Nobili and in Ethiopia with Pedro Paez. In summary, Shorter says, "The great Jesuit missionaries, Ricci, de Nobili, Paez and others, were not theoretically or theologically equipped, let alone supported, by the Church of their time, to carry their inculturation through successfully. But their abortive endeavours were a sign of the Church's yearning for a more fully developed Catholicity."[32]

The questions raised by these missionary experiences in the sixteenth and early seventeenth centuries were raised again in the nineteenth when there was an expansion of missionary activity and a number of new religious orders were founded explicitly for that purpose. To cite

---

30. Ibid., 155.
31. Ibid., 158.
32. Ibid., 163. Similar issues were faced by the Mendicant and Jesuit missionaries in the colonization of Latin America.

only one example, Cardinal Charles Lavigerie, who founded the Society
of Missionaries of Africa, the White Fathers, in 1868, insisted that his
missionaries learn the local language and speak it among themselves,
and that those they educate remain truly African, keeping their customs
and way of life; he urged them to keep descriptive accounts in a jour-
nal of their cultural traditions and legends.[33] In spite of such urgings,
Shorter concludes, the missionaries of the nineteenth century "were
hindered from real dialogue by their theology; not merely by an unde-
veloped theology of salvation and the Church, but by the very nature
of contemporary classicist theology itself."[34] It was not until Vatican II
that Roman Catholic theology began to free itself from this classicist,
ahistorical, and monocultural framework.

At the Second Vatican Council, the presence of many indigenous
bishops, the celebration of the liturgy in a variety of rites, and the cau-
cuses according to various language groups made cultural pluralism
an experiential fact. This was reflected in the documents, especially
*Gaudium et Spes* and *Ad Gentes*. The council explicitly recognized a
"plurality of cultures," saying:

> Various conditions of community living, as well as various patterns
> for organizing the goods of life, arise from diverse ways of using
> things, of laboring, of expressing oneself, of practicing religion, of
> forming customs, of establishing laws and juridical institutions, of
> advancing the arts and sciences, and of promoting beauty. Thus
> the customs handed down to it form for each human community
> its proper patrimony. (GS 53)

It further acknowledged that "God ... has spoken according to the culture proper to different ages" and that "the Church, too, has used in
her preaching the discoveries of different cultures to spread and explain the message of Christ to all nations.... But at the same time, the
Church, sent to all peoples of every time and place, is not bound exclusively and indissolubly to any race or nation, nor to any particular
way of life or any customary pattern of living, ancient or recent" (GS
58). Thus, the classicist, monocultural assumptions of the nineteenth
century were explicitly repudiated.

The Decree on the Missionary Activity of the Church, *Ad Gentes,*
urged the process of inculturation, saying that "the faith must be taught
by an adequate catechesis celebrated in a liturgy which harmonizes with
the genius of the people, and introduced into upright institutions and
local customs by appropriate canonical legislation" (AG 19). It encouraged what it calls "the young Churches" to borrow from the customs,

---

33. Ibid., 169.
34. Ibid., 172.

traditions, wisdom and learning, arts and sciences of their own cultures those things that "can contribute to the glory of their Creator." To achieve this, the council said, "theological investigation must necessarily be stirred up in each major socio-cultural area, as it is called. In this way, under the light of the tradition of the universal Church, a fresh scrutiny will be brought to bear on the deeds and words which God has made known, which have been consigned to sacred Scripture, and which have been unfolded by the Church Fathers and the teaching authority of the Church" (AG 22). It urged episcopal conferences in each region to pursue such a program of adaptation.

Thus, a new era in the inculturation of the faith was initiated by Vatican II. This initiative has been furthered by Popes Paul VI and John Paul II. We mentioned above the 1974 Synod on Evangelization and the exhortation *Evangelii Nuntiandi*, which Paul VI issued afterward on December 8, 1975. This is perhaps the most important papal statement on the subject of inculturation. Again, recognizing the particular churches with their own cultural heritages, the pope cautions against regarding the church as "a federated association of more or less heterogeneous individual churches, essentially different from each other," but then goes on to say that the individual churches "must make their own the substance of the evangelical message. Without any sacrifice of the essential truths they must transpose this message into an idiom which will be understood by the people they serve and thus proclaim it" (EN 63). Such a transposition must take place "in fields relating to the sacred liturgy, to catechetics, to the formulation of theological principles, to the secondary ecclesial structures and to the ministry. When we speak of idiom we must be understood to mean not so much an explanation of the words or a literary style as an anthropological and cultural adaptation" (EN 63). Pope John Paul II has continued this theme and, in 1982, established the Pontifical Council for Culture to encourage and oversee the process of inculturation.[35]

Despite all this official encouragement, our experience since Vatican II of the dialogue between faith and cultures has been ambiguous. More has been done in the field of liturgy than in other areas. The Constitution on the Sacred Liturgy, *Sacrosanctum Concilium*, was the first promulgated by the council (December 4, 1963) and implementation began immediately. It positively encouraged inculturation of the liturgy, saying:

> Provided that the substantial unity of the Roman rite is maintained, the revision of liturgical books should allow for legitimate variations and adaptations to different groups, regions, and peoples,

---

35. For a fuller discussion of the teachings of Paul VI and John Paul II on inculturation, see Shorter, *Toward a Theology of Inculturation,* chaps. 15 and 16.

especially in mission lands. Where opportune, the same rule applies to the structuring of rites and the devising of rubrics (SC 38).

It further suggested that "more radical adaptation of the liturgy" is needed in some places and assigned the "competent territorial authorities" to "carefully and prudently consider which elements from the traditions and genius of individual peoples might appropriately be admitted into divine worship." These recommendations should then be submitted to the Apostolic See (SC 40).

New orders for the Mass and for some sacraments were drawn up in India, Zaire, and the Philippines, among other locales. In 1975, the post-conciliar Consilium (commission for the implementation of the council) approved twelve points of cultural adaptation proposed by the bishops of India, but then told them that the period of experimentation was over. A similar attempt in Zaire begun in 1970 took until 1988 to win approval from Rome. In the Philippines, a culturally adapted order for the Mass, *Misa ng Bayang Filipino,* was submitted to Rome in 1976, but since it has not yet been approved, it is gradually disappearing.[36]

In the field of canon law, the experience has also been ambiguous. Pope John XXIII had initiated the revision of the Code of Canon Law in 1963, and the work began just before the close of the council. It was not until 1983, however, that the new revised code was promulgated. During the intervening period there was speculation that the universal code would be more in the manner of a basic constitution, with specifics left to the local or regional episcopal conferences — a move toward inculturation. That did not happen. The 1983 code, however, does authorize adaptation in some areas. In the formation of priests, for example, each nation is to have its own program for priestly formation (can. 242), and the students are to acquire a knowledge of the "general culture which is in accord with the needs of time and place" (can. 248). In the area of liturgy, the code assigns the task of preparing translations of the liturgical books to the local episcopal conferences, but these require the approval of the Apostolic See whose duty it is to "order the sacred liturgy of the universal Church" (can. 838). But the general reaction to the 1983 code, according to Shorter, is that it is not in harmony with non-Western cultures. He cites the instance of marriage, saying that the "Code ignores important African realities like the communitarian character of marriage and the parallelism of Church and customary rites."[37] His conclusion is that "Canon Law is possibly the most serious instance

---

36. Anscar J. Chupungco, O.S.B., *Liturgies of the Future: The Process and Methods of Inculturation* (New York: Paulist Press, 1989), 86–94.

37. Shorter, *Toward a Theology of Inculturation,* 69, citing Steven Bwana, "L'effet produit par le nouveau code en Afrique," Concilium 205 (1986): 133–40.

of cultural bias among the structures of communion in the Universal Church." An African synod of bishops in planned for the near future, and the possibility of an African code of canon law and liturgical rite is being considered.

Although we mentioned above Rome's ambivalence about national and regional episcopal conferences, the 1983 code gives them juridical standing as a "permanent institution" (can. 447, 449) These provide some intermediate structure between the individual bishop and the central Roman authorities. They can "exercise certain pastoral functions on behalf of the Christian faithful of their territory." But a working paper circulated by the Congregation for Bishops in January 1988 disputed their teaching authority and argued that national and regional episcopal conferences "express collegiality, but only in an analogical sense."[38] The overall tenor of the document was an effort to denigrate the place and function of episcopal conferences. There was strong negative reaction to the working paper from episcopal conferences around the world and nothing further has been heard about it as of this writing.

Recent experience in the area of doctrine has not tended to encourage inculturation in that area either. The very fact that the Vatican has drafted a Catechism for the Universal Church is evidence of this. While the introduction to the draft stated that it was intended to be used as a guide for the bishops, who could then adapt it to local conditions, it could have the effect of being a uniform standard against which all attempts at an inculturated theology would be judged. Again, the draft was widely criticized by theologians and bishops as a retrogression from Vatican II and recent scholarship. In this connection we can recall the reaction of the Vatican to liberation theology, the most developed of inculturated theologies, reviewed in the previous chapter.

In summary, the experience of inculturating the faith since Vatican II has reflected the ongoing tension between a conception of the church as a highly centralized and rather uniform organization and the conception of the church as a more diffuse communion of diverse local or particular churches, between the substance of the faith and the forms of its expression, between a desire for unity and a stifling uniformity. Such tensions pose both challenges and possibilities for the future.

---

38. Congregation for Bishops, "Theological and Juridical Status of Episcopal Conferences," Rome, January 12, 1988. For a theological response and evaluation of this document, see Avery Dulles, "The Mandate to Teach," *America* (March 19, 1988): 293–95, and "Episcopal Conferences: Their Teaching Authority," *America* (January 13, 1990): 7–9.

# CHALLENGES AND POSSIBILITIES

The possibility of a truly global, multicultural, polycentric church is upon us, but, as Rahner has said, it has only begun to be realized. The Christian community, both Protestant and Roman Catholic, has officially recognized this possibility and urged the process of inculturation in diverse regions. But the centralized Roman Catholic church has been reluctant to allow the experimentation necessary for this to occur. There is a legitimate concern for the unity of the church, but this is still confused with uniformity in liturgy, doctrine, and discipline. Cultural pluralism is a fact and should be viewed as a possibility to be realized, not a problem to be overcome.

How to encourage greater cultural pluralism and still maintain the unity of the church, both synchronically and diachronically, is *the* challenge. An awareness of how pluralistic the Christian tradition has always been would be a help. I think Robert Schreiter is correct when he points out the church's tradition can be seen "as a series of local theologies, closely wedded to and responding to different cultural conditions."[39] We can too easily forget that there were Alexandrian and Antiochene theologies, Anselmian and Thomistic theologies, as well as a plurality of liturgical rites, Syrian, Coptic, Roman, etc. Each of these strands has contributed to and enriched the tradition. We need not fear pluralism; we are its heirs.

If we accept such cultural pluralism in our past as well as in the present, how can we maintain continuity with the past and unity in the present? This can be achieved, I think, if we conceive of the relationship between past cultural expressions of Christianity and the diverse cultural expressions currently possible as one of "cultural dialogue" or, to use Dulles's terminology, "cultural reciprocity." Such a dialogical relationship "would recognize the originality of each culture, the inadequacy of each, and the consequent need for mutual criticism and openness."[40] Such a dialogue is based on analogy. As Roest Crollius says, "In order to encounter the other, one has to be someone and, at the same time, one should be able to find a point of meeting and understanding the other as other. Through this dialogue, one not only learns to understand the other, but acquires also a deeper understanding of oneself."[41] The meeting point of this dialogue is the Christian symbol system. We share this with our Christian forbears and across cultural boundaries. The fullness of meaning that can be borne by this symbol

---

39. Robert Schreiter, *Constructing Local Theologies*, 93.
40. Dulles, "The Emerging World Church," 8.
41. Ary A. Roest Crollius, S.J., "The Meaning of Culture in Theological Anthropology," in *Inculturation: Its Meaning and Urgency*, 64.

system cannot be known until it is refracted through a diversity of cultural expressions. Hence, it is not a question of preserving a substance of the faith that is uncontaminated by culture, but of discovering the many facets of that faith through a variety of cultural forms. Christianity has always been incarnated in a particular culture, but not isolated or secluded in any one. It remains communicable across cultures.

Such a process of intercultural dialogue is complicated today by the fact that wherever Christianity is found it has already been inculturated several times over. Thus, for example, the Catholicism that Mexican-Americans bring to the United States is a Catholicism inherited from pre-Reformation Spain adapted to and combined with the culture of pre-Columbian Mexico. Vietnamese Catholics bring a Catholicism filtered through French Catholicism of the eighteenth and nineteenth centuries, and so on. Hence, it is not the situation of Ricci bringing Western European Catholicism to the culture of China, but a situation in which all cultures are porous and have been so for some time. The United States is definitely a multicultural society, but this is also increasingly the case in other countries where there is massive migration of indigenous peoples from rural areas to large metropolitan centers such as Mexico City or Lima, Peru.

The process of inculturation today is further complicated by the impact of modern Western technology and communications. Not only is this true on the superficial level of Coca-Cola, blue jeans, and rock-and-roll music, but modernity involves a "profound transformation of individual and social consciousness."[42] Even though some cultures have consciously tried to insulate themselves, international radio and television have made this practically impossible. Quechua or Aymara-speaking *campesinos*, recently arrived in the *pueblos jovenes* (new villages) of Lima, can be found watching reruns of "Dallas" on television sets in hovels without running water. How to inculturate the faith for people who are undergoing such rapid cultural change would be a major challenge even for Matteo Ricci!

For dialogue among inculturated particular churches to take place, we need to develop new structures. We have already mentioned the Synod of Bishops as one possible vehicle for such dialogue. There have also been exchanges between national and regional episcopal conferences as, for example, between those of Central America and the United States, which enabled the churches of North America to understand and be in solidarity with the Christians in the strife-torn countries of Central America and influence the policies of the U.S. government in that area. In this instance also, hundreds of laypersons such as the Maryknoll Lay

---

42. Marcello de Carvalho Azevedo, S.J., *Inculturation and the Challenges of Modernity* (Rome: Pontifical Gregorian University, 1982), 33.

Missioners, Jesuit Volunteers, and others have carried on the dialogue at the grassroots level of the church. Such mutual exchange raises the consciousness of both churches and provokes deeper insight into the Christian faith they both share.

When engaging in such cross-cultural dialogue, we need to keep in mind that every culture has its limitations and that Christianity challenges each culture. Every form of inculturated Christianity is partial and limited and can be enriched by the critique from other forms. Roman Catholicism in the West could be greatly enhanced by dialogue with Eastern Orthodoxy. Catholicism as inculturated in the United States has something to contribute to a Euro-centered form of Catholicism. Through such dialogue and mutual criticism we may discover a Christianity far deeper and richer than that possessed by any particular church.

We need also to remind ourselves that, despite all the difficulties, and all the challenges to the emergence of a multi-cultural, global church, the church has historically demonstrated, as Dulles says, a "capacity, so astonishing to the ancient world, of bringing Jews and Gentiles, Greeks and barbarians, into a single people. In Christian antiquity the sense of worldwide fellowship was assiduously cultivated by adherence to a single rule of faith, concelebration of the liturgy, eucharistic communion, letters of peace, mutual hospitality, and charitable assistance."[43] We can do the same today. The challenge of maintaining unity while recognizing cultural pluralism is accompanied by the possibility of a deeper and fuller presence of Christ in world.

## RECOMMENDED READINGS

Schineller, Peter, S.J. *A Handbook on Inculturation*. New York: Paulist Press, 1990.
Schreiter, Robert. *Constructing Local Theologies*. Maryknoll, N.Y.: Orbis, 1985.
Shorter, Aylward. *Toward a Theology of Inculturation*. Maryknoll, N.Y.: Orbis, 1988.

---

43. Dulles, "The Emerging World Church," 9.

# Chapter 10

# The Church
# in the United States

We noted in the previous chapter that inculturation is an ongoing process that applies not only to non-Western cultures but to the First World as well. In this chapter, then, we will turn to the cultural context in the United States and, in particular, to the Roman Catholic community here. We mentioned some of the characteristics of our cultural context in chapter 1: the affluence and generally middle-class character of the United States, our individualism and emphasis on autonomous freedom, and the dominance of the "therapeutic" outlook on life. We also cited the immigrant character of the Roman Catholic community as well as the tension experienced between being Roman Catholic and being American. Now we will discuss more recent developments in the culture that have affected Christian communities in the United States and the post–Vatican II Roman Catholic community in particular, and the challenges and possibilities confronting us now and for the future.

## SOCIAL AND CULTURAL DEVELOPMENTS

We have seen that throughout its history the self-understanding of the Christian community has been affected by events outside the community as much as by developments within the community. This remains true for the contemporary church as well. The self-understanding of the Roman Catholic community in the United States has been shaped not only by the major event of the Second Vatican Council but also by developments in society as a whole. Catholic historian Jay Dolan is correct when he says, "In fact, it is fair to say that World War II had as much influence on the reshaping of contemporary American Catholicism as did the Second Vatican Council. Another way of putting this is to state that social and cultural forces were as important as theological developments in transforming American Catholicism."[1] He suggests that the changes in American society since World War II rank in influence with those experienced in the Industrial Revolution. Following World War II, there was a massive expansion of the economy, such that the "gross national product soared 250 percent between 1945 and 1960" and "per capita income was 35 percent higher than even the boom year of 1945."[2] This new affluence brought a new middle class, of which Catholics were a large part. Through the 1970s and 1980s, however, this economic development slowed considerably and the 1980s in particular witnessed a widening gap between the rich and the poor and the middle class lost ground.[3] The Reagan years were an economic disaster for all but the wealthy in the United States.

"There is a congruence between class and race," as Dolan also notes. The overwhelming majority of the poor are black or Hispanic. "Poorly housed, poorly educated, and struggling to survive they made up the underclass of American society."[4] Despite the move of many blacks into the middle class in the 1970s, there remains a seemingly permanent underclass in the urban centers composed of poor blacks and recent immigrants from Central and South America and Southeast Asia. The result has been a society divided along economic and racial lines, a two-tiered society. Dolan contends that a two-tiered church has also emerged. "One level is white, middle-class, and suburban; the other is brown and black, lower-class, and urban. Neither one talks very much to the other and the lower class church feels especially alienated from the rest of the American Catholic Church. Bridging this gap and effectively responding to the needs of lower-class, black and brown Catholics is perhaps the greatest challenge church leaders face as American Catholicism enters the closing years of the twentieth century."[5] The numbers support the significance of this claim: of the 57 million Roman Catholics, approximately 3 percent are black, or 2 million, and approximately 30 percent or 16 million are Hispanic. Another 3 percent identify themselves as "nonwhite." The result is that two-thirds of Roman Catholics are white, middle-class and probably suburban, and the others feel themselves "guests" in a "host" culture.

We have already mentioned another major social change, that is, the

---

1. Jay P. Dolan, R. Scott Appleby, Patricia Byrne, and Debra Campbell, *Transforming Parish Ministry: The Changing Roles of Catholic Clergy, Laity, and Women Religious* (New York: Crossroad, 1990), 308.

2. William H. Chafe, *The Unfinished Journey: America since World War II* (New York: Oxford University Press, 1986), viii, cited in Dolan, ibid., 308–9.

3. *New York Times*, January 11, 1991, reported that "for the most affluent fifth of all households, wealth rose 14 percent from 1984 to 1988, after adjusting for inflation."

4. Dolan, *Transforming Parish Ministry*, 309.

5. Ibid., 311.

feminist movement in the United States. Since the 1960s there has been
an organized movement to overcome the discrimination against women
in all areas of public life, business, politics, government, and the pro-
fessions. Great advances have been made in these areas and there have
been major attitudinal shifts concerning the roles of both women and
men in family life. Many more women have careers outside the home,
and men are sharing more of the burdens of family rearing and domestic
chores. This movement has impacted on the renewal of women's religious congregations in the Roman Catholic church. "As they abandoned
the cloister women religious took on the independent spirit of their sisters in the women's movement and sought a more just and equitable
place in the church."[6] As mentioned in chapter 7, this has led to the
question of women's ordination to the presbyterate, but also to placing
women in other positions of responsibility and decision making in the
church.

In addition to these economic, racial, and gender factors, another
major development in society in the United States has been the dramatic
rise in the overall educational level, especially in higher education. In
1950, there were 2.6 million persons enrolled in higher education; in
1960, 3.6 million; in 1970, 8.6 million; and almost 12.4 million in 1982.[7]
Among mainline religions, there was only a small portion of educated
members in the 1950s, but by the 1980s a third or more were college
educated. The G.I. Bill was a major factor in this postwar expansion of
higher education, and Roman Catholics were among those who bene-
fited most. The number of Catholics with a college education has more
than doubled in the last twenty years. As of 1984, 17 percent were college graduates and another 24 percent had some college education (a
total of 41 percent).[8]

This rapid rise in the level of education has had a number of consequences for the mainline Christian communities and for Roman Catholics in particular. First, as Robert Wuthnow points out, education seems
to be a "fundamental basis of attitudinal divergence in American culture." "The better educated were more likely in their own minds to
identify themselves as religious liberals. And their views on church matters, social and moral questions, and political issues all tended to set
them off from religious conservatives. Those without college educa-
tions, on the other hand, were much more likely to identify themselves

---

6. Ibid., 312.

7. Robert Wuthnow, *The Restructuring of American Religion* (Princeton, N.J.: Princeton University Press, 1988), 155, and Wade Clark Roof and William McKinney, *American
Mainline Religion: Its Changing Shape and Future* (New Brunswick, N.J.: Rutgers University Press, 1987), 65.

8. George Gallup, Jr., and Jim Castelli, *The American Catholic People: Their Beliefs,
Practices, and Values* (Garden City, N.Y.: Doubleday & Co., 1987), 5.

as religious conservatives, to hold more traditional religious views, and to espouse a wide range of social and political attitudes that reflected a conservative orientation."[9] This division between religious liberals and religious conservatives he believes to be "one of the powerful symbolic barriers around which American religion has become restructured." There are other bases for the division between liberals and conservatives within the Roman Catholic tradition, theology for example, but education is certainly one of them.

A second consequence of the rising educational level has been a greater freedom to criticize and disagree with ecclesiastical authorities, a greater sense of individual freedom to choose — what Wade Clark Roof and William McKinney have termed "the new voluntarism." Speaking specifically of Catholics they say, "Members of this community are making far greater choices of belief and belonging; in birth control, abortion, and sexual styles, more and more young Catholics regard these matters as private and thus beyond the realm of church authority. . . . So embedded in young Catholics today are the values of personal autonomy in forming one's conscience that formally stated doctrinal and moral imperatives appear to have little or no impact upon many of them."[10] This is the attitude that Andrew Greeley some years ago characterized as "the communal Catholic." Such Catholics are "loyal to the Catholic collectivity and at least sympathetic toward its heritage. At the same time, they refuse to take seriously the teaching authority of the leadership of the institutional church. Such communal Catholics are Catholic because they see nothing else in American society they want to be, out of loyalty to their past, and they are curious as to what the Catholic tradition might have that is special and unique in the contemporary world."[11]

A third consequence for Roman Catholics of the educational revolution was its impact on priests and religious women. Dolan says, "I would argue that education was the single most important catalyst for change among sisters and priests for the simple reason that it opened up new horizons for them. . . . The code word was 'professionalization,' but the reality was educational advancement."[12] Thousands of nuns were encouraged for the first time to get advanced degrees in an area of specialization, and a similar number of priests participated in clergy renewal programs to update themselves in Scripture and catechetics.

All of these social and cultural factors — economic, class, race, gender, and education — have contributed to the rise of "special purpose

---

9. Wuthnow, *The Restructuring of American Religion*, 168.

10. Roof and McKinney, *American Mainline Religion*, 55–56.

11. Andrew M. Greeley, *The American Catholic: A Social Portrait* (New York: Basic Books, 1977), 272.

12. Dolan, *Transforming Parish Ministry*, 314.

groups" and the decline of denominationalism. This is the thesis of Robert Wuthnow's work to which we have referred previously. By special purpose groups he means such organizations as the Moral Majority, Religious Roundtable, the National Christian Action Coalition, the Fellowship of Christian Athletes, Bread for the World, Marriage Encounter, Pax Christi, and so on. These are groups that cut across denominational lines and mobilize resources for specific objectives. They do not usually develop into denominations themselves. There are about eight hundred nationally incorporated special purpose groups, about three hundred founded since 1960.[13] Wuthnow argues that "rather than religion's weight being felt through the pressure of denominations, it may be exercised through the more focused efforts of the hundreds of special purpose groups now in operation."[14] Many parishes sponsor such groups as a form of service to their various constituents, but membership in such a group does not necessarily replace participation in the parish. Frequently, however, participants in a special purpose group discover that they have more in common with the other members of the group than with their fellow parishioners. Wuthnow argues that "perhaps more than anything else, rising levels of education have worked as a social solvent. As the population has become better educated, denominational barriers have ceased to function as hermetic categories of religious identification."[15]

These social and cultural factors — increased economic affluence, division along racial, ethnic, and gender lines, rising educational level, and decreasing denominational identity — all have impacted on all the religious communities in the United States. Let us turn now to their implications for the Roman Catholic community.

## CATHOLICISM AND CULTURE IN THE UNITED STATES

First, the Roman Catholic community definitely moved into the mainstream of social and cultural life in the United States. As Roof and McKinney summarize: "After World War II Catholics made such spectacular gains in education, occupational status, and income that by the 1970s their overall status levels were roughly equal to those of Protestants. With upward mobility and rapid assimilation, Catholics moved into the mainstream socially, culturally, and religiously. They have come to resemble other Americans in many respects: in social attitudes, child-

---

13. Ibid., chap. 6.
14. Ibid., 121.
15. Ibid., 97.

rearing values, political party affiliation, and religious patterns. Young Catholics, especially now, attend worship services, join churches, and drop out of churches much the same as Protestants."[16] It has become a middle-class, or to use Johannes Metz's term, a "bourgeois" church.

Second, although this is true for the majority (67 percent) of Roman Catholics, a sizable minority of blacks and especially Hispanics have not been integrated and do not feel a part of this community. Despite three *Encuentros* (encounters, meetings), in 1972, 1977, and 1986, and the bishops' pastoral on Hispanic ministry, *The Hispanic Presence: Challenge and Commitment,* in 1983, "there continues to be," as Allan Deck says, "a chasm between what is being preached and proposed and what is really happening."[17] Thus, Roman Catholicism has also become a two-tiered church.

Third, in addition to this division along racial and ethnic lines, the feminist movement has contributed to the alienation of many women and led to further division over the issues of justice for women within the church. We have already mentioned the implications of this for ministry in chapter 7.

Fourth, the dramatic rise in the level of education, combined with Vatican II's renewed emphasis on the laity, has led to greater expectations of participation in the life and governance of the church on the part of laypersons, as well as greater lay leadership. It has also contributed to the increasing independence from church authority in matters of family and sexual morality.

Fifth, the Roman Catholic community too is divided between religious conservatives and religious liberals. There was a definite polarization after Vatican II. The religious conservatives, represented by the *Wanderer,* the *National Catholic Register, Opus Dei,* and the Right to Life movement have mercilessly attacked bishops and theologians they perceive to be forsaking the Catholic tradition and adapting too much to the modern world. The religious liberals or progressives, represented by the *National Catholic Reporter* and many bishops and theologians, perceive the conservatives as trying to reverse Vatican II and return to a preconciliar ghetto mentality and an ahistorical approach to theology.

These various divisions are experienced on all levels of the Catholic community, within the national bishops' conference, within dioceses, parishes, universities, and seminaries. It is important to recall, however, that such diverse responses to the culture have characterized the community from the beginning. Jay Dolan observes:

---

16. Roof and McKinney, *American Mainline Religion,* 15–16.
17. Allan Figueroa Deck, S.J., *The Second Wave: Hispanic Ministry and the Evangelization of Cultures* (New York: Paulist Press, 1989), 3–4.

> Even before masses of immigrants started coming to the United
> States, Roman Catholicism was experiencing a fundamental con-
> flict in its relationship to American society. Some Catholics wanted
> a church that would be thoroughly American. Rooted in Ameri-
> can soil, it would be independent of any foreign interference; its
> clergy would be in tune with the "American way of life"; church
> and state would be separate and religious toleration would be
> a virtue, not a vice; and English, not Latin, would be the lan-
> guage of church prayer. . . . Other Catholics, however, . . . wanted to
> transplant a European model of Roman Catholicism to the United
> States.[18]

The first group were represented by John Carroll, John England, John
Ireland, Orestes Brownson, Isaac Hecker, and John Courtney Murray.
The latter were at first led by French and German-born clergy, and
later by Michael A. Corrigan, archbishop of New York, and Bernard J.
McQuaid, bishop of Rochester.

David O'Brien has discerned a similar division in the history of the
American Catholic Church. The first he terms "republican," which, at
its best, "recognized the tension between religious and civic allegiances
and attempted to mediate between them, asking what America had to
teach the church and what the church could offer to America."[19] The
second he calls the "immigrant tradition," which, "assisted by the ul-
tramontane movement in Europe, gave church needs and interests the
priority. . . . In the United States the threats posed by external hostility
and internal diversity, in a setting in which money and personnel were
always inadequate, reinforced the drift toward a more self-interested
form of public presence."[20] In addition to these two, which correspond
closely to Dolan's two traditions, O'Brien argues that a third strand,
"evangelical" in style, has emerged in the twentieth century. This group,
epitomized by the Catholic Worker movement founded by Dorothy Day
and Peter Maurin in 1933, "sought a reintegration, personal, communal, and public, by means of a complete commitment to the gospel,
expressed in profound religious faith, an interiorization of the spiritual
life, and a dedication to serving the poor and healing the wounds be-
setting society."[21] Though marginalized and small in number, O'Brien
believes that "evangelical Catholicism would begin to spread in the
wake of Vatican II, the race crisis, the war in Vietnam, and the deepening
specter of nuclear annihilation."

---

18. Jay P. Dolan, *The American Catholic Experience* (New York: Doubleday & Co.,
1985), 294.
19. David O'Brien, *Public Catholicism* (New York: Macmillan, 1989), 5.
20. Ibid., 6.
21. Ibid., 7.

Whether or not one accepts Dolan's or O'Brien's analysis and terminology, it is clear that historically the Roman Catholic community has
responded to American culture in diverse, even conflicting, ways. There
have always been those who took a basically positive view of the American experience and tried to appropriate it within the Catholic tradition,
and those who have emphasized the negative aspects of that experience,
saw it as a threat to Catholicism, and tried to insulate the faithful from it.

In the two recent pastoral letters of the U.S. bishops, on nuclear
weapons and peace in 1983, and on the economy in 1986, we can see
evidence of two styles, the evangelical and the republican, since both letters appeal to Gospel values and to the language of natural law, human
dignity, and human rights, the former directed to Christians, and the
latter to the general public. By distinguishing but combining these two
styles, O'Brien feels that the bishops have helped to clarify the relationship of the Catholic community to American public life.[22] The reaction
of many Roman Catholics to these letters, however, suggests that the
longstanding diversity of traditions in relating to culture in the United
States perdures.

The very fact that these two pastoral letters were critical of the U.S.
nuclear weapons policy and of the present economic arrangements suggests that Catholicism no longer feels the need to demonstrate its loyal
Americanism. It is no longer a guest in the host culture of Protestantism.
Some observers have argued that the time has come for a more positive contribution from the Catholic tradition to American public life.
William Lee Miller and Richard John Neuhaus, from quite different perspectives, have suggested that now is the "Catholic moment," when the
rich Catholic tradition of the common good and of reasoned argument
in public life could contribute to a renewal of a more communitarian
public philosophy and a critique of excessive individualism.[23]

When we ask, on the other hand, what the American experience
can contribute to Catholicism, we think immediately of John Courtney
Murray's insightful appropriation of the separation of church and state,
religious pluralism, and tolerance for the Decree on Religious Liberty of
Vatican II. The American experience was the basis for this major shift in
the self-understanding of the Roman Catholic community. The American
style of open and public discussion used by the bishops in the preparation of their recent pastoral letters has enhanced their authority in the

---

22. Ibid., 249–50.
23. William Lee Miller, *The First Liberty: Religion and the American Republic* (New
York: Knopf, 1986); Richard John Neuhaus, *The Catholic Moment: The Paradox of the
Church in the Postmodern World* (San Francisco: Harper & Row, 1987); and the critical
review of both books in David Hollenbach, "Religion, Morality, and Politics," *Theological
Studies* 49, no. 1 (March 1988): 74–80.

eyes of most Catholics and the public in general, although it has not been equally appreciated in Rome.

In summary, then, we can see that social and cultural factors in the United States have had a great impact on Roman Catholicism here. Although retaining some of its immigrant character and continuing to receive a second wave of immigrants, the Catholic community has become mainstream American. It is a large, vigorous, and vital church that is beginning to have a greater impact on American public life. This is in keeping with the various stages of inculturation — translation, assimilation, and transformation — we saw in the previous chapter. Whether or not Roman Catholicism, or even a more unified ecumenical Christian community through special purpose groups, can actually *transform* American culture remains to be seen.

## U.S. CATHOLICISM AND THE GLOBAL CHURCH

Although the Roman Catholic community in the United States has always maintained contact with the universal church, especially with Rome and with the European countries from which so many immigrants came, two factors have occasioned an increasing sense of responsibility for the church beyond our national boundaries. The sheer fact that the United States is a global superpower means that the American Catholic community automatically has influence as well as responsibility. Within the country, Roman Catholics are the largest single denomination and hence can exercise considerable political leverage. Within the Roman Catholic church, the American church, because of its size and wealth, can also carry considerable weight.

Second, Vatican II in speaking of the collegiality of bishops reminded them that they are "obliged by Christ's decree and command to be solicitous for the whole Church" (LG 23). Such solicitude has, perhaps, been most clearly exercised with regard to Central and South America. The response of the church in the United States to the request of Pope John XXIII in 1961 to send one-tenth of the U.S. clergy to help alleviate the severe shortage of priests in Latin America was overwhelming. Both diocesan and religious priests and religious men and women poured across the border. Ivan Illich set up a training center for them in Cuernavaca, Mexico. Many immersed themselves in working with the poorest and most oppressed and discovered in the process that part of the problem was the policy and practice of the U.S. government itself and of the multinational corporations such as United Fruit Company and W. R. Grace & Co., owned and operated by Americans. Thus, a network of information and contacts that transcended cultures and national boundaries developed and provided the North American religious leaders with information and perspectives at variance with the official line of the State Department on a variety of issues. The slaying of four American religious women in 1980 and of six Jesuit educators and their housekeeper and her daughter in 1989 further catalyzed the Catholic community in the United States to bring pressure to bear on the government about its policy in Central America, El Salvador especially. In addition, there have been regular meetings between representatives of the episcopal conferences of Central America and the United States.

Recent relations between the American Roman Catholic community and the Vatican have not always been characterized by "solicitude." The National Conference of Catholic Bishops, encouraged by Vatican II, has been much more proactive in recent years. Raising their voice in significant pastoral letters, they have had an impact on sister churches in other regions. We have mentioned in the previous chapter the reaction this has provoked from Rome. The Vatican has questioned the authority of episcopal conferences to teach and suggested that this was not an authentic form of episcopal collegiality.[24]

Rome has also instigated investigations of individual bishops, such as Bishop Walter Sullivan in Richmond and Archbishop Raymond Hunthausen in Seattle, reprimanding and humiliating them.[25] The Vatican ordered investigations of Catholic seminaries and religious life in the United States during the 1980s. Both investigations were co-opted by the U.S. bishops and conducted according to American procedural standards. The findings in both investigations were quite positive, much to Rome's dismay.

The Vatican has ordered ordinaries to withdraw the *imprimatur* from books without bringing any clear charges against the authors and has denied the eminent moral theologian Charles Curran the right to teach as a Catholic theologian, again without any fair procedure. These and other activities on the part of Vatican officials caused such a strain in relations that the American hierarchy requested a special meeting with the pope and curial officials, which was eventually held March 8 to 11, 1989. All the U.S. archbishops met for several days with the pope and curial officers and tried to explain American social and cultural differences. One respected prelate concluded afterward that Rome still does not understand nor respect the American church intellectually or culturally. Rome does not understand or appreciate the open, free, participative style of discussion and decision making. They felt that the open hearings that the bishops conducted in preparing their recent pastoral letters

---

24. "Theological and Juridical Status of Episcopal Conferences," Congregation for Bishops, Rome, January 12, 1988.

25. See the statement of the Catholic Theological Society of America, "Do Not Extinguish the Spirit," 1990, which includes documentation.

would diminish episcopal authority, whereas Americans generally felt that the authority was enhanced by having listened to all sides.

Despite these strained relations, the American Catholic church remains strongly loyal to Rome and is in no danger of going its own way, much less of schism. But, as we saw in the previous chapter, if there is to be a truly global church, much more allowance must be made for local and regional diversity. "Cultural reciprocity" will allow the American Catholic community to learn from other churches, but also to contribute from its own cultural experience.

## CHALLENGES AND POSSIBILITIES

All of the lines of division mentioned above offer challenges to the American Catholic community. But perhaps the most difficult challenge on the local level, the level of the parish, is that of racial and ethnic divisions. Many parishes are not just "two-tiered," but are multicultural, including Anglos, Hispanics, Vietnamese, Filipinos, blacks, and others within the same parish. Some parishes have liturgies in three or four languages on a Sunday. This complex situation has led some to call for a return to something like the national or "personal parish" as a pastoral strategy to serve these groups, especially the large number of Hispanics. Allan Deck has argued that "the Hispanic community was to some extent deprived of the strong local institutional base that national parishes provided for generations of Catholic ethnics."[26] They have lacked "the security and clarity that comes from having one's own turf," he says. It may be that each immigrant group needs this as a stage in the process of assimilation to the wider culture. The so-called leakage of Hispanic Catholics to Protestant fundamentalist groups suggests that the present parish set-up is not satisfying their needs. Yet the deliberate attempt to foster base communities among Hispanic Catholics has not met with much success either.[27]

If the presence of large numbers of recent immigrants, especially the second wave of Hispanics, is a challenge to the American Catholic community, it also offers new possibilities. As the Pastoral Letter on Hispanic Ministry says, "Hispanics in our midst are an as yet untapped resource as a cultural bridge between North and South in the Americas . . . which will necessarily entail an ever greater understanding of and linkage with Latin American society and Church."[28] Such a linkage could well have an impact not only on the church, but also on how the United States deals

26. Deck, *The Second Wave*, 59, and "Proselytism and Hispanic Catholics: How Long Can We Cry Wolf?" *America* (December 10, 1988):485–90.

27. Deck, *The Second Wave*, 70–73.

28. *The Hispanic Presence: Challenge and Commitment*, NCCB, 1983, 25. See also,

with its southern neighbors. Further, the church in the United States could be enriched by the spirituality and strong sense of the transcendent in Hispanic Catholicism. It could very well be a counterbalance to the secularizing tendencies we mentioned in chapter 1.

The challenge posed by multicultural parishes and the arguable need for new immigrants to have some turf of their own raises the larger question of how successful the traditional territorial parish can be as a form of Christian community in a pluralistic, highly mobile, individualistic, and therapeutic society. Can a way of being church that originated in an agrarian, village, and feudal social context remain viable today in the United States?

The recent study of parishes sponsored by the University of Notre Dame concluded that "despite some problem areas, the post–Vatican II Catholic parish in the United States is basically healthy. It plays a central role in the lives of its parishioners and continues to change to accommodate a changing people and a changing church."[29] But the study passed over the problem areas rather lightly. It only mentioned in passing the growing shortage of priests that we discussed in chapter 7. It dealt only with "core Catholics," defined as "non-Hispanic Catholics who were registered members of parishes,"[30] thereby eliminating all Hispanics and the estimated fifteen million Catholics not registered in parishes. Even within this selected sample a large minority, "possibly 40 percent," do not feel that the parish is a real community for them, and 46 percent said they seldom speak with the pastor.[31] The study also mentions the fragmentation of the parish along interest and age lines, reporting that the two activities that bring people together are Mass and bingo.[32] Of course, the experience of parish life varies considerably from one parish to another, but it would seem that there are enough anomalies in the present structure to call it into question. We need to recognize that there have always been various forms of ecclesial life, various ways to be "church," and to use our imaginations to develop the forms most suitable to the contemporary context in the United States.[33]

A second challenge to the American Catholic community arises from its move into the mainstream and middle class, and that is its ability to be critical of the negativities in the American experience: consumerism, materialism, racism, sexism, and individualism. Can a church that has

---

Joseph Gremillion and Jim Castelli, *The Emerging Parish: The Notre Dame Study of Catholic Life Since Vatican II* (San Francisco, Harper & Row, 1987), 97.

29. Gremillion and Castelli, *The Emerging Parish*, 200.

30. Ibid., 30.

31. Ibid., 60.

32. Ibid., 70.

33. See T. Howland Sanks, S.J., "Forms of Ecclesiality: The Analogical Church," *Theological Studies* 49, no. 4 (December 1988): 695–708.

been absorbed into American society still raise a prophetic voice challenging these "isms"? Some have seen the bishops' pastorals on peace and the economy as a move in this direction, and O'Brien believes that the "evangelical" stream of Catholicism has grown in response to them. But others have argued that the bishops' critique of U.S. nuclear policy and of the economy was muted by the middle-class character of the church as well as by the articulate voices of the right.

On the other hand, George Gallup and Jim Castelli found that on the economy, war and peace, and social issues, American Catholics generally are more liberal than has been supposed. They conclude that although "Catholics are 'conservative' on some key social issues: abortion, the death penalty, school prayer, pornography, busing, and the legalization of marijuana... Catholics clearly come down on the 'liberal' side of other key social issues: most notably women's rights, gun control, civil rights for minorities and homosexuals, and the decriminalization of possession of small quantities of marijuana."[34] Thus, the Catholic people, and not only the bishops, have the potential for exercising a prophetic voice in American society. Such a voice will remain weak, however, unless the Catholic community can overcome the various divisions mentioned above.

Can the church appropriate the best of American social and cultural experience and bring it to bear on the universal church? This is a third challenge. We have already mentioned the contribution of the American experience of separation of church and state, religious pluralism, and tolerance to the Decree on Religious Liberty of Vatican II. Monika Hellwig has suggested a few other aspects of American experience that could be gifts to the worldwide church. She mentions "the optimistic spirit of enterprise in American culture," which "explores and develops the resources of the world and of the universe," and which could act to "correct a certain rather melancholy and passive sense of what it means to be Christian."[35] "A second rather significant aspect of American culture which is or can be a gift to the church," she says, "is a legal system derived from British common law," especially its procedural principles that are devised to guarantee justice for all. She feels that the present system within the Roman Catholic church is "patently less just and less consonant with the goal of the reign of God" and could profit from the American experience.[36] Hellwig also suggests that the American tradition of freedom of conscience, freedom of speech and assembly, freedom of the press, and academic freedom could also be

---

34. Gallup and Castelli, *The American Catholic People*, 115.

35. Monika Hellwig, "American Culture: Reciprocity with Catholic Vision, Values and Community," in Cassian Yuhaus, C.P., ed., *The Catholic Church and American Culture: Reciprocity and Challenge* (New York: Paulist Press, 1990), 64–66.

36. Ibid., 66–68.

gifts to the global church. While Americans can tend to be self-righteous and self-congratulatory, we should, with due modesty and humility, not undervalue the possible contributions from our social and cultural experience to the universal church.

Finally, can there be an American contribution specifically to ecclesiology, to the theological self-understanding of the Christian or Catholic community? Although the division between religious conservatives and religious liberals entails diverse ecclesiologies, particularly concerning the activity of the church in the world, the American experience inclines most U.S. Catholics to have an "elective affinity" with certain ecclesiological traditions, especially concerning its internal organization. The experience of freedom of speech, assembly, and the press, mentioned above, is most compatible with the charismatic element of the church, the freedom of the Spirit to "breathe where it wills."

The democratic experience of participation in governing the community resonates with the conciliar or synodal tradition more than with the monarchical strand in ecclesiology. The experience of checks and balances and the separation of powers makes Americans suspicious of any concentration of power in one person or one body. The experience of religious pluralism and toleration incline Americans toward ecumenism and to greater pluralism and diversity of theologies and practices within the Catholic community itself. The multicultural experience reinforces this tolerance and encourages cultural reciprocity.

These aspects of American social and cultural experience do not constitute a distinctively American ecclesiology, but do provide the basis for an affinity with certain strands in the tradition. The way the tradition has been appropriated, however, has definitely been shaped by American culture. American Catholicism is an inculturated Catholicism and, as such, should not be presumed to be the standard for the rest of the church. That would be another form of cultural imperialism.

In summary, then, we have seen that recent social and cultural developments in the United States — increased economic affluence, a growing gap between rich and poor, division along ethnic and racial lines, the feminist movement, a dramatic rise in educational level — all have contributed to the development of a two-tiered church divided also between religious conservatives and religious liberals, with a decrease in denominational identity and a growth of special purpose groups. All of these factors have implications for the Roman Catholic community in the United States. The American Catholic community has moved into the mainstream and the middle class and is no longer a guest in a host culture. It has assumed greater importance in the universal church, has learned from it, and has something to contribute. It may yet be a prophetic force in the transformation of American society, but that remains to be seen.

## RECOMMENDED READINGS

Dolan, Jay P. *The American Catholic Experience*. New York: Doubleday & Co., 1985.

Dolan, Jay P., R. Scott Appleby, Patricia Byrne, and Debra Campbell. *Transforming Parish Ministry: The Changing Roles of Catholic Clergy, Laity, and Women Religious*. New York: Crossroad, 1990.

O'Brien, David. *Public Catholicism*. New York: Macmillan, 1989.

Roof, Wade Clark, and William McKinney. *American Mainline Religion: Its Changing Shape and Future*. New Brunswick, N.J.: Rutgers University Press, 1987.

Chapter 11

# The Church, the Churches, and the World Religions

If there is one picture that has captured the human imagination in the late twentieth century it is the photograph of the earth from outer space: that blue-green orb surrounded by whispy white clouds floating in the deep dark blue of space. Whether or not the human race is alone in the universe, that photo makes it strikingly clear that we are inescapably together on spaceship earth. The sense of human solidarity, of global awareness, of a shared destiny is epitomized in that photograph.

This increased consciousness of human solidarity and of the unity of the race has been spurred by the rapidity of communications — we have almost instantaneous knowledge of events anyplace around the globe — and the ease and frequency of travel. No one is isolated in her or his own culture, nor insulated from contact with persons of different cultures, races, or religious traditions. The threats to our shared destiny from the possibility of nuclear annihilation and from ecological disaster make this quest for global unity not just a leisurely academic exercise but one of urgent action.

For Christians, this new sense of and search for greater global unity raises the question of divisions within the Christian community as well as divisions between Christians and other great religious traditions. To what extent are the various religious traditions responsible for some of the conflicts around the world? Think of Hindus and Sikhs in India, of Muslims and Jews in the Middle East, of Protestants and Catholics in Northern Ireland, of Shi'ite Muslims in Iran and neighboring countries. If religions are not the causes of these various conflicts, they at least serve as legitimations and additional irritations between the warring factions. Do not Christians, and all religious people, have the obligation to try to overcome these obstacles to peace and human solidarity?

The unity of the Christian community itself has been a hallmark and a concern from the very beginning of the church. From the New Testament (cf.1 Cor. 11:18–19; Gal. 1:6–9; 1 John 2:18–19), through the patristic period, and throughout its history, as we have seen, there have been challenges to its unity that have forced the church to develop various criteria of unity. Unity has been manifested in different ways at different periods in the life of the Christian community: unity of faith, or the *regula fidei*, unity with the local bishop, communion with other churches, especially Rome, unity of the apostolic tradition, and, later, unity in practices, structures, and law. The issue has been raised again in our time in a changing context and with new urgency, particularly for Roman Catholics following the ecumenical openness of Vatican II.

In this chapter, then, we will discuss recent developments in the movement toward Christian unity (ecumenism) and in the relationships with other world religions (interreligious dialogue) insofar as these impact on the self-understanding of the Christian community. Our purpose is not to trace the history of these developments, although we will mention these briefly, but to delineate the challenges and possibilities that the present context poses.


# ECUMENISM BEFORE VATICAN II

Before discussing the new impetus given the ecumenical movement by Vatican II, we should remember that the leadership in the ecumenical movement in the twentieth century came primarily from Protestants. The missionary experience of the nineteenth century and developments in biblical studies both made the divisions originating centuries earlier in the European context somewhat anachronistic. Many date the birth of the modern ecumenical movement from the World Missionary Conference held in Edinburgh in 1910, where a Chinese delegate proclaimed, "You have sent us missionaries who gave us the knowledge of Jesus Christ, and for this we are profoundly grateful to you. But you have also brought us your divisions. . . . Deliver us from all the 'isms' which you attach to the preaching of the Gospel among us."[1] The credibility of the Christian witness outside of Europe was clearly undermined by perpetuating and exporting these historical divisions. The growth of the historical-critical methods of biblical scholarship fostered collaboration across denominational lines and led scholars to look beyond doctrinal divisions to their roots in Scripture.

---

1. Jacques Desseaux, *Twenty Centuries of Ecumenism*, trans. Matthew J. O'Connell (New York: Paulist Press, 1983), 46.

In an attempt to deal with these doctrinal divisions, the first World Conference on Faith and Order was held in 1927 in Lausanne, Switzerland. Two years earlier there had been the first Universal Conference on Life and Work in Stockholm, 1925, to relate the Christian faith to social and political issues. At a meeting in Utrecht in 1938, it was proposed that these two movements unite to form the World Council of Churches. This union was delayed by World War II, but was finally inaugurated at Amsterdam in 1948, and there have been regular assemblies since then, most recently in Canberra in 1991.[2]

There were also ecumenical stirrings among the Orthodox and Roman Catholics in the 1920s. The Orthodox patriarch of Constantinople, Joachim III, sent an encyclical letter, January 2, 1920, to all the churches of the world urging exchanges and contacts on all levels. The Catholics and Anglicans held the famous Malines Conversations, sponsored by Cardinal Désiré Mercier from 1921 to 1926, with the intent of eliminating prejudices and misunderstandings on both sides. The Orthodox were represented at the first Assembly of the World Council of Churches in 1948, but entered into full participation only in 1960. Although some Roman Catholics were invited to that assembly as observers, the Vatican forbade any Catholics to attend. It was not until the Second Vatican Council that the Roman Catholic Church as an organization entered into the ecumenical movement.

## DOCUMENTS OF VATICAN II

The Second Vatican Council had an ecumenical thrust from its inception, since John XXIII had made the pursuit of Christian unity one of his goals in summoning the council. We have already seen in chapter 6 the monumental shift from the simple identification of the true church of Christ with the Roman Catholic church found in *Mystici Corporis* to the language of "subsists in" found in *Lumen Gentium* 8. The council members were sensitive to this ecumenical concern, and after several documents dealing with church unity were submitted, they decided in December 1962 that there should be one Decree on Ecumenism to be drafted by the Secretariat for Christian Unity. This was then supplemented by a separate Decree on Eastern Catholic Churches

2. For a standard history of the ecumenical movement see *A History of the Ecumenical Movement, 1517–1948*, vol. 1, ed. Ruth Rouse and Stephen Charles Neill (Philadelphia: Westminster, 1967); *The Ecumenical Advance: A History of the Ecumenical Movement, 1948–1968*, vol. 2 (Philadelphia: Westminster, 1970); and W. A. Visser't Hooft, *The Genesis and Formation of the World Council of Churches* (Geneva: World Council of Churches, 1982).

and a Declaration on the Relationship of the Church to Non-Christian Religions.[3] We will deal with each document briefly.

The Decree on Ecumenism, *Unitatis Redintegratio,* begins with some "Catholic Principles on Ecumenism" in which the council acknowledges blame for previous separations on both sides. It accepts the "separated brethren . . . with respect and affection," and says that they "have a right to be honored by the title of Christian, and are properly regarded as brothers in the Lord by the sons of the Catholic Church" (UR 3). The council further recognized that "very many, of the most significant elements or endowments which together go to build up and give life to the Church herself can exist outside the visible boundaries of the Catholic Church: the written word of God; the life of grace; faith, hope, and charity, along with other interior gifts of the Holy Spirit and visible elements" (UR 3). Such elements and actions are "capable of providing access to the community of salvation," but "it is through Christ's Catholic Church alone, which is the all-embracing means of salvation, that the fullness of the means of salvation can be obtained." Thus, the council admitted that there could be salvation outside the Catholic church, even though it alone has the *fullness* of the means of salvation.

The document urged "all the Catholic faithful to recognize the signs of the times and to participate skillfully in the work of ecumenism." This should include the elimination of "words, judgments, and actions" that make mutual relations difficult, "dialogue between competent experts from different Churches and Communities," cooperation in projects for the common good, and, finally, renewal and reform within the respective churches (UR 4). This last task is the primary duty of Catholics. The council urged unity in essentials but at the same time allowed "a proper freedom in the various forms of spiritual life and discipline, in the variety of liturgical rites, and even in the theological elaborations of revealed truth" (UR 4).

In the second chapter, "The Practice of Ecumenism," the council called for "that continual reformation of which she [the church] always has need, insofar as she is an institution of men here on earth," admitting that there have been "deficiencies in conduct, in Church discipline, or even in the formulation of doctrine (which must be carefully distinguished from the deposit itself of faith) . . . " (UR 5). Rectifying such deficiencies requires a "change of heart." In this spirit, the council members "beg pardon of God and of our separated brethren" for past

---

3. The Decree on the Missionary Activity of the Church (*Ad Gentes*) touches in passing on the cooperation between various denominations and on interreligious dialogue, but it does so only tangentially and is not directly pertinent to our discussion here. The Declaration on Religious Freedom (*Dignitatis Humanae*), although not dealing explicitly with ecumenism, had a reassuring effect on many Protestants because of its implications for the nature of the church.

sins against unity. They encouraged common prayer services for unity, but were cautious about common worship (UR 8). Further, they urged study and dialogue to understand the outlook of other churches and recommended that theological education, especially for future priests and bishops, be from an ecumenical perspective (UR 9) The council reminded Catholic theologians that, when comparing doctrines, "they should remember that in Catholic teaching there exists an order or 'hierarchy' of truths, since they vary in their relationship to the foundation of the Christian faith" (UR 11). This notion of a "hierarchy of truths" has been of immense significance in the dialogues that followed the council.

In chapter 3 the document discusses the two main divisions that have occurred in the past, with the East and with Protestants. It refers to "family ties" with the sister churches of the East and recognizes that they have a heritage from which the whole church can draw. This diversity of traditions is recognized with approval, saying, "From the earliest times, moreover, the Eastern Church followed their own disciplines, sanctioned by the holy Fathers, by synods, even ecumenical Councils. Far from being an obstacle to the Church's unity, such diversity of customs and observances only adds to her comeliness, and contributes greatly to carrying out her mission..." (UR 16). This legitimate variety applies also to "differences in theological expressions of doctrine" and allows that these could "be considered as complementary rather than conflicting." Finally, "After taking all these factors into consideration, this sacred Synod confirms what previous Councils and Roman Pontiffs have proclaimed: in order to restore communion and unity or preserve them, one must 'impose no burden beyond what is indispensable' (Acts 15:28)" (UR 18). Some would argue that this last statement has been forgotten twenty-five years after the council.[4]

The council approved a separate but complementary Decree on Eastern Catholic Churches, *Orientalium Ecclesiarum*. Sometimes referred to as Uniate churches, these churches have separate rites but are united with Rome. This decree reassured the Eastern Catholic churches that they "can and should always preserve their lawful liturgical rites and their established way of life, and that these should not be altered except by way of an appropriate and organic development." Moreover, "their rights and privileges...which flourished when the East and West were in union should be re-established" (OE 6 and 9). It then proceeded to restore some of these ancient rights and practices.

The Declaration on the Relationship of the Church to Non-Christian Religions, *Nostra Aetate*, originated with a request from Pope John XXIII that the council "make a statement on the Jews and asked Cardinal Bea

---

4. See, for example, Heinrich Fries and Karl Rahner, *Unity of the Churches: An Actual Possibility* (Philadelphia: Fortress Press, 1985).

to see to it."[5] But some did not want the council to say anything about the Jews lest it offend Arab governments. Further, bishops from some areas of the world where Jews are few were more concerned with other great religions. Hence, the document was expanded and presented a worldwide view, but did not deal with any religious tradition in depth.

The document gives primary consideration "to what human beings have in common and to what promotes fellowship among them" and recognizes that the various religions all seek "answers to those profound mysteries of the human condition" (NA 1). The Catholic church, it says, "rejects nothing which is true and holy in these religions" and looks upon them with sincere respect. The Catholic church urges its members that they "prudently and lovingly, through dialogue and collaboration with the followers of other religions, and in witness of Christian faith and life, acknowledge, preserve, and promote the spiritual and moral goods found among these men, as well as the values in their society and culture" (NA 2).

With regard to the Jews, the council recalls "the spiritual bond linking the people of the New Covenant with Abraham's stock." It states clearly that the passion and death of Jesus "cannot be blamed upon all the Jews then living, without distinction, nor upon the Jews of today," and deplores "the hatred, persecutions, and displays of anti-Semitism directed against the Jews at any time and from any source" (NA 4). Many felt that this statement was not strong enough to atone for centuries of anti-Semitism within the church. It was, nonetheless, an official condemnation of such practices and attitudes.

Taken together, these three documents of the Second Vatican Council mark a major change in the fundamental self-understanding of the Catholic Christian community. No longer does the church understand itself as the exclusive means of salvation, nor as identical with the true church of Christ, but now recognizes other Christian communities as sisters and brothers deserving the title Christian. They are bound in unity by a shared baptism and many other elements for building up the church, such as the Scriptures. It recognized that there have been diverse ways in which revelation has been received and that a plurality of ways of being Christian has existed from the earliest times. Different theological formulations are accepted as being complementary, rather than conflicting. These diverse traditions are to be accepted with esteem and respect and are not an obstacle to unity. This is an obvious change from the previous expectation that separated churches must "return to Rome" and accept a uniformity imposed by Rome. The emphasis was on what we have in common with other Christians and with all humans,

---

5. Robert A. Graham, S.J. in the introduction to the document in Abbott, *Documents of Vatican II*, 656.

rather than on the differences that divide us. Such an emphasis provides a basis for dialogue and collaboration.

## DEVELOPMENTS SINCE VATICAN II

### Ecumenism

Not only the documents of Vatican II, but the experience of the council itself and the inevitable involvement of the World Council of Churches and the individual churches gave rise to an explosion of ecumenical activity on many levels. We cannot detail them all here, but will mention some significant examples.

On the highest level, even before the council was over, the meeting in Jerusalem in January 1964 of Pope Paul VI and the ecumenical patriarch of Constantinople, Patriarch Athenagoras, was of immense symbolic significance. The silence that had prevailed between these two major branches of Christianity since the Council of Florence was at last broken in the cradle of Christianity and the "two pilgrims," in the words of their joint communiqué, "fixed their eyes on Christ."[6] Other symbolic gestures, such as the return of relics and the lifting of the mutual excommunications of 1054, followed.[7] Three years later Pope Paul VI visited Istanbul and Patriarch Athenagoras returned the courtesy with a visit to Rome. The archbishop of Canterbury, Dr. Michael Ramsey, also visited Rome in 1966.

In addition to such symbolic gestures, whose importance should not be underestimated because of the profound effect on the atmosphere and attitudes of all, structures were set up to continue the dialogue and collaboration. A Joint Working Group was established with the World Council of Churches and preparations were made for bilateral dialogues with the various Protestant churches. The "dialogue of charity" between the Orthodox churches and the Roman Catholic Church blossomed into a theological dialogue officially inaugurated in November 1979 by Patriarch Dimitrios I and Pope John Paul II.[8] It seems to many that this pope has placed much greater emphasis on the dialogue between East and West than on the dialogues with the Western Protestant churches.

These bilateral dialogues are, perhaps, the most significant and amazing development in the ecumenical movement in recent years. Amazing, because of the extent of the agreement on theological issues

---

6. Joint Communiqué of Pope and Patriarch, January 6, 1964, in *Towards the Healing of Schism: The Sees of Rome and Constantinople*, ed. and trans. E. J. Stormon, S.J. (New York: Paulist Press, 1987), 64.

7. Ibid., 126–31.

8. For a record of these contacts up until 1984 see *Towards the Healing of Schism*.

that had been the major points of disagreement, such as justification by faith, baptism, Eucharist and ministry, and papal primacy. Without attempting a complete survey of the results thus far, let us mention a representative sample.

The question of justification by faith was certainly at the heart of the division in the sixteenth century between Lutherans and Catholics. Official dialogues between Lutheran and Catholic biblical scholars and theologians in the United States began in 1965 and produced documents on the Nicene Creed, baptism, the Eucharist, and papal primacy among others. After five years of research, position papers, and discussions, the dialogue partners declared substantial material agreement on justification by faith in 1983. Not since the Colloquy at Regensburg (where agreement on this doctrine had been reached, as noted in chapter 5) has there been such convergence.

The dialogue acknowledged that there are different "thought structures" among Catholics and Lutherans, but said that these "need not be church-dividing."[9] In the Common Statement they summarize their agreement: "It must be emphasized that our common affirmation that it is God in Christ alone whom believers ultimately trust does not necessitate any one particular way of conceptualizing or picturing God's saving work. That work can be expressed in the imagery of God as judge who pronounces sinners innocent and righteous, and also in a transformist view which emphasizes the change wrought in sinners by infused grace."[10] Thus the statement of Vatican II that diverse theological formulations could be considered as complementary rather than conflicting was exemplified in this common statement on justification by faith.

The lengthy and detailed background papers that support the Common Statement make it clear that this was not a superficial or cosmetic agreement. The dialogue partners recognized that it was now possible to extricate the theological issue of justification by faith from other "nontheological sources of division" with which it had been intertwined in the sixteenth century, such as the power of princes, social and economic issues, and the churches' struggle for worldly power. Hence, a profound theological agreement is now possible. The common statement of agreement was submitted to the respective churches "with the hope that it will serve them as they face the need to make appropri-

---

9. *Justification by Faith: Lutherans and Catholics in Dialogue VII*, ed. H. George Anderson, T. Austin Murphy, and Joseph A. Burgess (Minneapolis: Augsburg, 1985), 70. For the German counterpart see Karl Lehmann and Wolfhart Pannenberg, *The Condemnations of the Reformation Era: Do They Still Divide?* (Minneapolis: Fortress, 1990).

10. Ibid., 72.

ate decisions for the purpose of confessing their faith as one."[11] Such "appropriate decisions" have not yet been taken.

On the fundamental theological questions and practices of the Eucharist and ministry there has also been remarkable agreement between Lutherans and Catholics. The dialogue sessions that ended in 1967 on "The Eucharist as Sacrifice" concluded: "Despite all remaining differences in the ways we speak and think of the eucharistic sacrifice and our Lord's presence in his supper, we are no longer able to regard ourselves as divided in the one, holy, catholic, and apostolic faith on these two points."[12] With regard to ministry, both sides agreed that there is a "God-given Ministry" that is entered into by ordination for a "life-time of service and is not to be repeated," although this ministry has been structured differently in the two traditions. Nonetheless, "we are agreed that the basic reality of the apostolic Ministry can be preserved amid variations in structure and implementation, in rites of ordination and in theological explanation."[13] A much broader discussion of "Baptism, Eucharist and Ministry" took place in Lima, Peru, 1982, among representatives from all the major Christian denominations and, again, produced remarkable agreement on these fundamentals of the Christian faith.[14]

For an example of the recent agreement concerning papal primacy, we turn to the final report of the Anglican–Roman Catholic International Commission, 1981, since the position of the papacy was the major issue in the historical origin of their separation. Over a twelve-year period, these dialogues produced two statements on authority in the church, the Venice Statement (1976) and the Windsor Statement (1981) with some "Elucidations" in between. The 1976 statement recognized that "primacy and conciliarity are complementary elements of *episcope*," although at times one has been emphasized at the expense of the other with a resultant serious imbalance. Nonetheless, it said that this general pattern "needs to be realized at the universal level. The only see which makes any claim to universal primacy and which has exercised and still exercises such *episcope* is the see of Rome, the city where Peter and Paul died. It seems appropriate that in any future union a universal primacy such as has been described should be held by that see."[15]

---

11. Ibid., 74.

12. *The Eucharist as Sacrifice: Lutherans and Catholics in Dialogue III*, published jointly by Representatives of the U.S.A. National Committee of the Lutheran World Federation, and the Bishops' Committee for Ecumenical and Interreligious Affairs, 1967, 198.

13. Paul C. Empie and T. Austin Murphy, eds., *Eucharist & Ministry: Lutherans and Catholics in Dialogue IV* (Minneapolis: Augsburg, 1979), 13–15.

14. *Baptism, Eucharist and Ministry*, Faith and Order Paper No. 111 (Geneva: World Council of Churches, 1982). For the controversial Vatican response to the Lima document, see "Baptism, Eucharist and Ministry: An Appraisal," *Origins* 17 (November 19, 1987): 401–16.

15. "Anglican–Roman Catholic Conversations, Final Report, 1981," in Harding Meyer

This represented a consensus on the basic principles of primacy, though problems and difficulties remained. The commission identified four particular difficulties: "the interpretation of the Petrine texts, the meaning of the language of 'divine right,' the affirmation of papal infallibility, and the nature of the jurisdiction ascribed to the bishop of Rome as universal primate."[16]

After five years of further study, they were able to come to a common understanding of the first two. They believed that universal jurisdiction must be balanced with an understanding of local conditions, a respect for cultural diversity, and a rightful freedom of conscience. Anglicans wanted assurance that their distinctive theological, liturgical, and other traditions would be respected in any future union, but felt that the agreed-upon statement provided that assurance. Concerning infallibility, they expressed reservations about the Marian dogmas having sufficient basis in Scripture, but both sides recognized that the importance of these dogmas had been exaggerated and appealed to the notion of the "hierarchy of truths" mentioned above. Finally, the commission said that some difficulties would not be resolved "until a practical initiative has been taken and our two Churches have lived together more visibly in the one *koinōnia*."[17] They concluded by calling for such practical initiatives. Once again, they have not been forthcoming.

There have been many bilateral dialogues and conversations and not all of them would demonstrate as much agreement as the samples just cited.[18] But in general, there has been remarkable progress in theological understanding of the basic issues separating the major Christian bodies. Unfortunately, this theological convergence has not been widely disseminated nor have the churches officially responded to it. The appropriate decisions and practical initiatives called for by the various dialogues have not occurred either.

Of course, the unity of the Christian churches does not depend on theological agreement alone. Such theological progress must be received and understood not only by church officials but by the people in the pews as well. They, in turn, must have some experience that this theology illuminates and corroborates. There remains the dialectical relationship between theory and practice to which we have referred throughout this volume.

---

and Lukas Vischer, eds., *Growth in Agreement: Reports and Agreed Statements of Ecumenical Conversations on a World Level* (New York: Paulist Press, 1984), 97. For an almost identical statement from the Lutheran–Roman Catholic dialogue, see Paul Empie and T. Austin Murphy, eds. *Lutherans and Catholics in Dialogue: Papal Primacy and the Universal Church* (Minneapolis: Augsburg, 1974), 28.

16. Ibid., 106.

17. Ibid., 115.

18. For the views of some other denominations on the role of the papacy see Peter J. McCord, ed., *A Pope for All Christians?* (New York: Paulist Press, 1976).

On the level of practical experience, at least in the United States, there have also been amazing developments. Pulpit exchanges, common prayer, spiritual retreats, covenanting between parishes and between dioceses of different denominations, training of seminarians in ecumenical consortia, students from different denominations studying together in the same graduate schools, working together for civil rights, peace, and social justice — all such activities provide the plausibility structure for greater unity among Christians. Such experiences have broken down longstanding stereotypes and prejudices and led to greater mutual understanding and respect. The atmosphere and attitudes have changed dramatically since Vatican II. No longer do Catholics think that Christian unity means a "return to the true church of Rome," and no longer do Protestants (with the exception of people like Ian Paisley in Ireland) think that Rome is the "whore of Babylon." Despite this progress, the ecumenical movement seems to be "on hold," and much remains to be done, as we will see below.

## Interreligious Dialogue

More difficult and more threatening to the self-understanding of the Christian community is the increasing awareness of and interface with the other great religious traditions of the world, Buddhism, Hinduism, Islam, and Judaism. The historical consciousness we have spoken of throughout this book, as well as the appreciation of the positive elements in these other religious traditions, make claims of superiority or exclusivity of any one tradition appear questionable. We know that religions are deeply embedded in their cultural matrices, that linguistic forms are always limited in their ability to deal with the most profound questions of human existence, and that each tradition has only a partial grasp of the mystery of the universe. Further, we see the need for people from different religious traditions to work together in the pursuit of international peace and justice, to alleviate the massive suffering in the world, and to overcome ethnic, racial, and tribal divisions for the good of all.

With all of these factors motivating various religious leaders, there has been a plethora of meetings, dialogues, conferences, and discussions between scholars, religious leaders, local communities, and people on all levels, some bilateral, some multilateral, some substantive, some more symbolic. For example, in January 1968, Roman Catholic, Orthodox, and Protestant representatives met with a group of Muslims at Selly Oak Colleges in England; Jews and Christians met in Lugano, Switzerland, in October 1970, at the invitation of the International Jewish Committee on Inter-religious Consultations and the World Council of Churches on the theme "The Quest for World Community"; a World

Conference on Religion and Peace met in Kyoto, Japan, in October 1970;[19] leaders of all the major world religions met in Assisi in October 1986 at the invitation of Pope John Paul II to pray together for world peace; a major conference between Christians from a variety of denominations and Buddhists took place in Berkeley, California, in the summer of 1987 and produced six volumes of working papers; there have been numerous smaller dialogues between Christians and Buddhists in Sri Lanka, Burma, Cambodia, Laos, Thailand, and Japan;[20] the International Jewish-Catholic Liaison Committee held twelve official meetings between 1971 and 1985, and Pope John Paul II prayed and spoke in the Great Synagogue of Rome in April 1986, to mention only a small sample of such meetings.

It is not possible, nor is it our purpose here to summarize the results of so many diverse dialogues; we are concerned only with the impact of such contacts on the self-understanding of the Christian community. How are we to understand ourselves in the light of our respect and esteem for the truth embodied in these other religious traditions? Can we maintain traditional Christian claims to the uniqueness of Jesus and the exclusivity of salvation in his name only (Acts 4:12)? If God works salvation through other religions, how are Christians related to them? What is the purpose or mission of the Christian community if the Spirit is working in other religious communities? Is conversion to Christianity no longer a goal of missionary activity? Should there be such evangelizing activity at all? What of the mandate to "Go, therefore, and make disciples of all nations, baptizing them in the name of the Father, and of the Son, and of the holy Spirit, teaching them to observe all that I have commanded you" (Matt. 28:19–20)? Before examining the ways in which contemporary Christian theologians are approaching these questions, let us turn briefly to the special relationship between Christians and Jews.

As we have seen, it was this special relationship that prompted Pope John XXIII to request a statement that developed into *Nostra Aetate.* The background for dialogue between Christians and Buddhists and Hindus is mutual ignorance, but the background for dialogue between Jews and Christians is "more than two thousand years of bitterness

---

19. S. J. Samartha, *Courage for Dialogue: Ecumenical Issues in Inter-religious Relationships* (Geneva: World Council of Churches, 1981), 3–6.

20. *Buddhism and Christianity,* ed. Claude Geffré and Mariasusai Dhavamony, Concilium 116 (New York: Crossroad, 1979), 99–117. For the present state of this ongoing dialogue see Paul O. Ingram, *The Modern Buddhist-Christian Dialogue: Two Universalistic Religions in Transformation* (Lewiston, N.Y.: Edwin Mellen Press, 1988); John B. Cobb and Christopher Ives, eds., *The Self-Emptying God: A Buddhist-Jewish-Christian Conversation* (Maryknoll, N.Y.: Orbis, 1990).

and misunderstanding."[21] Hence, while Christians and Jews have much more in common, this two-thousand-year history makes dialogue all the more difficult.

Ever since Augustine enunciated the basic position that Jews should not be physically harmed but tolerated because they confirm the truth of Christianity in their own Scriptures and provide a living warning to Christians of what happens when one rejects Christ, there has been mistrust and even contempt between the two faiths.[22] Christians have basically understood themselves as having replaced the Jews as God's Chosen People, the "New" Covenant having superseded the "Old" Covenant. Although it was never official Christian doctrine, the "Jews" were held responsible in the popular mind for the death of Jesus. Although the Crusades were directed against Muslims, many crusading armies took out their venom on Jews as well. Luther's notorious treatise, *On the Jews and Their Lies*, 1543, was, in the words of one historian, "one of the most scurrilous displays of anti-Jewish venom ever written."[23] The silence of many Christians and church leaders during the Holocaust is perceived by many Jews as a continuation, if not a culmination, of earlier anti-Semitic attitudes. The memory of such a long and painful history cannot be erased overnight, but much has happened since Vatican II.

In addition to *Nostra Aetate,* the World Council of Churches and many particular denominations have repudiated and condemned any idea that the Jews can in any way be held guilty of the crucifixion or are a people accursed and have expressed repentance for any "teaching of contempt" for Jews.[24] Many bilateral and multilateral dialogues and conferences have been held. With regard to Catholics specifically, the International Jewish-Catholic Liaison Committee was founded in 1971, and since then has held twelve meetings until 1985, dealing with various major subjects.[25] Among these there are five that remain basic for Jewish-Christian relations today: Are Christians still seeking the conversion of the Jews, and, if so, how is this "mission" to the Jews compatible with true dialogue? How do Christians relate to the State of Israel, and is criticism of its policies always rooted in anti-Semitism? Can Christians and Jews understand and accept how differently they read the same

---

21. Walter Harrelson and Randall M. Falk, *Jews and Christians: A Troubled Family* (Nashville: Abingdon Press, 1990), 16.

22. For a brief overview of this history see Marc Saperstein, *Moments of Crisis in Jewish-Christian Relations* (London: SCM Press, 1989).

23. Ibid., 33.

24. Ibid., 52–53.

25. See International Catholic-Jewish Liaison Committee, *Fifteen Years of Catholic-Jewish Dialogue: 1970–1985,* Selected Papers (Rome: Libreria Editrice Vaticana, 1988), and Eugene J. Fisher, A. James Rudin, and Marc H. Tannebaum, eds., *Twenty Years of Jewish-Catholic Relations* (New York: Paulist, 1986).

Scriptures?[26] Although there have been drastic changes in the official attitude of Christians toward Jews, are there still limits to toleration, mutual trust, acceptance, and dialogue? And, most basically of all, how does each faith community understand Jesus of Nazareth?[27]

Once again, it is beyond the scope or purpose of this book to deal with all the issues raised by recent interreligious dialogues. We are interested in the consequences this new experience of a plurality of major religious traditions has for our understanding of the church. Christians are only beginning to come to terms with this fact, but there have been some groping attempts toward a theology of world religions.

## TOWARD A THEOLOGY OF WORLD RELIGIONS

The last ten years have seen a virtual explosion in the literature dealing with a theological understanding of the world religions.[28] We cannot survey all the recent writings on this topic, but some consensus is emerging on the issues at stake and the possible options for Christians.

The major issues are primarily the traditional Christian claims that Jesus as the Christ is unique and that salvation comes only in his name, i.e., with Christology and soteriology, rather than with ecclesiology. But secondarily, the place and purpose of the church in the salvific process is called into question, if we recognize that other religions can be vehicles of salvation for their members. In the Christian tradition there have been two approaches to this question. The ancient dictum, dating from the time of Cyprian, *Extra ecclesiam nulla salus* (outside the church there is no salvation), expresses the Christian view that has come

---

26. On this point, see the stimulating work of Norbert Lohfink, S.J., *The Covenant Never Revoked: Biblical Reflections on Christian-Jewish Dialogue,* trans. John J. Scullion, S.J. (New York: Paulist Press, 1991).

27. For an excellent, balanced discussion of these issues, see Harrelson and Falk, *Jews and Christians,* and Paul M. van Buren, *A Theology of the Jewish-Christian Reality,* part 1, *Discerning the Way* (San Francisco: Harper & Row, 1980), part 2, *A Christian Theology of the People Israel* (San Francisco: Harper & Row, 1983), part 3, *Christ in Context* (San Francisco: Harper & Row, 1988).

28. See, for example, Alan Race, *Christians and Religious Pluralism: Patterns in the Christian Theology of Religions* (Maryknoll, N.Y.: Orbis, 1983); Paul F. Knitter, *No Other Name?: A Critical Survey of Christian Attitudes toward the World Religions* (New York: Orbis, 1985); Hans Küng, Josef van Ess, Heinrich von Stietencron, Heinz Bechert, *Christianity and the World Religions: Paths of Dialogue with Islam, Hinduism, and Buddhism* (Garden City, N.Y.: Doubleday & Co., 1986); Leonard Swidler, ed., *Toward a Universal Theology of Religion* (Maryknoll, N.Y.: Orbis, 1987); John Hick and Paul F. Knitter, eds., *The Myth of Christian Uniqueness: Toward a Pluralistic Theology of Religions* (Maryknoll, N.Y.: Orbis, 1987); and Lesslie Newbigin, *The Gospel in a Pluralist Society* (Grand Rapids: Eerdmans, 1989); Jacques Dupuis, S.J., *Jesus Christ at the Encounter of World Religions,* trans. Robert R. Barr (Maryknoll, N.Y.: Orbis Books, 1991). Most of these volumes also contain extensive bibliographies.

to be called "exclusivist."[29] This view sees little or no salvific value in
other religions and affirms the necessity of membership in the church
for salvation. Even in this view, however, salvation was allowed to those
who did not receive sacramental baptism, but were received into the
church through "baptism in blood," martyrdom, or "baptism by desire"
(*in voto*) for those who intended to be baptized but died before having
done so. A second strand of the traditional Christian view of salvation,
now referred to as "inclusivist," admits the salvific power of other religions but affirms that this is in and through the redemptive work of
Christ although this is not realized by members of these other religious
traditions. They are, in the words of Karl Rahner, "anonymous Christians."[30] This view tries to hold in tension the universal salvific will of
God and the uniqueness of the revelation in Christ. Salvation is possible in other religious traditions, but the ultimate norm of salvation and
the fullness of salvation is only in and through Jesus Christ. This view
is found in Vatican II (GS 22) and was articulated by Pope Paul II in his
encyclical, *Redemptor Hominis* (n. 14).

Today, many Christian theologians are attempting to formulate a position they are calling "pluralist." This is a "move away from insistence
on the superiority or finality of Christ and Christianity toward a recognition of the independent validity of other ways."[31] Salvation can take
place in other religious traditions without any, even covert, relation to
Christ. This view emphasizes God's universal salvific will and that grace
is operative in many ways. The Christian church is not the exclusive
channel of grace or salvation. It is one among many paths. In this view,
"Christianity is seen in a pluralistic context as *one* of the great world
faiths, *one* of the streams of religious life through which human beings
can be savingly related to that ultimate Reality Christians know as the
heavenly Father."[32] Each religious tradition is unique, but not absolute
or superior to the others.

Such an affirmation of thoroughgoing pluralism, or "pluralism as
parity," in Langdon Gilkey's phrase, requires a reinterpretation of Christology and soteriology, but Hick and others believe there have been
similar developments in Christian self-understanding before, and that
a pluralistic vision does not require a "radical departure from the diverse and ever-growing Christian tradition, but its further development
in ways suggested by the discovery of God's presence and saving activity
within other streams of human life."[33] Paul Knitter argues that there was

---

29. Race, *Christians and Religious Pluralism*, chap. 2.
30. Ibid., chap. 3.
31. Hick and Knitter, *The Myth of Christian Uniqueness*, viii.
32. John Hick, "The Non-Absoluteness of Christianity," in Hick and Knitter, *The Myth
of Christian Uniqueness*, 22.
33. Ibid., 33.

a variety of interpretations of Jesus and development of the early Christian understandings of Jesus even *within* the New Testament, and there is no reason why such continuous reinterpretation should cease now.[34] He suggests that today we need a "theocentric" (or, better, a "soteriocentric")[35] Christology focusing on Jesus' proclamation of God and the kingdom of God. Hick suggests an "inspiration" Christology centered on the understanding of Jesus as God's inspired eschatological prophet. Both believe that Christians can continue to confess Jesus as savior and witness to this truth in their lives "without making any judgments whether this revelation surpasses or fulfills other religions."[36]

Not all Christian theologians wrestling with these questions would take such an open view. Lesslie Newbigin, for example, argues that such a pluralist view is an uncritical acceptance of "modern historical consciousness" that is the "product of a particular culture and can claim no epistemological privilege." He says that "to affirm the unique decisiveness of God's action in Jesus Christ is not arrogance; it is the enduring bulwark against the arrogance of every culture to be itself the criterion by which others are judged."[37] He argues for a position that affirms the uniqueness of the revelation in Jesus Christ, but allows the possibility of the salvation of non-Christians. At the same time he denies that non-Christian religions are "vehicles of salvation," but allows for the "gracious work of God in the lives of all human beings."[38] He does not explain how these seemingly contradictory affirmations cohere.

This brief survey of various ways Christian theologians are beginning to deal with religious pluralism is by no means complete. This is a discussion that is only at its initial stage and will surely continue to occupy us in the future. Some would say that religious pluralism is the central problem confronting Christianity in our time, comparable to the confrontation with science in the nineteenth and early twentieth centuries.[39] In any case, it has definite implications for our self-understanding as a Christian community.

How can the church carry out its mission to proclaim the Gospel to all nations and engage in open and honest dialogue at the same time? This was seen as a conflict by the World Council of Churches at its assembly in Nairobi, 1975, and the WCC's 1979 *Guidelines on Dialogue* did not resolve it. More recently, Pope John Paul II addressed the issue in his encyclical, *Redemptoris Missio,* 1991, subtitled, "On the

---

34. Paul Knitter, *No Other Name?,* 173–82.
35. Paul F. Knitter, "Toward a Liberation Theology of Religions," in Hick and Knitter, *The Myth of Christian Uniqueness,* 187.
36. Ibid., 205.
37. Lesslie Newbigin, *The Gospel in a Pluralist Society,* 166.
38. Ibid., 182–83.
39. See, for example, Alan Race, *Christians and Religious Pluralism,* 6.

Permanent Validity of the Church's Missionary Mandate."[40] In this encyclical, the pope does not see interreligious dialogue and the mission of the church to proclaim the Gospel to be in conflict. Rather, he says, "Interreligious dialogue is a part of the church's evangelizing mission. Understood as a method and means of mutual knowledge and enrichment, dialogue is not in opposition to the mission *ad gentes* [to the nations]; indeed it has special links with that mission and is one of its expressions" (no. 55). He affirms that God is present "to entire peoples through their spiritual riches, of which their religions are the main and essential expression even when they contain 'gaps, insufficiencies and errors' " (no. 55). Perhaps the most succinct statement of his position is the following paragraph:

> In the light of the economy of salvation, the church sees no conflict between proclaiming Christ and engaging in interreligious dialogue. Instead, she feels the need to link the two in the context of her mission *ad gentes*. These two elements must maintain both their intimate connection and their distinctiveness; therefore they should not be confused, manipulated or regarded as identical as though they were interchangeable. (no. 55)

Although the pope once again, along with Vatican II, asserts that the church "alone possesses the fullness of the means of salvation," he goes on to say that "other religions constitute a positive challenge for the church: They stimulate her both to discover and to acknowledge the signs of Christ's presence and of the working of the Spirit as well as to examine more deeply her own identity and to bear witness to the fullness of revelation which she has received for the good of all" (no. 56). Finally, he says that "dialogue is a path toward the kingdom and will certainly bear fruit, even if the times and seasons are known only to the Father (cf. Acts 1:7)" (no. 57). Despite this generally positive view of interreligious dialogue, he warns against "incorrect theological perspectives" which are "characterized by a religious relativism which leads to the belief that 'one religion is as good as another' " (no. 36). Thus, the pope would seem to be in the inclusivist school, although urging interreligious dialogue as part of the church's mission and witness.

Those attempting to articulate the relationship of Christianity to the other world religions are still formulating the questions and examining the possibilities and have achieved no consensus at this time. Such discussions among theologians are at the early stages, as we have said. The increasing experience of ordinary Christians confronting other religious traditions suggests that these discussions are not just academic

---

40. *Origins* 20, no. 34 (January 31, 1991): 541–68.

exercises, however, and the issues raised for Christianity will not go away.

## CHALLENGES AND POSSIBILITIES

The pursuit of Christian unity was given a major new impetus by the Second Vatican Council, which raised the expectations and hopes of Catholics as well as all other Christians. A new atmosphere of mutual respect, cooperation, and dialogue developed rapidly and much progress has been made, especially on the level of theological discussion. "From the viewpoint of dogma," Heinrich Fries and Karl Rahner have argued, "a unity of the churches is already possible today with this kind of epistemological tolerance."[41] By "epistemological tolerance" they mean that the mainline churches need not affirm all dogmatic propositions held by each of them, but could reserve judgment on those that are considered important to one but not to another. In other words, if we invoke the "hierarchy of truths" of which Vatican II spoke, there is already sufficient dogmatic agreement to warrant an actual unity among the mainline Christian churches. They further argue that we have all learned that we can live with a greater degree of pluralism of discipline, liturgy, and church structure than previously had been thought.[42] The surprising agreement in the Lima document is evidence of this.

But Christian unity does not depend on doctrinal agreement alone. The wide areas of agreement between Lutherans and Catholics and between Episcopalians and Catholics in the bilateral dialogues among the theologians has not produced much movement on the part of the official leaders of any of the denominations. The Lima document was "received" by many denominations, and there are six volumes of *reactions* to it, but no *action!* There are a variety of nontheological factors that must also be dealt with: economic and political issues, matters of style and taste, that are just as important, perhaps more so, from a human perspective, as theology. Just as such nontheological factors were operative in the breach between East and West and at the time of the Reformation as we have seen, so the same will be true with any movement toward Christian unity. As was true then, the personalities of church leaders will also be a factor. Think only of the difference between Pope John XXIII and Pope John Paul II and their impact on the ecumenical movement.

The possibility of Christian unity remains a real one, but the challenge to the churches is to initiate concrete, specific actions on all levels,

---

41. Fries and Rahner, *Unity of the Churches,* 38.
42. Ibid., 47

local as well as denominational. Local church leaders, lay as well as clerical, will have to make Christian unity a high priority and they will have
to help educate the average church member. We have seen historically
that attempts at church unity from above do not succeed. How to move
the whole People of God in this direction remains a major challenge.

Interreligious encounter and dialogue pose even greater challenges
than does intra-Christian ecumenism. There is not as much common
ground or history to begin with, and the linguistic and cultural barriers
are much greater. Nonetheless, much progress has been made in the
last twenty-five years. At this stage, the goal is mutual understanding
and cooperation, not religious unity. While the dialogues between religious leaders and scholars may serve this purpose and may be mutually
enriching in our respective spiritual lives, it may be that the greatest
possibilities lie in cooperative efforts in the social and political sphere.
Knitter suggests that the worldwide experience of poverty and oppression may be the context for and the source of further interreligious
encounter and dialogue. He says, "If the religions of the world, in other
words, can recognize poverty and oppression as a common problem, if
they can share a common commitment (expressed in different forms)
to remove such evils, they will have the basis for reaching across their
incommensurabilities and differences in order to hear and understand
each other and possibly be transformed in the process."[43]

Such common action on behalf of the poor and oppressed is in keeping with most religions' notion of salvation or liberation. Aloysius Pieris
says, "I submit that the religious instinct be defined as a revolutionary urge, a psycho-social impulse, to generate a new humanity. . . . It is
this revolutionary impulse that constitutes, and therefore defines, the
essence of *homo religiosus*."[44] Whether or not this is true, it does appear
that the possibility for common action in the face of massive poverty
and social injustice cannot responsibly be ignored by any religiously
committed person. As for Christians, how they come to understand
their mission in and for the world may provide the key to interpreting their traditional claims to uniqueness and exclusivity. I will suggest
how Christians could understand their mission in the world without
converting all other peoples to Christianity in the Conclusion.

It would be premature to predict the outcome of this new encounter
between Christianity and the world religions. Christians cannot set
a priori limits on the working of God's grace in the world, nor need
we assume that the dialogue "will diminish the revelatory importance

43. Paul F. Knitter, "Toward a Liberation Theology of Religions," in Hick and Knitter,
*The Myth of Christian Uniqueness*, 186.
44. Aloysius Pieris, "The Place of Non-Christian Religions and Cultures in the Evolution
of Third World Theology," in Virginia Fabella and Sergio Torres, eds., *Irruption of the Third
World: Challenge to Theology*, (Maryknoll, N.Y.: Orbis, 1983), 134.

of Jesus Christ."[45] It could be that, just as the confrontation between Christianity and science in the nineteenth and early twentieth centuries resulted in a better and deeper understanding of God and creation, so this new encounter may free us for a deeper understanding of Jesus Christ and his role in the salvation of the world. Whatever the outcome, Christians can understand themselves today only in the context of the plurality and parity of the other great world religions.

## RECOMMENDED READINGS

*Baptism, Eucharist and Ministry*. Faith and Order Paper No. 111. Geneva: World Council of Churches, 1982.

Fries, Heinrich, and Karl Rahner. *Unity of the Churches: An Actual Possibility*. Philadelphia: Fortress Press, 1985.

Harrelson, Walter, and Randall M. Falk *Jews and Christians: A Troubled Family*. Nashville: Abingdon Press, 1990.

Knitter, Paul, *No Other Name?: A Critical Survey of Christian Attitudes toward the World Religions*. Maryknoll, N.Y.: Orbis, 1985.

---

45. Avery Dulles, S.J., *Models of Revelation* (Garden City, N.Y.: Doubleday & Co., 1983), 192.

Chapter 12

# *Conclusion*

Our reflections on the life and self-understanding of the community called church lead to some general conclusions. First, the Christian community has throughout the course of history lived amid a series of polar tensions: between unity and diversity, between the particular churches and the church universal, between being a community of the holy and being a school for sinners, between being a church open to the world and a sect apart from the world, between adapting to the cultural and social context and raising its prophetic voice to challenge that context, between the Spirit-led or charismatic aspect of the community and its need for structure and institutionalization, between preserving its apostolic heritage and reading the signs of the times, between being in the world and having here no lasting home. At various times, emphasis may have been on one of the poles rather than the other, but these tensions have remained throughout the life of the community and we should not be surprised that they continue in the present.

Second, living creatively with these tensions has led to both continuity and change in the church in the course of its history. These differences within similarity demonstrate that "church" is an analogous notion. It is not univocal, nor is it completely equivocal. It bears meanings that are partly the same and partly different. Across both time and space, there has been enough commonality to maintain its identity as a Christian community, yet enough flexibility to survive constant challenges, both internal and external. Knowing this history, we should not be threatened with change today, nor easily let go of our heritage. The church is and always has been an analogous notion. Its outward expressions, forms, and structures have been historically conditioned and will continue to be so. New ways of being church, new forms of ecclesiality, are emerging even today.[1] These must always be tested against the com-

---

1. T. Howland Sanks, S.J., "Forms of Ecclesiality: The Analogical Church," *Theological Studies* 49 (1988): 695–708.

munity's basic self-understanding and mission, but the Spirit of the Lord will continue to lead the community in new and unexpected directions. The church is a living community, not a museum piece.

Third, any dynamic organization needs to remind itself continuously of its purpose or mission. Amid all the changes, the church must have its guiding vision clearly in mind. Underlying all the challenges we have discussed in the last part of this book, this is the major one facing us today: to be clear about our mission in and for the world. For Roman Catholics, the Second Vatican Council marked the end of an era when the primary emphasis of the church was on preserving and conserving, on protecting the faith and the faithful from contamination by the world. The church was guided by what Gregory Baum has recently termed the "logic of maintenance."[2] By that he means that the institution was preoccupied with maintaining itself rather than with the end or purpose for which it was founded. He contrasts this to the "logic of mission," in which an organization determines its activities and structures in the light of its mission, rather than self-preservation.

*Gaudium et Spes* called for a new way of conceiving of the church's presence and activity in the world today. To help us understand this mission, I want to recall some early Christian images. In the Sermon on the Mount, Jesus addresses his disciples directly, saying,

> You are the salt of the earth. But if the salt loses its taste, with what can it be seasoned? It is no longer good for anything but to be thrown out and trampled underfoot. You are the light of the world. A city set on a mountain cannot be hidden. Nor do they light a lamp and then put it under a bushel basket; it is set on a lampstand, where it gives light to all in the house. Just so, your light must shine before others, that they may see your good deeds and glorify your heavenly Father. (Matt. 5:13–16)

Again, describing the kingdom of heaven, not the disciples directly, Jesus says, "To what shall I compare the kingdom of God. It is like yeast that a woman took and mixed with three measures of wheat flour until the whole batch of dough was leavened" (Luke 13:20–21).

Salt, leaven, and light. These images all suggest not opposition to the world, but permeation, pervasion, insertion. The mission of the followers of Jesus is to be active *in* the world, not to withdraw from it or to control it. Nor do these images suggest that the mission is to make all the world Christian. Salt does not turn all the food into salt, and leaven does not change all the dough into yeast. Further, if salt, leaven, and light are effective, they no longer stand out from that which they permeate but

---

2. Gregory Baum, *Compassion and Solidarity: The Church for Others* (New York: Paulist Press, 1990), 42–43.

blend in with it. They transform from within. These images do not focus on Christian uniqueness or distinctiveness, but on the contribution Christians can make in the transformation of the whole.

Salt, leaven, and light seem to be appropriate images for understanding the mission of the church today. In a pluralistic, relativistic, and privatized world, in a world of massive suffering and oppression, the Christian community must look outward, beyond itself. It cannot afford to be preoccupied with its internal problems or self-preservation, although it must practice internally what it preaches if it is to be a credible witness to the Gospel. But concern for the neighbor in the widest sense, as expressed in Matthew 25, service to all humanity as expressed in *Gaudium et Spes,* must take precedence. If we understand ourselves as salt, leaven, and light, there can be no opposition between our faith and our daily lives. As a Christian community we have been called to be not only a community of disciples, but also a community of apostles, those sent forth in service to all humanity. Our task, then, is not to *survive* but to *serve,* not to *worry* but to *witness,* not to *hide* but to *hope,* and to bring hope to others. As Gustavo Gutiérrez has said, "This time is dark only for those who do not believe the Lord is present in it."

# Index